Urban Photography
in Argentina

Urban Photography in Argentina

Nine Artists of the Post-Dictatorship Era

David William Foster

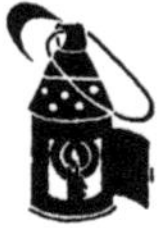

McFarland & Company, Inc., Publishers
Jefferson, North Carolina, and London

David William Foster is also the author of
Bibliography in Literature, Folklore, Language and Linguistics:
Essays on the Status of the Field (McFarland, 2003)

LIBRARY OF CONGRESS CATALOGUING-IN-PUBLICATION DATA

Foster, David William.
    Urban photography in Argentina: nine artists of the
post-dictatorship era / David William Foster.
       p.   cm.
    Includes bibliographical references and index.

    ISBN-13: 978-0-7864-3121-2
    softcover : 50# alkaline paper ∞

    1. Photographers — Argentina.   I. Title.
TR139F68   2007
770.92'282 — dc22   2007016285

British Library cataloguing data are available

Cover photograph by Gabriel Díaz.

Manufactured in the United States of America

McFarland & Company, Inc., Publishers
Box 611, Jefferson, North Carolina 28640
www.mcfarlandpub.com

To my wife Virginia,
who encouraged me to pursue
my passion for photography, and,
as always, to my students

Table of Contents

Preface

"Trabajar en lo visual con frases hechas y arriesgar por el camino de la obviedad: primer plano, gran angular, fondo, mensaje social"— Marcos López, Pop latino, *no pag.*

"[The photograph is not] supposed to repair our ignorance about the history and causes of the suffering it picks out and frames. Such images cannot be more than an invitation to pay attention, to reflect, to learn, to examine the rationalizations for mass suffering offered by established powers. Who caused what the picture shows? Who is responsible"— Sontag, 117.

Argentina has always been a country of photographers, and there is a long tradition of commercial, journalistic, documentary, and art photography, with the sort of international recognition such a production merits. In the 1990s Sara Facio, certainly the dean of Argentine photography, whose publishing operation La Azotea publishes many of the newer practitioners, began to curate a permanent collection of Argentine photography at the Museo Nacional de Bellas Artes (see array of younger photographers represented in Mangialardi and Bécquer Casaballe; see also Facio, *Fotografía argentina actual* and *Fotografía argentina dos*).

Yet, while the work of the majority of current Argentine photographers is available, if not always in published book form, at one site or another on the Internet, there is little in the way of interpretive academic studies. I included a chapter on Facio — the work she has done on her own, as well as her famous collaborations with Alicia d'Amico — in my book *Buenos Aires: Perspective on the City and Cultural Production*, and it remains the only in-depth critical examination of her work, despite extensive brief notes, catalog presentations, and blurbs in overviews of photography (Facio is given due space in *Image and Memory: Photography from Latin America 1866–1994*, which is the only extant survey of Latin American photography). But in the case of Argentina, one is struck by the fact that, although there are over 1,000 Internet sites for Grete Stern, the German photographer who was formed in the Bauhaus movement, but whose major work, especially her feminist photomontages, were done in Argentina in the mid–twentieth century, she has yet to be accorded the detailed critical commentary the originality of her work deserves (see Foster, "Dreaming in Feminine").

In mid–1999, the International Center of Photography in New York held an exhibit of eleven Argentine photographers, "Myths, Dreams, and Realities in Contemporary Argentine Photography," curated by Anne Wilkes Tucker (see exhibit catalog of the same name).[1] Although I had never worked critically with photography as a scholar, I had, for family reasons, an exposure to professional photography. Since I was struck by the eloquence of this exhibit (rather limited, for the number of photographers involved, as the ICP was still in its small upper-East Side quarters), it occurred to me that this work could be integrated into my work on other forms of cultural production in Argentina in the context of the military dictatorship of right-wing nationalism (1966–73) and the neofascist military regime in the 1960s, 1970s, and 1980s, followed by the period of redemocratization in the late 1980s.

My previous work had concerned itself with a significant amount of graphic material, in the form of a study, *Contemporary Argentine Filmmaking*, which looked at films that had been produced since the return to constitutional democracy in 1983; many of them examined issues from the period of the military dictatorship. Moreover, I had also worked on another genre of nonprint culture, the Argentine theater, which in 1981 had mounted the first large-scale refutation of censorship and the culture of neofascism. But I had focused predominantly on print culture, whether what is conventionally understood as literature (mostly the novel and short fiction) or, to calque a word from Argentine Spanish, "contestatorial" journalism (writing that analyzed from a critical point of view sociopolitical events, such as the writing on the Malvinas [Faulkland Islands] invasion or on the so-called Dirty

War of repression during the early years of the neofascist dictatorship following the military coup of 1976). I had also, along the way, published a book on Latin American graphic humor, which refers to material with a certain amount of sociopolitical commentary, but not of the level of focused analysis that underlay the work on Argentine cultural production of the military period and the subsequent return to constitutionality.

Photography, like film, is a very public form of cultural representation. This allows it to be displayed in many sorts of spaces in conjunction with many sorts of other productions (i.e., photography as an adjunct of sociological analysis, as in the case of the Jelin-D'Amico collaboration on poverty in Buenos Aires, or Facio and d'Amico's photographs illustrating Julio Cortázar's text on the city of Buenos Aires). But the public nature of photography also means that it is easily censored, and one can, therefore, speak of a hiatus of critical photography in Argentina: concomitantly, one can refer to the way in which this hiatus is filled by the celebratory photography of someone like Pedro Luis Raota, who functioned as something like the official photographer of the dictatorship (Luís and Luís provide an overview of Raota's work; for a sample of Raota's work, see Raota).

This study, then, is only a modest intervention in the complex and extensive history of photography in Argentina. Rather, it is more an examination of the role of photography in the continuing development of culture in Argentina following the military dictatorship,[2] the project of redemocratization, the imposition of a neoliberalist economic policy, the collapse of that policy in the context of corruption and high but officially ignored social costs, and the abiding political instability of democratic institutions. It would be foolhardy to believe that, with fully democratic elections in 1983 and the transition from dictatorship to constitutionality, Argentina's problems were solved. Indeed, they were only beginning, not because democracy created problems (of course, in one sense, it did), but rather because it allowed for the attempts at a full public debate over where Argentina was in its national history and in what ways problems could be addressed. There has been a lot of critical work for cultural production to take on in post–1983 Argentina, between those who believed that a new day had come for the country and those who believed that it was business as usual;

between those who believed that institutional ineptness essentially perpetuated authoritarian structures and those who believed that such structures could be adequately deconstructed; between those who subscribed to Argentina's potential allegedly to be a First-World country and those who believed that such triumphalism only perpetuated a hypocrisy that covered over the unimpeachable misery that failed institutional practices encouraged; and between those who felt it was more important to project an international image of a vibrant society restored and those who sensed the imperative to recognize the many social subjects who were being ignored by such projections.

The work of the principal photographers in this study represent the way in which this work has been taken on by the current generation of photographers, in the same way in which my earlier studies charted examples of this work in the realm of filmmaking and print literature.

Marcelo Brodsky, for example, has used photography to intervene in the ongoing debate about what has been called the Argentine Holocaust: the disappearance and massacre of 30,000 Argentine citizens during the period of repression. Brodsky brings to his work the resonances for Jewish culture of a term like "holocaust," as well as the issue of remembering, which is captured in the title of the project with which he was involved and is the title of his first published volume, *Buena memoria*. What is particularly interesting about Brodsky's work is that he combines print texts with photographs, and his own photography with that of others, in order to participate in a community of critical analysis of Argentine social history relating to the repression. Brodsky is also a major participant in the project in progress to create a Parque de la Memoria, and one of his roles is to assure the representation of the Jewish experience in recent Argentine sociopolitical history (concerning the Parque, see Huyssen).

Gabriel Valansi also invests in the resonances of the Holocaust, but his emphasis lies not with identifying the period of repression as an Argentine Holocaust (although he may well want to make such a claim), but rather with the way in which projections of authoritarian repression remain in the way in which marginal sectors that make up the growing Argentine lower class experience social repression through their inability — and their loss of some form of previous ability — to participate in the mythology of First-World Argentina. If neoliberalism was every bit as devastating as the military dictatorship, the collapse of neoliberalism has only served to increase social and economic marginalization. Valansi's work has not been published in conventional book form. Rather, the immense large-canvas type photographs that he has produced, focusing on nighttime scenes of the detritus of a fragile system, contrast eloquently with the scope of those scenes. Yet these giant photographs work to insist that the reality they capture is not an insignificant detail of the nocturnal cityscape, but a major index of Argentine life in the megalopolis.

Eduardo Gil eloquently examines the hidden face of Argentine society in *(argentina)*, a title that is doubly eloquent, both by lowercasing the proper name of the country, as though it were a common noun and not the special flag-waving, anthem-singing national entity, and then by suggesting its marginal quality by the enclosing of that name in parentheses. Quite appropriately, this device must provide fits for electronic bibliographic systems. Moreover, I use the structurally ambiguous "hidden away" advisedly, since part of Gil's project is to deal with mentally institutionalized individuals, many of whom are often indices of the failures of a society toward its citizens, a society that then proceeds to hide them away, such that they become the hidden face of a society. In the time-honored way in which cultural production asks us to see what we think does not exist or wish to deny exists, *(argentina)* asks us to scrutinize human beings made insignificant by their circumstances.

Gaby Messina has had, as yet, only one major show, but it is a fascinating one, addressing as it does the question of senior citizens in Argentina, and especially the status of women. By addressing a topic that is not highly important in terms of social symbology — Argentina, like most societies of late capitalism, is markedly youth-oriented — while investing in that topic the photographic codes of fashion photography, Messina introduces a truly impressive gallery of great Argentine women, not in the sense of their sociopolitical notoriety, but in terms of the highly personal world they inhabit: they may not always dominate it and it is not always a desirable world (especially in the case of those confined to geriatric homes), but it is a world, a room à la Virginia Woolf, most have worked to make their own.

Another major way of warehousing supposedly inconvenient social subjects is by incarcerating them, and the images in Adriana Lestido's *Mujeres presas* come from a women's prison in La Plata, the capital of the Province of Buenos Aires. One is immediately struck by the abjectness of these women, beyond the simple fact of their being imprisoned (for reasons never stated): some are elderly, while others are apparently somewhat crazed or acutely alienated; many have extensive tattooing, suggesting a harsh underworld experience prior to their incarceration, or, at least, compliance with the long-standing practice of prison tattooing; one series deals with a woman forced to give the young child she has had with her in prison up for adoption. In the case of both Gil's and Lestido's photography, it is difficult to sustain any rational sense for the triumphalism of the avowals of a First-World society. Moreover, one senses that the triumphalism of the 1990s in neoliberal Argentina was not all that different from the triumphalism in the latter half of the 1970s during the height of the military dictatorship. Gil and Lestido rank high among those who sense the absurdity and the cruelty of such triumphalist sentiments, sentiments that have no truck with the human castoffs that populate their sparse but eloquent photographic treatises.

The most visible faces of economic devastation in Argentina are those of the street children. Gabriel Díaz's *Muertes menores* includes images of little deaths, in the sense that the children he photographs experience a sort of death in small doses through the economic and social marginalization they experience and the problems that come with it, such as malnutrition, sexual exploitation, exposure, drug addiction, and the generalized abuse of the street. But these are also "small deaths," to the extent that the subjects involved are the smallest units, the children, of a society. Someone once said that you can tell a lot about a society by the way it treats its children, and one can well imagine what Díaz thinks about institutional Argentina. What has emerged as his most well known photograph is of a young adolescent, apparently from the margins of the northern Argentine provinces, sniffing glue under one of the allegorical eagles that decorates the monument in front of the national Congress. Díaz's photographs have a strong element of staginess about them, such that one might say he stacks the deck for maximum rhetorical effect. Yet that would be an ungenerous characterization, since a couple of hours spent walking the streets of Buenos Aires will reveal unstaged incidents no less dramatic than Díaz's photographs.

Another photographer who uses staged images, but in much different ways, is Marcos López. López, additionally, works with color (all of the preceding photographers, except for Brodsky, work essentially in black and white), and it is often a visual universe of primary and garish colors. Moreover, López works with intricately composed scenes, often with so much detail that it is difficult for a commentary to know where to begin (so much for Barthes's theory of the punctum, the privileged point of entrance into the photographic universe). Although López works with a sharp sense of humor, dealing in the ridiculous, the absurd, the ludicrous, and the hilarious, his photography too involves a sense of social commentary. His emphasis on kitsch, on recycled cultural values, allows him to make highly intriguing statements about the themes and the commitments that underlie contemporary Argentine society in, like Valansi, both a consumerist sense and one of a postmodern pastiche that the trivial aspects of everyday life must have a perverse sort of poetry because it lacks any apparent transcendental one. In addition to examining the question of the use of kitsch in general in López's photography, I also look at a specific thematic cluster of his images, those that promote a porose relationship between homosociality (understood as the special bonding between men in the construction of a dominant masculinist society, at the expense of women and any other social subject constructed as "insufficiently masculine") and homoeroticism (understood as the erotic attraction — with or without specific accompanying erotic practices — between men).

Returning to black and white, Silvio Fabrykant is best known as a publicity photographer, working with some of the most important personalities in politics and culture since the return to constitutional democracy in 1983. However, and demonstrating how context influences our understanding of cultural production, the insertion of what might otherwise be seen as circumstantial portraits into the context of a major gallery display that directly fronts the masculine identity of the subjects allows for the opportunity to view them in terms of important issues in gender studies. As I have noted and is evident in my approach to much of the work in the volume, gender has been of paramount importance in my work on Latin American culture, and it is in these terms that I was attracted to Fabrykant's collected portraiture.

Finally, and continuing with work in black and white, Gabriela Liffschitz (now deceased), who was not part of the International Center of Photography exhibit, questions consumerist values in a radically different register. In Liffschitz's case, it is the consumption of the female body that is at issue. What is truly innovative about Liffschitz's work, especially in the context of Argentine machismo, is that she has had the courage to photograph her own cancerous body and its own fleshly embodiment of the devastations of modern society as they affect the individual exposed to the noxious elements of the city. I do not know what the sources of Liffschitz's cancer were, but one does know very well that cancer is typically a disease of the urban experience. Moreover, Liffschitz not only exposes her own experience with cancer, but she does so in such a way as to affirm the female body, and even more so when that body no longer fulfills the expectations of the masculinist gaze.

The assertive audacity of Liffschitz's photographs; the outrageousness of López's; the insistently testimonial nature of Gil's, Lestido's, and Díaz's work; the long-range sociohistoric projects of Brodsky's and Valansi's complex images constitute a body of work that I have found to be as significant as the cultural production in other genres I have worked with in addressing the continuing social and political issues of recent Argentine history. Although the analyses that follow undertake to understand how the photographs function semioticly in the creation of visual meanings, they do so first and foremost within the context of ongoing processes of Argentine artists to provide a deeply critical interpretation of national life.

Seven of the eight photographers featured in this study are included as representatives of Argentina in *Mapas abiertos: fotografía latinoamericana 1991–2002*. Only Liffschitz is excluded, perhaps because her work was considered too clinical. Of the seven, six are represented by the reproduction of one or more of their works. Eduardo Gil is mentioned several times, but none of his photographs are included.

I always find it imperative to thank above all others my students, who patiently accompany me in the discovery of a proper critical voice for examining diverse sorts of cultural production. Various research programs at Arizona State have contributed to the execution of this project, but primarily my home department, Languages and Literatures, as well as Jewish Studies. This is the opportunity to thank my father, now deceased for over half a century, but who, when I was a child, unknowingly awoke in me an interest in photography — even though this is the first opportunity I have had to do something with that interest. Eduardo Caro, Ramona Ortiz, Angela González-Echeverry, Felipe Montoya, Mauricio Duarte, Fernando Pezzino, Eduardo Muslip, and Kyle Black have all served as research assistants and associates on various stages of this project. Cindy Webster provided much-needed reality checks on some of my discussions. Elia Hatfield assisted me in preparing the final version of the photographic dossiers. But I most need to thank the photographers themselves, who met with me and discussed my interest in their art; I especially thank Eduardo Gil, who has served as the point person in contacting most of the other photographers. Sara Facio, a true doyenne of Argentine photography, has always been extremely gracious in her interest in my work, and, finally, my Argentine sister, Elida Messina, has contributed in ways too multiple to enumerate.

Some of this material has been previously published in different forms.

A summary of the chapter on Marcelo Brodsky appeared as "Marcelo Brodsky's *Buena memoria*," *Annual Newsletter* [Arizona State University, Jewish Studies Program] 4 (2003–04): 3.

A shorter version of the essay on Adriana Lestido appeared as "Women's Society in Prison: Adriana Lestido's *Mujeres presas*," *Journal of Latin American Urban Studies* 6 (Fall 2004): 1–18.

The essay on Gabriel Messina was written in Spanish in a somewhat shorter version for an as-yet unpublished homage to my colleague L. Teresa Valdivieso.

A shorter version in Spanish of the part of the essay on Marcos López dealing with kitsch appeared as "El kitsch argentino: la fotografía de Marcos López," *Guaraguao; revista de cultura latinoamericana* 8.18 (verano 2004): 79–101. The material on homosociality/homoeroticism appeared as "Homosocialism ⟷ Homoeroticism in the Photography of Marcos López," *Dissidences* 1 (2005). On the Internet: http://www.dissidences/MarcosLopez.html, 08/30/05.

The essay on Gabriela Liffschitz first appeared as "Defying the Masculinist Gaze: Gabriela Liffschitz's *Recursos humanos*," *Chasqui* 32.1 (May 2003): 10–24.

A shorter version of the essay on Gabriel Valansi appeared as "Gabriel Valansi: Neoliberal Nights in Buenos Aires," *Fisura; revista de literatura y arte* 1.3 (febrero 2003): 27–33. Also in *Significação; revista brasileira de semiótica* 18 (2002): 89–113.

The essay on Silvio Fabrykant appeared in Spanish as "Masculinidades argentinas: *Hombres* de Silvio Fabrykant," *Arizona Journal of Hispanic Cultural Studies* 9 (2005): 87–97.

1

Photography and Memory in Marcelo Brodsky's *Buena memoria*

There is a measure of ambiguity about the title of Marcelo Brodsky's 1997 project, *Buena memoria: un ensayo fotográfico*. This volume brings together images of the Buena Memoria project, Brodsky's own commentary on it, and a series of texts by prominent Argentine writers of the generation of the 1976–83 neofascist dictatorship in Argentina, novelists Martín Caparrós and José Pablo Feinmann (also a prominent screenwriter), and poet Juan Gelman. The conjugation of all of these elements provides for a complex cultural product that involves much more than only photographs for exploring the individuals of a group of disappeared persons.

The Buena Memoria Project centers on the class photograph of students in the 1er Año, 6ta División, 1967 of the prestigious Colegio Nacional of Buenos Aires, Argentina's premier college preparatory institution and historically one of the best in Latin America. In 1967, the group of students in question was in its first year of studies, and the photograph is of those who belonged to the sixth class division that would basically have completed classes together as a single coterie during all six years of the program of study. Argentina was, in 1967, in the second year of the military dictatorship that assumed power in 1966 and that would allow for elections in 1973. Between 1973 and 1976, Argentina experienced a transitional, basically weak and inept democracy, built around the legendary return in 1973 of Juan Domingo Perón from eighteen years of exile. The aging and ailing Perón's inability to effectively govern Argentina upon his return, and his death in 1974, precipitated the social dissolution that would lead to the unabashed neofascist military regime of the 1976–83 period.

The students pictured in *Buena memoria* would have graduated in 1972, and many of them evidently became involved in a range of political and social activities that led to the disappearances recorded by the project; one of those who were "disappeared" in this manner was Brodsky's brother Fernando (Brodsky provides personal and family details in his interview with Guagnini). It is important to note that there is no necessary correlation between those involved in protest activities and those who were disappeared. The complete lack of any form of institutional justice or constitutional guarantees, and the coherent administration of a penal system, meant that one could end up arrested, tortured, imprisoned, and killed for the most tenuous of reasons, without any proof ever forthcoming — not then and not now — as to the exact circumstances. The Argentine Dirty War — the height of the repression and the disappearances between the 1976 coup and the end of the decade — has often been compared to the Jewish Holocaust at the hands of the Germans (see *Ese infierno* 296–300 for one such comparison). In the case of the latter, there was a concrete, albeit appalling, motivation: the fact of being Jewish (in addition, to be sure, of other categories that were also the object of the Final Solution). During the Argentine Dirty War, beyond the deliberately vague designation of "subversive," which could and did cover so many forms of social conduct, there never was a coherent way of understanding the basis on which any one individual might be disappeared. One often heard the affirmation "Por algo será" (There must be some reason), but the State never felt it needed to provide any (the place to begin to understand these issues is *Nunca más* [1984], the report of the National Commission on the Disappeared).

Thus, it is imperative not to draw specific conclusions from the group of disappeared ex-students featured in Brodsky's project, at least in terms of specific political action programs. This observation is important, because Fernando Brodsky, like many of his fellow students at the Colegio Nacional, was Jewish: the Colegio was one of the major Argentine institutions for Jews to gain social mobility in a society that still has some marked record of anti–Semitism. Moreover, this anti–Semitism was particularly pronounced during the periods of military dictatorship, and Jacobo Timerman and others (Feitlowitz, 97–109, for example) have made the point that Jews were particularly singled out for persecution by the forces of repression. The intensely reactionary Catholicism that marked the military dictatorships led as a matter of course to an anti–Semitism that saw in the Jews of Argentina — the largest Jewish population in Latin America and one of the top six in the world, although one that has been shrinking steadily in recent decades — a direct threat to its concept of an appropriately Christian national reorganization. It is only on this basis that Jewish students, prominent at the Colegio Nacional, are also prominent in the inventory of the disappeared of the 1er Año, 6ta División.

What is ambiguous about Brodsky's title is the conjunction of the adjective *buena* with the noun *memoria*. To be sure, there is nothing problematical in memories being good, since good memories are one of the great defenses against the depredations of daily life. However, *Buena memoria* is manifestly not about good memories: the cover of Brodsky's book includes a fragment from the Colegio Nacional class picture, with the photographer's superimposed annotations on the details of the disappearance and murder of class members. *Buena memoria* is an exercise in the recovery of memory, not necessarily a suppressed memory, but a memory that has slipped away (concerning the issue of memory in contemporary Argentine society, see Pianca; on the subject of mourning, see Avelar; on the subject of historical trauma like the Argentine Holocaust, see Seligmann-Silva). Horacio González makes an eloquent assessment about the recycling of such a photograph as this class picture:

> The issue is imaging then that the photograph harbors a terrible secret, perhaps in accord with the basic principles of a well-known argument that would place in what is familiar a secret, horrifying map. Marcelo Brodsky's art seeks to free, from within the photograph, the hidden itinerary of a destiny, as if we were before an ultra-realist act, of an almost physical nature. As if the image were a fragile substitute for a reality it represents completely but which for some unknown reason had forgotten to reveal itself [14].

There is a specific ideological weight attached to classmates, especially those that were part of the group with which one graduated from high school. High-school graduation is considered in most Western societies as a major turning point in one's life, and the festivities and commemorations of high school graduation serve to monumentalize that event and to hypostatize the coterie of individuals associated with it. If there is a nostalgic return to youth associated with high-school reunions, or, at least, with the contemplation of their evocative power, it is not likely to be perceived as a return to an innocence considered to have been lost under the weight of harsh and disappointing lived experiences.

Rather, one returns to a moment of the first fullness of personal identity: completing high school is usually taken to mean the first step in forging a personality, a routine of life, and a place in the world, themes that one recalls with satisfaction or despair as one actually progresses through the trajectory of her or his life. Moreover, for these youths there was the exceptional promise of being graduates of the best prep school in the country. As a channel of opportunity for youths of real and exceptional talent, the Colegio Nacional has also been important as a factor in social mobility, and it is important to note that the children of immigrant families are especially well represented in the 1967 roster, since in Argentina an individual with a non–Hispanic surname is likely to be from a family associated with the mass immigration to that country in the late nineteenth and early twentieth centuries.

Thus, indeed, the ambiguous nature of the title is grounded on a dramatic irony: one might expect the return to the class picture made sacred to be beneficent, but it cannot under the circumstances of the book. No amount of wishful thinking, no amount of the nostalgia-driven revision of the past can overcome the brutal facts of the fate of some of the members of the 1967 class. There is, therefore, less of a dynamic of an optional, occasional return to the emotional oasis of the past that class pictures typically provide; rather, what is operant here is the imperative to return to that past and connect it to a historical trajectory that is part of a nightmare of history in which these individuals are frozen, with all of the sense of congealed human experience we have come to associate with the semiotics of photography. Brodsky's title resemanticizes the master photograph of this exposition, a photograph which, in fact, is not even his. And in the process of resemanticizing that photograph, his project resemanticizes the sociocultural experience of the class photograph, building for it a historical meaning quite supplementary to its original intent. In this sense, this is a photography of found objects, but where the object is, rather than a material constituent of the world the photographer records, another photograph that the photographer can make his own by virtue of the way in which he inscribes political process, that of memory as a response to the destructive forces of a historical holocaust.

Another dimension of Brodsky's title is the vagueness of the word *buena* and the way in which such a vagueness slips toward the oxymoronic because of its imprecise meaning. What might, in fact, constitute an appropriately "good memory"? Admittedly, a good memory is that of the consoling nostalgia of a past — and, likely, idealized — camaraderie. And equally so, it is the recollection of the sense of fulfillment represented by the orderly completion of academic studies in a social context promising emotional and material rewards for such a completion. But, given Argentine history subsequent to the time of the photograph and the graduation of the classmates it portrays, which the repeated frustration of democratic government, the grim and increasingly appalling application of regimes of neofascist tyranny, the roller-coaster cycles of the Argentine economy, the circumstances of disappearance, death, exile, against the backdrop of something like a collective psychosis, the promise of a functioning society for which the Colegio Nacional could be taken as a dominant icon could no longer be immediately apparent. Since this photograph can no longer be a synecdoche of the icon of the Colegio Nacional, itself in turn an icon of national aspirations, the question remains as regards into what system of meaning it might now be inserted.

My point is that there is an unstable calculus of meaning between *buena* and *memoria*, since it is unclear what memory is to be evoked nor why it is to be considered a good one. While it is true that, from an immediate point of view, the title can be read oxymoronically — the memory to be evoked, the disappearance and death of young citizens, can never be a "good" one — the important matter is to address the construction of an appropriately "good memory." It is for this reason that Brodsky's project is much more than a collection of photographs. The material object of his book does not consist strictly of photographs that are arranged together under a global title to produce a reality effect in terms of their interpretation of a specific sociohistorical universe: it is not a book of photographs about something.[1] It is, rather, a book about a photograph, one that Brodsky himself did not take, but one on which he has created an interpretational project and produced a book about in order to further interpret it. As a consequence, *Buena memoria* functions on four levels: (1) it is the material reality that has been embedded in (2) a photograph (even if it is the staged reality of a class picture); (3) it is the project that inserts that photograph in an interpretive context; and (4) it is a book publication that raises the stakes on that interpretation by supplementing it with an array of ancillary cultural products — specifically, other photographs and literary texts — in order to widen its sphere of meaning.

The novelist Martín Caparrós, in his comments on this project, makes the brilliant observation that the missing young women and young men of the 1967 class photo have experienced a double disappearance. Certainly, they were victims of the apparatus of disappearance of the military dictatorship, an apparatus that we could once again evoke in terms of the "processing of social subjects" that the system of persecution involved. So, then, let us evoke it just once more: arrest, torture, incarceration, death, disappearance of the remains, with going underground and exile partial optional paths in the logic of this sequence. At any point in this sequential chain, the individual ceases to exist for his or her respective social spheres, the hypostatized school class being only one — and, at that, perhaps a particularly tangential one — of them. Caparrós's point, however, is that the ignorance and denial of the circumstances of their lives constitute another level of disappearance, and we are as much distracted from contemplating the choices they made that led to their disappearance as we are from the disappearance itself:

> Eso significaba algo: era muy difícil discutir aquella política — era muy difícil hablar desde la sacralización de la democracia sobre una época en que la democracia era, cuando mucho, un valor instrumental — y, para no hablar de ellos como sujetos que habían tomado una opción política, era mejor transformarlos en víctimas, en objeto de la decisión de otros — unos señores malos que los habían ido a buscar a sus casas porque los malos son así y hacen esas cosas —.
>
> En esa acción de los malos, los nuestros se convertían en desaparecidos y en nuestros relatos sin historia nosotros volvimos a desaparecerlos: les quitamos sus vidas. Hablamos de cómo fueron objeto de

secuestro, tortura, asesinato y no hablamos casi de cómo era cuando fueron sujeto, cuando eligieron para sus vidas un destino que incluía el peligro de la muerte, porque creyeron que tenían que hacerlo. Aquellas versiones de la historia eran, entre otras cosas, una forma de volver a desaparecer a los desaparecidos [10].

Attentive to the details of grammar, Caparrós demonstrates by implication how the neologism *desaparecidos* is built on a past particle that functions in an underlying passive syntagm. The missing are the patients of an action done to them by others, "porque los malos son así." The problem for Caparrós is the denial of social subjectivity that comes from ignoring these patients as agents of their own active syntagm, in the sense that there were those things that they forthrightly choose to do, "cuando eligieron ... el peligro de la muerte." It is the restoration of the agency of these former classmates that is the point of Brodsky's memory project (an excellent collection of essays on the question of memory in contemporary Argentina is Dreizik).

Far from simply remembering who these individuals were and reminding their classmates and subsequent generations of classmates who they were and the fact that they were disappeared, *Buena memoria* seeks to restore their social subjectivity. The issue of social subjectivity is particularly noteworthy in this context, since the sort of bourgeois life, a life of talent, application, study, determination, recognition, and material and symbolic success, is what the Colegio Nacional is all about and what, presumably, the bulk of the students were aspiring to by going through its rigorous, demanding academic programs. This training led for many to ancillary aspirations (one can argue in another context whether the political commitment of these graduates was of a whole with the sociopolitical parameters of the Colegio or was an exceptional alternative to it), but theirs were aspirations driven by the considered decisions and deliberate enterprise one would assume to be associated with the students of an institution such as the Colegio Nacional.

The foregoing explains the ways in which Brodsky sets out to contextualize the found object of the class photograph. The annotations he makes on it, the texts with which he surrounds it, and the photographs of his own with which he supplements it. What I will now be calling the base photograph is presented reiteratively throughout, and it is accompanied by other photographs that are ancillary to it. Brodsky himself was a member of the 1967 6ta División class, and although the photograph was not taken by him, he figures prominently in it. In fact, the fragment of the photograph that appears on the cover of *Buena memoria* highlights two classmates, one of which (on the left) is Brodsky himself. The base photograph, which is repeated both in its entirety, in fragments like the cover image, and in terms of the framing of individual classmates whose lives and fates are subsequently analyzed, is complemented by other photographs. These ancillary photographs involve other school events of the period and include the members of a science class or a soccer match (both page 11); a school camping excursion (13). They also involve Brodsky family images from the period, such as a photograph of Brodsky and his brother (15); snaps taken at birthday parties (16, 17); the children during a family trip (17); brother Fernando sitting meditatively on his bed (14). And, finally, they involve photographs relating to Brodsky's memory project, the section entitled "Puente de la Memoria" (52–63) and other installations concerning students of the Colegio Nacional who were disappeared (10, 12). There are also three final appendixes to *Buena memoria* that I will comment on separately; they add further layers of meaning with reference to the base photograph.

Buena memoria is so complexly layered that it is difficult to speak of a central core. However, let us identify as such what is the central thrust of this collection of texts and images, which are the stories of disappeared Colegio Nacional students, with specific reference to those from Brodsky's own *promoción* or class. Thirty-two students appear in what I am calling the base photograph, eighteen of whom are boys (**Fig. 1.1**). Brodsky describes his work with this photograph in the following fashion:

Cuando regresé a la Argentina después de muchos años de vivir en España, acababa de cumplir cuarenta y quería trabajar sobre mi identidad. La fotografía, con su capacidad exacta de congelar un punto en el tiempo, fue mi herramienta para hacerlo.

Empecé a revisar mis fotos familiares, las de la juventud, las del Colegio. Encontré el retrato grupal de nuestra división en primer año, tomado en 1967, y sentí necesidad de saber qué había sido de la vida de cada uno.

Decidí convocar a una reunión de mis compañeros de división del

Colegio Nacional de Buenos Aires para reencontrarnos después de veinticinco años. Invité a mi casa a los que conseguí localizar, y les propuse hacer un retrato de cada uno. Amplié a un gran formato la foto del 67, la primera en que estábamos todos juntos, para que sirviera de fondo a los retratos y pedí a cada uno que llevara consigo para el retrato un elemento de su vida actual [...].

Resolví trabajar sobre la foto grande que me había servido para fotografiar a mis compañeros de división y escribir encima de la imagen una reflexión acerca de la vida de cada uno de ellos. La misma se completó posteriormente con un texto más extenso que acompaña los retratos [21].

The effect of this creative process is very much of a series of carefully composed images. In the first place, the idea of using the base photograph as a backdrop to the individual photographs Brodsky will take of each of those classmates who had been located and who had agreed to participate imposes a context of juxtaposition. It is not just the then-and-now of similar photograph exercises, such as one might compile to show the development of a child or to contrast a grounding event and its commemoration, paradigmatically a wedding and a fiftieth anniversary. The rather mechanical process of juxtaposition, in

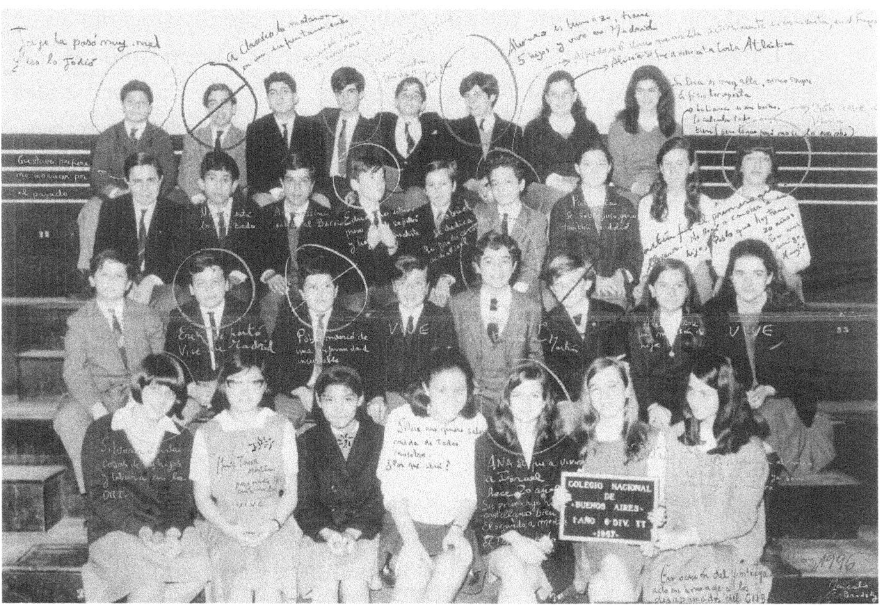

Fig. 1.1 (Marcelo Brodsky).

which one assumes as a matter of course there will be significant changes — with the nature and extent of those changes the whole point of the exercise — may produce interesting but not unexpected results. Where Brodsky's approach becomes both unique and exceptionally eloquent is in the absences that are recorded. Brodsky focuses on twenty-seven of the thirty-two students. However, two of those students are among the disappeared; no account is given of the other five. Now, it is not unexpected in realizing this sort of where-are-they-now? project to fail to contact everyone involved. The vagaries of life also result in old friends, long-lost relatives, and former classmates being irretrievably lost (one notes the recurring offer of Internet web sites that promise to help one find the individuals of one's past).

In the case of Brodsky's universe, the missing individuals exemplify much more than the "normal" vagaries of life, since they involve the specific workings of Argentine society relating to the period of the Process of National Reorganization and the Dirty War. Where the Dirty War did not contribute actively to the irretrievable disappearance of an individual, the general outlines of the Process forced many individuals into exile and a severance from their past roots. One of the arguments of the right against the documentation of the disappearances of the Dirty War is that the individuals registered as disappeared (as, for example, in the Anexo of *Nunca más*) were really self-imposed exiles who are enjoying a new identity somewhere outside Argentina or, perhaps, even still within the country. Many individuals did, of course, choose exile rather than fall into the hands of the forces of repression, and Brodsky himself exemplifies a generation of Argentines who were able to live and work outside Argentina, free from the danger and impossibility of doing so within the country. Exile, therefore, becomes a directly pertinent reason in the case of this project for the absence of a follow-up record for individuals, and the known disappearance of other individuals — Claudio and Martín, to be specific — accounts for the significant impossibility of the complete coverage of the sort of project Brodsky set up.

The fact that the base photograph, used as the backdrop for the follow-up pictures, is annotated becomes another element in the staged representation of experience. One assumes that it is as customary in Argentina as it is in other countries for class photos to be annotated with the names of one's classmates, with comments about them — serious, jocular, captious — and perhaps with slogans and dedications. Most photographs are social events, or integral to social events. Given what I have already said about the importance of class photographs, in the context of the monumentalization of the camaraderie of youthful academic experiences, what one might call the enhancement of a social photograph by written texts is not surprising. In this case, however, the written texts, rather than being contemporaneous with the photograph itself, are subsequent to it and record the weight of the twenty-five years of transpired history between when the photograph was taken and when Brodsky inserts his annotations. Martín Bercovich, according to the legend of the fragment of the base photograph that focuses on him, "fue secuestrado y está desaparecido desde el 13 de mayo de 1976" (42). This comment belongs to the level of the published book. On the level of the base photography, Brodsky's text, written in red grease pencil to accompany the bisected red circle around Martín's face that indicates his disappearance — his "prohibition" as part of the social realm of the living controlled by the apparatus of neofascism — reads: "Martín fue el primero que se llevaron. No llegó a conocer a su hijo, Pablo que hoy tiene 20 años. Era mi amigo, el mejor" (42). What Brodsky does in the case of Martín, as he does also in the case of Claudio Tisminetsky, the other classmate disappeared by security forces, is to include additional photographs from the period, since he cannot resort to the procedure of juxtaposing the picture from then with the image of who/what they are now. What is particularly touching about this strategy in the case of Martín is that it is a picture taken by Brodsky of Martín taking a picture of the former, "con su Kodak justo igual a la mía" on what appears to be an outdoor excursion (43).

Brodsky was already taking pictures at that time, and thus his own pictures from the period, most notably of his disappeared brother Fernando, are part of a continuum with the pictures taken of former classmates in the early 1990s. In this way, there is a whole series of textual strategies: (1) old and new photographs; (2) photographs by Brodsky and others; (3) texts by Brodsky and others; (4) texts by Brodsky on the photographs from that time to accompany photographs taken later. These all become a dense network of spaces: (1) the Colegio; (2) Brodsky's home; (3) the sites of the excursions and outings. They all become a dense network of times: (1) the moment of the original photograph; (2) Brodsky's annotations; (3) the events of twenty-five years — or less — in the lives of the classmates; (4) the moment of the complementary photograph; (5) the various expositions of this material; and, eventually, (6) its publication in book form. Each of these axes of time and place produce new and intersecting contexts or horizons of meaning, although there is always the microcontext of the vast enterprise to recover and revalidate memory within the framework of the perceived devastations of the Argentine Holocaust (whether or not with direct reference to the lives of Jews in Argentina under the military). The restoration of meaning to a lost/disappeared generation, even as it is made up of those who survived the Dirty War and its operations, has been going on since the return to constitutional democracy in Argentina, as part of concepts such as the redemocratization of Argentine culture (see Foster, *The Redemocratization*), the *Nunca más* investigations, and a myriad of exhibits such as *Cantos paralelos* (which traveled internationally; Ramírez) and *Arte y política de los años '60* (Giudice).

One could compile a huge bibliography of the diverse forms of cultural production —films, novels, theatrical works, essays — that have dealt with the issue of memory in Argentina, with the identification of the disappeared and, in Caparrós's terms, the integrity of their social subjectivity, in tandem with the passive nature of an emphasis on human rights abuses and the victimization of individuals. This is still an ongoing sociohistorical issue in Argentina, and Brodsky's work is an integral part of it.

An important semiotic element of Brodsky's follow-up pictures of his classmates is the request that their new, individual photos be taken with them holding some article that refers to their present life. The process of metonymy involved here signals many things. In the first place, it signals what they are in their current life — not to mention the fact that they *are* something. This is so since the disappeared classmates, not only because they cannot be present, but because they are disappeared, cannot be present with something from a current life, which, obviously, Claudio and Martín, at the very least, no longer have. Moreover, these articles signal what those who show them have become beyond and as a consequence of their training at the Colegio

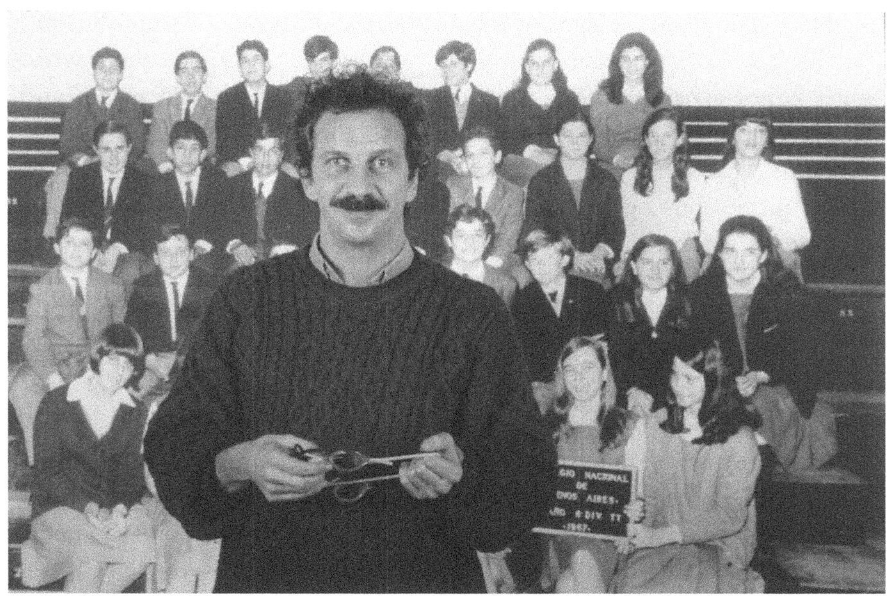

Fig. 1.2 (Marcelo Brodsky).

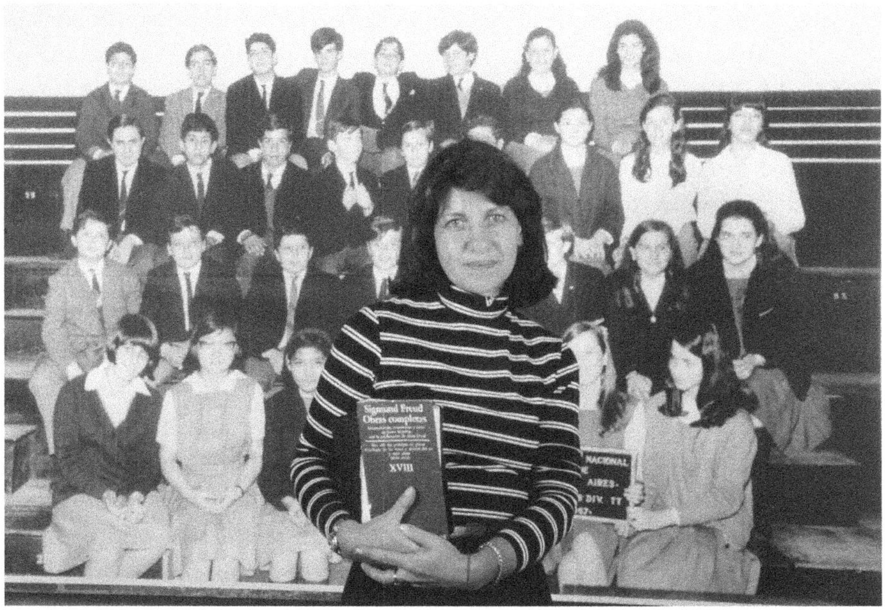

Fig. 1.3 (Marcelo Brodsky).

Nacional. They are signs of the profession, of the access to profession, that the Colegio Nacional training was meant to provide them with. It is not always obvious what the instruments they hold mean, and several do not have anything specific to show. For example, Juancho holds what looks like several pairs of scissors, but no explanation of his profession is given (51; **Fig. 1.2**). By contrast, Pablo, on the same page, is shown in his office at the Rockefeller Center, where he works for an international press agency. Etel holds a volume of the complete works of Freud in Spanish, but we are not told why (50; **Fig. 1.3**);Li-lia-na, who is a programmer, holds up a pocket calculator (39). And, not surprisingly, Brodsky's self-portrait (41) signifies his profession as a photographer (41): he directs an image agency.

The texts that accompany each follow-up photograph supplement and complement the grease-pencil annotations on the base photograph. Thus, in the case of Erik, on the base photograph, the pertinent fragment of which is always repeated on the double-page layout, the handwritten annotation reads "Erik se hartó[.] Vive en Madrid" (40), while in the follow-up photograph, he holds the base picture (we cannot see the handwritten comments on this scale), and the text accompanying the latter photograph speaks of his work in Madrid in his studio making silkscreens and woodcuts. The result of these conjunctions is a world of both accomplishment and frustration, of aspirations and their interruptions by grim historical facts. In reality, given all that transpired in Argentina during the twenty-five years between graduation and the follow-up photographs (more, given the four or five years between the base photograph and graduation), that Brodsky was able to track down so many former classmates and persuade them to participate in the project indicates how much, after all, Buenos Aires is still very much of a self-contained world. One does not wander far from Buenos Aires, and even when one does choose exile, roads eventually lead back to Buenos Aires, despite the large number of Argentine academics and professionals who have settled permanently abroad. This tight link is underscored in the photograph of Etel, where the accompanying texts, both the one handwritten on the base photograph and the one accompanying the follow-up photograph, refer to how her children are now themselves students of the Colegio Nacional. The latter reads: "Siempre se sorprende de cómo pasa el tiempo. Se vio a sí misma en la puerta del Colegio esperando a sus hijos salir del examen de ingreso y sintió que era ella la que estaba bajando las escaleras tras la prueba..." (50).

The tight link between then and now, between the generation of the base photograph and the generation of the children of those former students represented in the photograph, is borne out by the participation of the *Buena Memoria* project in a series of installations on the disappeared on the Colegio and the way in which these installations count on the active interest of contemporary students in the images and texts they contain. The appendix "Muestra en el claustro" reports on the installation of the base photograph and its accompanying visual and written texts in the entrance foyer of the Colegio:

> Como parte del acto [de memoria], se armó una exposición de fotos de la época [de la dictadura], para transmitir a los actuales alumnos del Colegio lo que había pasado. Las fotos eran algo que quedaba de los noventa y ocho compañeros [desaparecidos], una herramienta para convertirlos en personas concretas, próximas. Debíamos saber de qué y de quién estábamos hablando.
> Decidí incluir en la muestra fotográfica la foto grupal de 1er Año, modificada con mis textos y los retratos actuales de mis compañeros.
> Las fotos permanecieron expuestas en el Colegio durante unos días.
> La luz cenital del sol que atravesaba los enormes ventanales del claustro daba en la cara de los estudiantes que se detenían a observar, y producía un reflejo sobre el vidrio que protegía la foto intervenida.
> El retrato de esos reflejos constituye una parte fundamental de este trabajo, ya que representa el momento de la transmisión de la experiencia entre generaciones [54].

Aside from the emphasis on the intergenerational context of this photo — the former classmates become parents of the classmates who now study and comment on the exhibit — the placement of the exhibit in the Colegio Nacional adds new layers of meaning. In one sense, the classmates in the base photograph, particularly the missing ones, are returned to their lives prior to their disappearance, death, exile, and, in general, lives negatively affected by the events of the intervening years. The disappeared are converted into "personas concretas" via the reinsertion into the pre–Process/Dirty War history, which is a way of reconferring on them a full humanity. And it is this humanity that the current students of the Colegio Nacional contemplate, as they recognize in them and in the backgrounds, implied and explicit, their own current backgrounds in the halls of the Colegio Nacional. This is a circuit of meaning which those of us who see the exhibit, either as a physical installation or via the printed page, do not experience, but its presentation in *Buena memoria*, with the photographs of the current student-spectators and their accompanying written comments, is not difficult to grasp as another and particularly eloquent level of meaning. The implication is clear: these students are the new Argentine generation, one being raised within the relative parameters of constitutional democracy. It is less a question of remembering the best of the past or of vowing not to repeat the worst of it, but of creating a continuity of human society which is precisely what institutions like the Colegio Nacional exist to promote and deepen.

The photograph taken of the students examining the Puente de Memoria installation, which is the overall name of the various exhibits at the Colegio Nacional, not just Brodsky's, underscores the intergenerational relationship that the exhibit sought to establish (**Fig. 1.4**). The camera is situated behind the current students, who are examining the base photograph, which is under glass. The camera captures a fragment of the base photograph (the first row of classmates). Because of the position of the camera, the age of the photograph, and the intervening class, the images of the children in 1967 are faded and fuzzy. But we do make out four of them, with the even fuzzier grease-pencil annotations accompanying each one. Sharper and in vivid color are the images of four contemporary students who are examining the photographs and their accompanying annotations. The look of concentration and concern — one has a wrinkled brow — are evident correlatives of the seriousness with which they are studying this material. In other images, the students can be seen interacting more actively with the base photograph, as, for example, on page 56, we can see one student's hand blurred in motion as she points out details to another. A nice touch is that the children in the photograph are wearing the formal school clothes of the mid–1960s (from, at least, the sort of clothes required for the division photograph). The modern students are wearing casual clothes, and one is sporting the sort of white T-shirt with assertive lettering that is part of everyday school wear today. Moreover, the lettering is in English and asserts the sort of in-your-face declaration that would never have been possible during the military dictatorship of the

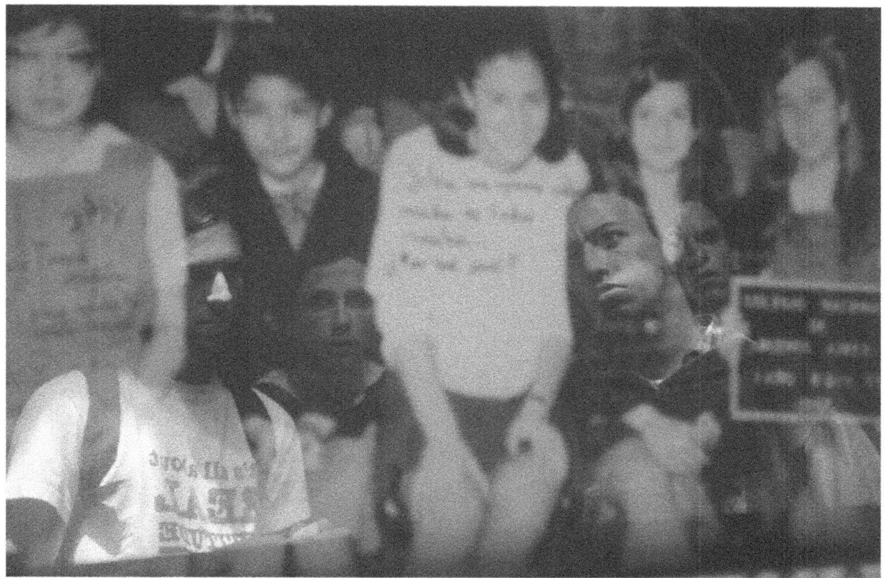

Fig. 1.4 (Marcelo Brodsky).

mid–1960s: "It's all about REAL *attitude.*" On the one hand, the T-shirt, its abrasive message, and the fact that it's in English signal the enormous distance between these youths and their peers of an earlier generation, quite apart from the difference of circumstance: regular school day vs. formal class portrait.

On the other hand, the blending of the two generations in the single photograph underscores the continuity between human generations and the reverence for that continuity that the project seeks to promote. Of note in this regard is the image on page 57, where the face of one of the contemporary students is captured being framed by the sign board that identifies the year and division which is held by one of the young women of the base photograph. This detail is enhanced by the annotation, on the base photograph, that we read regarding one of the 1967 students: "Silvia no quiere saber nada de nosotros. ¿Por qué será?" It seems evident that the modern students, by contrast, do want to have something to do with their classmates from the past. As one student writes in her text published alongside this photograph, "Ellos eran más peligrosos que nosotros porque tenían ideas muy claras y solidarias y estaban más unidos que nosotros. Tratemos de lograr eso sin

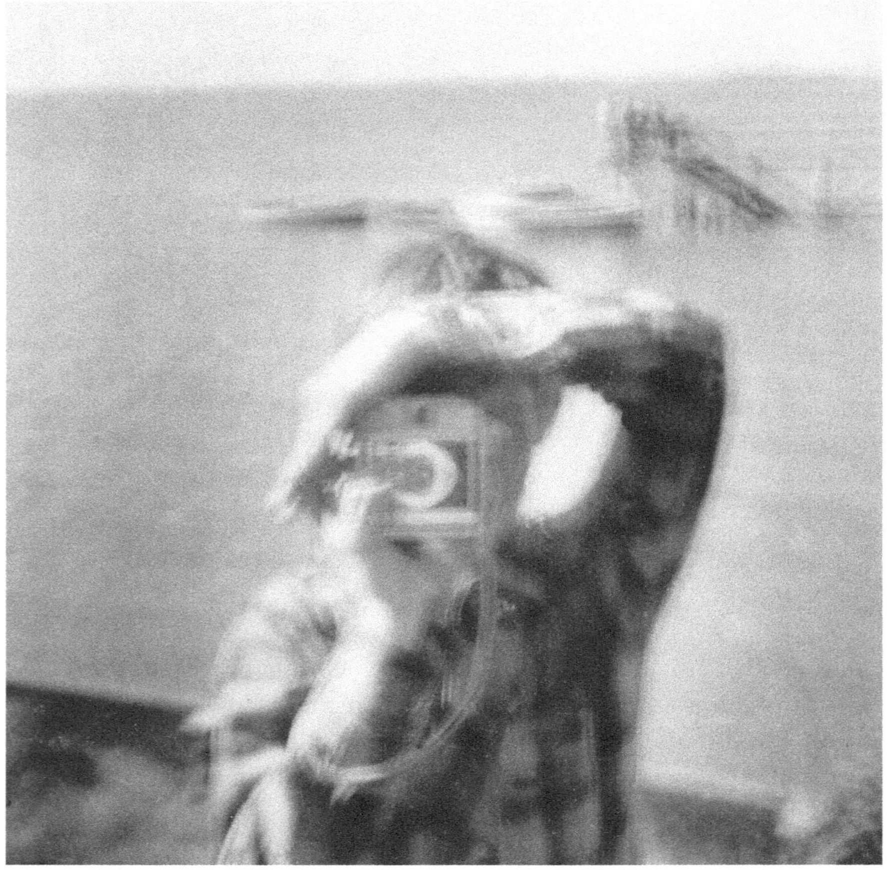

Fig. 1.5 (Marcelo Brodsky).

que nos vuelvan a reprimir de esa manera o de cualquier otra forma" (57). The hortatory he is a controlling predicate of the installation.

There is a second appendix to *Buena memoria*, "Martín, mi amigo," in which Brodsky returns to his disappeared classmate, Martín Bercovich, whom he had identified in the memory project as his best friend. Martín, like the young Marcelo, was also a photographer, and, as I have already commented, the impossible photograph of Martín twenty-five years later is replaced by one taken by Brodsky of Martín taking his (**Fig. 1.5**), Brodsky's, photograph. This photograph is repeated in an enlarged version on page 66 of *Buena memoria*; page 67 contains a photograph of Martín on an excursion, his own camera hanging from a strap around his neck. These two photographs are presented with the header "Podíamos ser fotógrafos." This header is ironic on at least two levels. First of all, the two boys were already photographers, even if only in an unfocused and untutored way. Yet even without knowing that these photographs would record a disappeared Martín, they were already taken with one of the major impulses of photography in mind: to provide a graphic memory of shared personal experiences, and they stand as monuments to the deep friendship between the two young men. Brodsky, in addition to the testimony of their friendship provided by the photographs, also includes a side-bar poem dedicated to Martín, which concludes with the statement "Seguí andando, solo / con tu presencia a cuestas." The second irony is, indeed, the fact not only that Brodsky continued to be able to live his life, but that he did, indeed, become a photographer in the fullest sense of the word and that he is able to recycle the photographs Martín and he took of each other within a formal cultural product devoted to the memory of the disappeared. In this sense, the personal is most assuredly political. The personal relationship between the two young men and the casual artistic production it generated, their shared photographs, become part of a political statement made about the uses of cultural production and the use of a public cultural production to pursue the specific political objective of promoting a memory of the texture of human lives of the victims of a neofascist (and, here, undoubtedly anti–Semitic) military regime.

The focus on Martín is complemented by the third appendix, "Nando, mi hermano," in which Brodsky returns to the figure of his brother Fernando. Fernando was not a photographer, although their mother was, and her photographs are included, including one that won a local prize. Although some of these photographs are presumably Brodsky's from when he was just beginning to handle the camera, the source is not always identified. Thus, their presence here does not speak directly to Brodsky the adult as photographer, in the way that the follow-up pictures I have discussed above do. Rather, they are part of the overall project that results in *Buena memoria* as such a complex cultural projection of the Colegio Nacional students. In this sense, the photographs relating to Fernando constitute the most extensive record in *Buena memoria* of the texture of a human life that was snuffed out by the practices of the military dictatorship in the late 1970s.

If Brodsky's insistent point, as set forth by Caparrós above at the outset of this essay, is the imperative to replace the status as victims of these individuals with a reaffirmation of their personhood, then the intimate family photographs — and it is an intimacy confirmed on the multiple levels of the personal relationship of the subject to Brodsky, the importance of family life in Argentina, and the characteristically solid ties of Jewish family life — are integral to the brother Fernando's recovered human life. In this context, the pathos of the family snap on page 74 is intense. It is a full-page photograph, which bleeds off the page on all four margins, of the three Brodsky children in a rowboat on the river at the Club Náutico Hacoaj, one of the social clubs that dot the Río de la Plata estuary as it stretches out into the suburbs northwest of the city of Buenos Aires; note that in this case it is a Jewish club (**Fig. 1.6**). In the fashion of such photographs, the three Brodsky children are hamming it up for the camera; as the accompanying text states: "Salir en bote juntos era la actividad familiar por exelencia" (75). The joy of these children in each other's company is evident on their faces. Fernando is in the foreground, and his smile and the roguish look in his eyes are tremendously captivating. The look on the faces of the other two children are also equally enchanting, but it is, of course, Fernando on whom we are meant to focus. Since the dossier of photographs is about him, one assumes that this one was chosen over others because of his foregrounded presence in it.

The theme of the dark waters of the Río de la Plata occurs twice in this dossier, and it is picked up again for the book's last page. The river is characteristically dark and muddy because of the continental silt that flows into it. The Río de la Plata is really not a river, but an estuary that brings together the affluence of many rivers that come down across the continent from the highlands. As it empties into the ocean, the river deposits enormous quantities of silt, which necessitates the constant dredging of the port area of Buenos Aires. The silt content of the river means the waters are always murky, and there is the constant danger of submerged objects that cannot be seen. As Brodsky remarks in his note accompanying the photograph in the rowboat, "Nos acostumbramos a sus aguas oscuras, a no zambullirnos de cabeza porque podía haber un tronco flotando bajo el agua." The river contains much debris that comes down off the continent, and this is the reference to the *tronco* in Brodsky's comment.

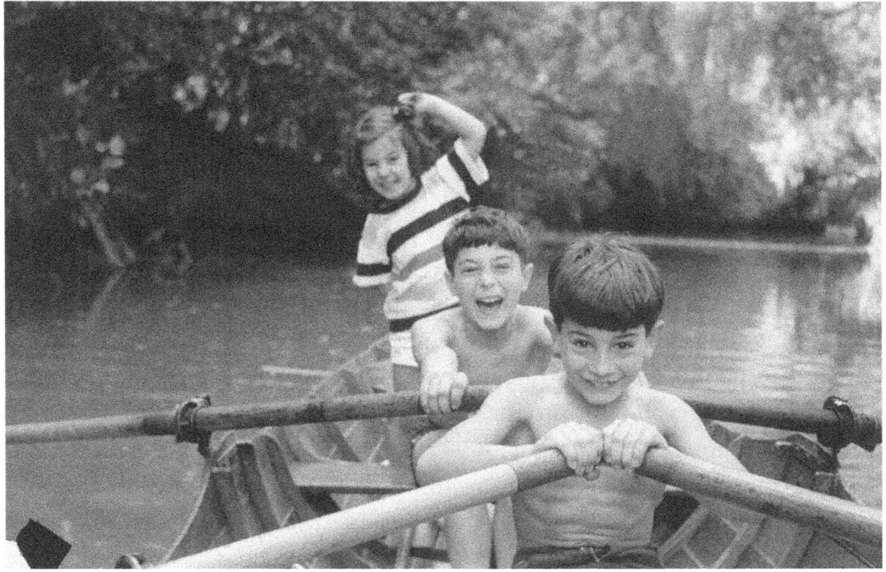

Fig. 1.6 (Marcelo Brodsky).

However, the river, during the height of the Dirty War in the late 1970s, also carried other debris in the form of the bodies of political prisoners who were dumped off the coast of the city from military aircraft, many of them still alive and heavily sedated. Brodsky refers directly to this detail of the repression by the double page 86–87 image, the right-hand panel of which is repeated as the last page of the book: "Al río los tiraron. Se convirtió en su tumba inexistente." The practice summarized here can be seen elaborated on in Marco Bechis's 1999 film *Garage Olimpo*, in which the overflight of the river is a recurring motif, although only at the end of the film do those spectators unfamiliar with the dumping practice of the military discover what the connection is between the overflights and the detention and torture center that gives its name to the film (it is a reconditioned automotive garage; hence the name). In turn, the double image of pages 86 and 87 and the image from page 87 that becomes the last page (88) are meant to tie in to the images on pages 84–85. Page 84 is a picture of Brodsky's uncle Salomón, who arrived at the turn of the twentieth century as a European immigrant; these immigrants arrived in the promised land of Argentina exclusively by boat, and for many their first photographs in the New World were related to the circumstances of their arrival: "Su imagen desafía el futuro, su postura lo espera todo" (84). This affirmation is the sort of paean one finds associated with the aspirations of immigrants, and it becomes pathetically frustrated by the sorts of violence many of them and their descendants found in the new country.

In the case of the Jewish immigrants, although Brodsky does not make specific reference to this fact, that violence often included anti–Semitism, which was a fundamental part of the neofascist military regime. Brodsky juxtaposes to the photograph of his uncle one of him and Fernando, also taken aboard a ship traversing the waters of the river. This photograph falls into the category of the cutely staged, as they are standing next to a sign that pointedly says "Prohibido permanecer en este lugar." There are many meanings available here, beyond that of the innocent joke of specifically taking a picture standing next to a sign saying that one could not be in that spot. "Este lugar" could also refer to the frustrated promise of Argentina: for those who suffered anti–Semitic violence, the point was that they were there where someone, institutionally or otherwise, was forbidding them to be, and the subsequent exile of many immigrant children meant a return to the Europe from which their ancestors had departed with so much hope almost a century before. But it can also mean the way in which the bodies dumped into the river were "forbidden to remain" there, like dead tree trunks that floated up against vessels out on the river or along the shore. This is the sense of the phrase "tumba inexistente," as many individuals died by being thrown from planes into the river, and some may have found a final resting place in the depths of the river. But many washed ashore, and there hangs over this entire account the question, was Fernando among them?

* * *

In 2001 Brodsky published *Nexo: un ensayo fotográfico*, which takes up again many of the themes of *Buena memoria*. Especially prominent is the space he once again devotes to his brother. But there is more of a general concern with the topic of memory, no longer tied specifically to the base photograph of the early volume. There is a concern for the recovery of items associated with repression and exile and the utilization of various strategies of photomontage to record those items and to place them in meaningful contexts. Of particular interest is the utilization of such photographs in an exposition like the base photograph of *Buena memoria* in installations at the Feria del Libro in Buenos Aires, along with photographs that record viewer reactions to the installations. These installations were made up of found books, books that had been buried in the ground to hide them from the raids of the forces of the regime, who considered many specific titles as prima facie evidence that those who had them in their possession could be legitimately eliminated as enemies of the state (see *Un golpe a los libros* for a study of print censorship during the dictatorship).

Also of extreme interest are the photographs that record the utilization of the remains from the 1994 bombing of the AMIA (Asociación Mutualista Israelí-Argentina — the Jewish community center) in the creation of the landfill along the waterfront of the Río de la Plata in the northern area of the city close to the Ciudad Universitaria, an area developed as a memorial to the disappeared of the Dirty War. The tie-in here is evident. Since the river played such an important role in the disappearance of an unknown number of victims of the repression, it is also significant that it became the dumping ground of yet another manifestation of the country's history of political violence, the bombing, during democracy, of the AMIA (and in 1992 the Israeli Embassy was bombed, also after the return to democracy).

If the military repression of the late 1970s had a strong strain of anti–Semitism, these two bombings were specifically anti–Semitic acts,[2] and it is fitting that there is also at that site, alongside the memorial to the victims of the disappearances, a memorial to the victims of the AMIA blast.[3]

2

Gabriel Valansi: Neoliberal Nights in Buenos Aires

Gabriel Valansi (b. 1959) works as both a professor of photography at the University of Buenos Aires and as an artistic advisor at the Museo de Arte Moderno de Buenos Aires. He is also a collaborator with the photography magazine *Fotomundo* (Buenos Aires, 1966–).[1]

Valansi's work is radically set off from that of the other participants in the International Center of Photography exhibit in New York. It essentially does not directly feature human figures; it concentrates on a nocturnal cityscape; and it is determinedly "anti-aesthetic" in the sense of using not only found objects, but ones that appear to have been abandoned as garbage — junk and no longer useful, damaged, and/or trashed objects (for theoretical works on trash/rubbish, see Thompson; Rathje; see Prignano for the Porteño context; Sánchez de Balcero provides, as a point of comparison, a study based on Bogotá).[2] Like other photographers in the ICP exhibit, Valansi makes almost exclusive use of black and white images, albeit ones of enormously high resolution that enable very large contact prints. Yet, ambiguity of image is essential to much of Valansi's work. While one can draw a certain global sense from the series, there are individual images that do not immediately lend themselves to objective identification, and they appear to fluctuate between impressionistic foregrounded patterns of light and a fragmentation of the outlines of images expected within conventional horizons of familiarity. Indeed, some perhaps might even find "surreal" appropriate here because of the possibility of perceiving a dreamlike landscape. These qualities are abetted by the nocturnal loss of foreground/background perspective. Although Valansi has also dealt with other themes, he possesses an established identity because of his work in the city of Buenos Aires in the deep hours of the night, and it is this cycle of work on which I will concentrate in the present analysis of his photography, in a 1998 series titled *Fatherland,* which in turn is part of a series of related projects, *Zeitgeist* (2000) and *Epílogo* (2000–2001).

To speak of the deep hours of the Porteño night is almost to speak of a No Man's Land, since one might well ask when is there ever a "deep night" in Buenos Aires, when is there a time of the night when the streets are empty of human comings and goings, when businesses are closed, and the intense combination of Argentine sociability and an imperative to live it out on the street declines. To be sure, one of the effects of neoliberalism in Argentina has been to sharpen class divisions and to produce an increasing class of individuals excluded from the sort of prosperity that has made Argentine public life so unique in Latin America — at least, a public life in terms of superavit consumption, the display of cultural accomplishments, and, simply, the enjoyment of the virtues of the flâneur. In a city in which in many sectors (especially the older commercial ones and the prosperous northern tier of neighborhoods that stretch west along the Río de la Plata), night only ends with the first weak light of morning.

This image of the City That Never Sleeps is, in any event, part of the public image of the city, and not one necessarily associated with tourism, because Buenos Aires has never been much of a city of international tourism. There are, certainly, tourists from the interior and tourists from surrounding Latin American countries, not to mention the happenstance tourism of a constituency of business types passing through the capital with a night or so at their disposal to see what the tango, etc., are all about. The Porteño barrios, all one hundred of them by legendary count, are not exactly deserted late at night. But the entire city is hardly an extension of the traditional image of the Great White Way of Avenida Corrientes — or of wherever the night life of Corrientes went with the decay of the old downtown and the emergence, with neoliberalism, of new nuclei of leisure, culture, and entertainment

(Puerto Madero, Retiro, La Recoleta, San Telmo, Flores, Palermo Chico, Palermo Viejo, La Costanera, Belgrano, and so on, not to mention places outside the city along the river; on Argentine nightlife in the city, see Gorbato).

Indeed, part of the context of this photography is the fact that neoliberalism cast a pall over the nightlife of the central core (a pall, it must be stressed, that began to be felt way back in the 1970s before the neoliberal process that began in the early 1990s). This involved not only encouraging its movement elsewhere, through the construction and promotion of new venues, but also as a consequence of the impoverishment of much of middle-class life neoliberalism brought with it, along with the subsequent profound devastation of overwhelming sectors of Argentine society since the closing months of 2001. In one sense, any perception of a deep night in at least the old central core of the city is an index of that process, to the extent that it is a direct consequence of it.

Moreover, Valansi's work, especially what I will be examining here, comes on the cusp of the transition from a still more-or-less functioning neoliberalism to what, without overstating the case, must now be identified as something like the Third-Worldization of Argentina. Argentina, and especially the capital Buenos Aires (huge sectors of the country were already increasingly impoverished by neoliberalism well before the last quarter of 2001), is now facing the prospect of having to live like the rest of Latin America. The most immediate manifestation of this is how the illegal workers from countries peripheral to Argentina who poured into Buenos Aires to sustain the underbelly of neoliberalism, as portrayed in Adrián Caetano's Dogma-style film *Bolivia* (2001), have fled the country for their respective homelands. If they are going to starve in the streets, they might as well do so back home; besides, there is the threat that the streets are going to be pretty much taken up by starving Argentines.

The series of images analyzed in this study is part of Valansi's 1998 exhibit *Fatherland*, at the FotoGalería del Teatro San Martín, the most important official cultural space of the Municipality of Buenos Aires. In an interview with Pablo Garber in *libroarte.com*, Valansi has the following to say about this series of forty photographs:

> "Fatherland" es una continuidad de [la] idea de "fines de fiesta", pero a
> la vez es un registro de lo que yo llamo "los holocaustos encubiertos",

que son esos holocaustos que no son mediáticos ni tienen resultados espectaculares, con muerte y desolación. Tienen un armado más sutil, y (entre comillas) son aceptados por el mundo libre, pero en definitiva siguen siendo holocaustos.... [La idea de "Fatherland" es] tratar de dar pistas, que tienen que ver con un registro "neutrónico", o sea, que no dejan muertos, ni cráteres, pero que existen. Y como la Argentina vivió sus holocaustos, y vive uno; intenté contar esa historia en "Fatherland".

Valansi makes specific reference to Robert Harris's 1992 novel *Fatherland* about the Holocaust, and this reference provides an enormous resonance to his work, in which he counts on a series of cultural references in the Argentine sociopolitical consciousness. In the first place, as I have already stated, Argentina has a special relationship to the Jewish holocaust, not just because Buenos Aires is home to many holocaust survivors, but because Argentina enjoyed historically a large German immigrant population. Adolf Eichmann's arrest there brought world attention to the Nazi influence in Argentina, which was not only strong throughout the 1930s and the war, but also — as is legendarily known — included Argentina becoming, during the first Peronista government (1946–52), a haven for Nazi war criminals like Eichmann (Camarasa, Goñi).

Additionally, the fact that the military regimes of recent decades (1966–73, 1976–83) were overtly modelled along neo-Nazi lines has kept alive a sense of a "fascist tradition" in Argentine (Viñas; *The Argentine Right*), the slang adjective *facho*, derived from the more academic *fascista*, is in daily use to describe an abiding authoritarian mentality and forms of behavior alleged to embody it. Valansi is himself Jewish, and so it is understandable that he would be particularly sensitive to not only a *facho* strand in the Argentine national ethos ("Lo que este país necesita es una mano dura" [What this country needs is a strong hand] is a common refrain), but as his adjective *encubierto* signals, to the ideological processes by which this mentality is ignored, argued away, hidden, or transformed into something else.

The return to constitutional democracy in Argentina and the much-touted trial of the military officers that made up the ruling Juntas, along with many of their most notorious subalterns, were evidence of a shift in the country's institutional climate. Yet the violence of the Menem years (the 1990s) was manifest — all too apparently, for example — in the virtually officially sanctioned persecution of journalists.

The also virtually officially sanctioned depredations of corruption, by agents of the government and segments of the business and banking communities and their shared cohorts, and the economic upheaval wreaked by neoliberalism may be interpreted as the sort of "hidden holocaust" that Valansi has in mind. It was hidden not that people did not know that violence was taking place, but rather because the mass of its victims — the common folk — were never consistently recognized as such. Indeed, the synergetic effects of unchecked neoliberalism and flagrant corruption have brought the country to a point of stagnation, exhaustion, and despair that are quite unprecedented. It is not that Argentina is alone in Latin America in terms of major social problems, but it is far easier to point to the photographable consequences of public violence in, say, Colombia than it is to the hidden violence in Argentina.

But yet Valansi's point would be that that violence is now not quite so hidden. Others may photograph the evidence of that violence in terms of the victims of street crime that has turned the once absolutely safe Buenos Aires into a place as dangerous as any other metropolitan center. There was for long the curious way in which Buenos Aires was always marvelously safe despite the repressive acts of what the activist Eduardo Luis Duhalde (not to be confused with the recent Argentine president of the same name) once called the "terrorist state," and this was not just because of the facile belief that fascism makes for safe streets. Others may also photograph the creeping way in which a megacity with narrow streets and many buildings now over a century old can, all of a sudden, began to show clear signs of decay; and at that, even at the height of the prosperity induced by neoliberalism in the early 1990s, public buildings were never very well maintained.

Valansi's photography takes a much more subtle approach to the recording of social reality in the context of the ongoing holocaust of economic violence. In the first place, human figures are absent from his work. There is the standing belief that "real" photography, with the exception of utilitarian photography that aims no more than to provide a record of a space, a building, a device, or a situation, is artistic to the extent that includes a human presence. The one exception that is generally accepted is nature photography, in which the beauty of flora and fauna may be prized to the extent that man — at least, modern man — is absent. Civilization is usually viewed, as is trenchantly apparent in denunciatory ecophotography of the sort practiced by the Brazilian Sebastião Salgado, as destructive of nature and the environment: this belief extends far beyond those in the ecological movement, such as to make even the kitschiest images of the landscape or animal life valued for their decorative and presumedly soothing qualities.

But what of the exclusion of human figures, especially in the built environment of the city, where the "human interest" presence is understood to give meaning to, often casually, urban backdrops? Certainly, there are urban monuments that have merited their own interpretive photographic record, especially ones that are related to major historical, social, and political events (e.g., the veritable kitschification of the Statue of Liberty, the Golden Gate Bridge, and — dare I say it? — the Twin Towers of the World Trade Center). A cliche of grade-B sci-fi movies is the eery sensation of the city devoid of human figures as a metaphoric harbinger for the disappearance from the planet of the human species. So, too, any photograph of a segment of urban reality in which human beings are not present is sensed to be at best nostalgic ("this was someplace where people once lived") or disturbingly dehumanized ("where are the people who [must] live here?"). The fact that the built human environment was built by human beings to serve specific human needs, while also being adapted, expropriated, reclaimed for complementary and supplementary needs, is both what may disturb some viewers because of the absence of human beings who depend on the built environment for livelihood and survival and what may make some viewers experience feelings of dehumanization. The absence of human beings would seem to negate the need for the building, and many routinely feel that abandoned buildings and sites need to be recycled, rebuilt, or cleared because they allegedly constitute eyesores, if not places of and for crime and assorted delinquency. It is, therefore, rather difficult to be convincing as regards a poetry of vacancy or the absence of human figures.

Yet, there is a poetics to be associated with viewing such spaces, to the extent that there is a fairly evident point to be made about their configuration as a consequence of the momentarily or perhaps even permanently absent humanity. Thus, archeologists routinely draw important conclusions about the nature of human life from the ruins left behind by disappeared people, and a sort of human geography allows us to view an urban scape and speculate as to features of the people who may live there, both in terms of how they have built that environment to meet their needs, and of how the already built environment shapes their understanding and satisfaction of their needs. And there is another way in which we can view the sort of vacant spaces being discussed here, which is in terms of why they are vacant. That is, in a version of the sci-fi films mentioned above, where vacancy has occurred because of some monstrous catastrophe of space aliens, a mystery virus, or whatever, something has caused these spaces to become vacant.

In the case of night scenes, certainly the vacancy occurs because of the routine abandonment of certain spaces as part of the established or conventional rhythm of social life. However, such vacancy is relative. In Buenos Aires there has customarily been a greater visibility of people out and about at night, with, concomitantly, a larger number of so-called night spots. So one of the interests in photographing the night becomes as much this greater utilization of public spaces at night as it is, through counterpoint, a perception of the decline of such utilization.

This is, precisely, what is at issue, at least in an initial approximation to them, in the bulk of the entries in the *Fatherland* exhibit, and I will now turn to these images in order to demonstrate how they constitute an interpretation of the effects of neoliberalism on Argentina — as viewed through the economically and sociopolitically centralizing city of Buenos Aires — and how that liberalism constitutes a hidden holocaust in a society for which "the party is over" (hence, the name *Epílogo* for a follow-up series to *Fatherland*).

Valansi's opening image (**Fig. 2.1**), the one that is the signature piece for the exhibition, is intriguingly mysterious. From a distance, the image appears to be an impressionistic pattern consisting of a dark background with a foregrounded pattern of glowing white spots. A line of smaller white spots snakes up the image vertically and elbows off to the left, only to return to a perpendicular position as it bleeds off the top of the image. Around this central line smaller clusters of dots organize themselves into a combination of rectangles and random

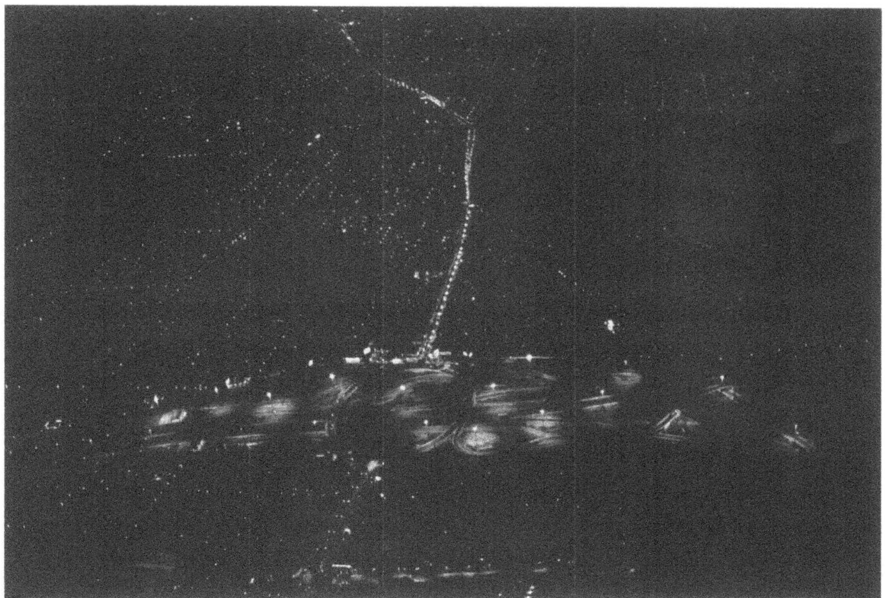

Fig. 2.1 (Gabriel Valansi).

clusters. Closer inspection, however, reveals that the spots are the lights that one would typically associate with a nighttime cityscape: high intensity street lights (or perhaps a combination of high intensity and medium intensity ones), lighted billboards, car lights (note, however, that it has only been the enormous increase in car traffic in the city that has brought the mandatory use of high beams), and some buildings. The pattern that emerges on the basis of the discovery that this is a nighttime cityscape is that of a part of the city in which a freeway, with its looping access ramps, constitutes the horizontal axis of the image, with an exit to an important arterial that travels up the image and bleeds off its top margin. The rectangular patterns are formed by lower intensity lights that border major and minor streets and mark the parameters of city blocks.

The relative irregularity of these patterns would seem to suggest that this is the central core of the city, as befits a city whose definitive foundation dates from 1580 (there was an abandoned attempt to found Buenos Aires in 1536). While a long way from being as randomly non-geometric as medieval European cities, it is made up of relatively small blocks that are often poorly lighted, whose geometry is often interrupted by diagonals, alleyways, and bisecting and irregularly drawn boulevards; the phenomenon of "streets that don't go through" is frequent in the central core.[3] Since the rectangles in the image are not punctuated very much by other points of light, one can believe that the time is very late. That is, there are few white spots that can be attributed to the lights of houses or businesses located within the blocks.

I am speaking in such detail about this perceived layout of the city, as the inaugural image makes a defining statement of the sequence of photographs as a whole. And that is done in terms of the juxtaposition between the freeway and the necessarily older arterial that feeds into it. I say older because it is likely the arterial was there before the freeway, especially in view of its irregular line.[4] But even if the freeway is a symbol of modernity, there are not all that many in Buenos Aires (just as there are, generally speaking, not many in all of Latin America): they are too expensive to build and maintain, and their installation is too disruptive of a residential, commercial, and industrial life that is often precarious enough without the effects of massive relocation.[5] There are some design and execution problems with the freeways the military imposed on the city beginning in the 1970s. Indeed, it is easy to believe that the freeways could only have been built by a tyrannical regime powerful enough to ignore common needs. Yet there is no question that these roads have been important for the commercial and industrial life of the city, especially in providing rapid access to the Ezeiza international airport, some twenty miles west of downtown and previously extremely difficult to get to because the traveler departing from the administrative and financial center had to cross the entire city before reaching the two-lane highway that completed the journey to Ezeiza.

Moreover, confirming the proposition that if you build freeways, the cars will come, the three- or four-fold increase in cars in Buenos Aires that came with neoliberalism would have been virtually impossible without the freeway, and the same is true of the residential development of the suburbs west, northwest and southwest of the city that have been prized as part of the American lifestyle whose incorporation — or implantation — was crucial to neoliberalism. Thus, where this image becomes eloquent is in juxtaposing the traditional arterial, which owes its irregular line to having developed in conformance to geographic irregularities and the gradual urban growth of the city, and the modern freeway, which cuts a brutal swath across the cityscape, creating massive disruptions and dislocations and often constituting an abiding environmental problem for the neighborhoods through which it passes. While it is possible to control fumes and noise, as many European and American cities assure they are doing with their freeway networks, the increase in traffic and concomitant traffic-related accidents is not something that can be controlled, since, quite the contrary, an increase in traffic is exactly what the freeway is meant to produce (one of the best examinations of the urban consequences of freeways is Davis's discussion of the issues surrounding the creation of freeways in that paradigm of the freewayed city, Los Angeles).

It is appropriate that Valansi use an image of the freeway as the signature piece of the *Fatherland* exhibit. Other manifestations of neoliberalism proper (e.g., the system specifically imposed at the beginning of the Menem government in the early 1990s, as dictated by the U.S. government and the International Monetary Fund) can rapidly disappear, as they have already begun to do so — i.e., specialty stores importing foreign goods. But the freeway is virtually a permanent monument, and short of falling so much into disrepair that it can no longer be used, it is unlikely that it will disappear merely because the economic system of which it is a part disappears. Moreover, the freeways were actually part of a promodernization project that goes back to the military regimes, well before neoliberalism proper, but yet is integral to the sort of ruthless capitalism, mediated by staggering corruption, that those regimes supported and that, under the aegis of constitutional democracy, the Menem government legitimated.[6]

The large-scale image of the city of the anchor photograph of *Fatherland* is complemented by several other views of the urban landscape in general. There is one, for example, that is a map of the midsection of the country, one that is also built on lights indicating population concentrations (**Fig. 2.2**; I do not know if this is a formal demographic representation, or if is a figurative one created by Valansi). The result is to show the enormous preponderance of the Provincia of Buenos Aires and, within it, of the city of Buenos Aires. Argentina is

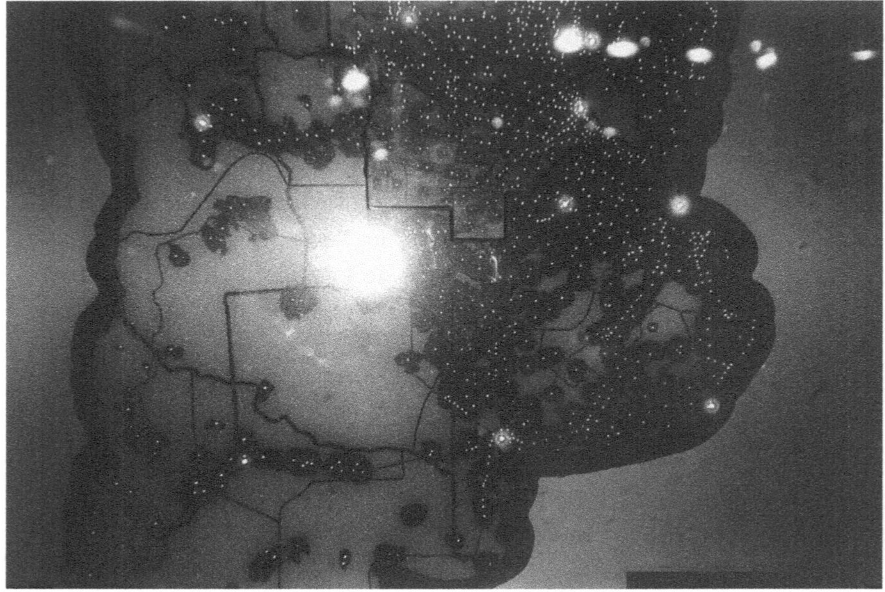

Fig 2.2 (Gabriel Valansi).

accused of living with its back to the rest of Latin America, but the Province of Buenos Aires lives with its back to the rest of Argentina. And the city of Buenos Aires lives with its back to the rest of the Province and the rest of the country and the rest of the continent. There is a long history of struggle relating to the role of Buenos Aires. The creation of La Plata in 1880 to serve as a decentralized capital of the Province was meant to address the power imbalance between Buenos Aires and the rest of the Province of Buenos Aires, and the designation of Buenos Aires in 1996 as an autonomous federal capital was intended to separate the responsibility of the city for its own administration, independent from the federal budget off which it had grown accustomed to living. In 1940 the social essayist Ezequiel Martínez Estrada published *La cabeza de Goliath*, in which he posited a master trope for the relationship between Buenos Aires and the rest of the country, that of the enormous head and the feeble body. This trope became all the more apparent with recent economic processes, because so much of the rest of the country experienced growing impoverishment alongside the overwhelming concentration of capital in Buenos Aires.

The migration of *cabecitas negras* from outlying provinces, mostly to the north, begun during the Peronista period and under very different ideological, social, and economic circumstances, nevertheless continued and intensified because there was no work to be had except in Buenos Aires.[7] It was complemented by the aforementioned sunsequent influx of *cabecitas negras* from surrounding Latin American countries.[8] In Valansi's photograph, the all-roads-lead-to-Rome concentration of lights in the Buenos Aires area is an echo of the liberalization of the metaphor, in the sense that it duplicates the very real way in which the railroad system of the nineteenth-century liberal economy was designed to carry Argentine exports to the port for shipment to Europe and the imported European luxury items to the mansions of the city and the rural estates of the wealthy exploiters/producers of those exports (the history of this development is told by Scobie). These lights are, in turn, complemented by the lights of other urban concentrations of the country, such as the subsidiary cities of Córdoba, Mendoza, Rosario.

However, the photograph is very effectively dominated by the reflection, in dead center, of the flash of the photographer's camera. This dead-centering of the flash has no function in terms of artistic symmetry. Rather, it is meant to correlate with—and predominate over—the lights of Buenos Aires and other urban, commercial, and financial centers, as the constituting punctum of the photographer's interpretation, by falling on the northern part of the Province of La Pampa, partially blotting out the spot on the map Valansi uses where the capital city of Santa Rosa is located. The Province of La Pampa is the Argentine heartland, and its name is the very geographic designation that is most famously associated with the land of Argentina, the vast Pampa that supports its historically most important and prosperous industry, cattle-ranching. Interestingly enough, in the schematic map of Argentina that I have at hand, prepared by the Instituto Geográfico Militar, this area is represented as minimally settled (*Atlas de la República Argentina*). This is true literally in the sense that it is part of a network of small towns that tie together the vast cattle ranches of this and the other provinces of the industry, La Pampa, Córdoba, Santa Fe, and Buenos Aires. In this sense, there is the evocation of the symbiosis linking Buenos Aires and the cattle ranches that is integral to so much of Argentine social and political history.

But there is another way of reading this image, and that is in terms of the devastation of the countryside by the neoliberal concentration of the metropolis and its satellite cities. In the case of the old liberal economy, there was something like a balanced exchange between the countryside and the port city (or port cities, since Rosario, up-river from Buenos Aires, is also a major shipping port). The countryside produced the export wealth, a percentage of which Buenos Aires got at the customs port; the imports this wealth bought were distributed between the wealthy *estancias* (the cattle ranches) and the city that served their interests. Indeed, it was customary for the cattle barons to have, in addition to their often quite magnificent country mansions [*Nuestras estancias*], fancy apartments or equally magnificent mansions in the city. The large-scale development of industry spurred by Perón beginning in the late 1940s upset this balance, beginning with the transfer of cheap labor of the *cabecitas negras* from rural areas (which included large numbers from the indigenous north) to the city, and, in the 1990s, the influx of cheap laborers from surrounding countries. It upset the balance because it represented only a minimal transfer for wealth back to the provinces: Buenos Aires became more and more of a universe unto itself, further exacerbating the trend that Martínez Estrada had perceived almost a decade before with his essay. The consequence has been the unchecked impoverishment of the countryside, so much so that despite any previous perception that Latin America really began with Argentina's borders with its neighbors, one could well maintain that it really begins with the Avenida General Paz that wraps around the southwestern, western, and northwestern edge of the city (the south is bordered by the Riachuelo tributary and ship canal, while the north and east are bordered by the Río de la Plata).

A third image continues the transposition of geographic images into photography for the purpose of imagining the centers of symbolic and real control of Argentine society (**Fig. 2.3**). Just as the train system funnels into Buenos Aires and fans out from Buenos Aires as part of the historical control of the entire country by the port city, the subway system, whose origins date back to the heyday of Argentine prosperity at the beginning of the twentieth century (the first line was opened in 1910), shows the same sort of pattern as regards the executive and financial center of the city vis-à-vis the outlying neighbor-

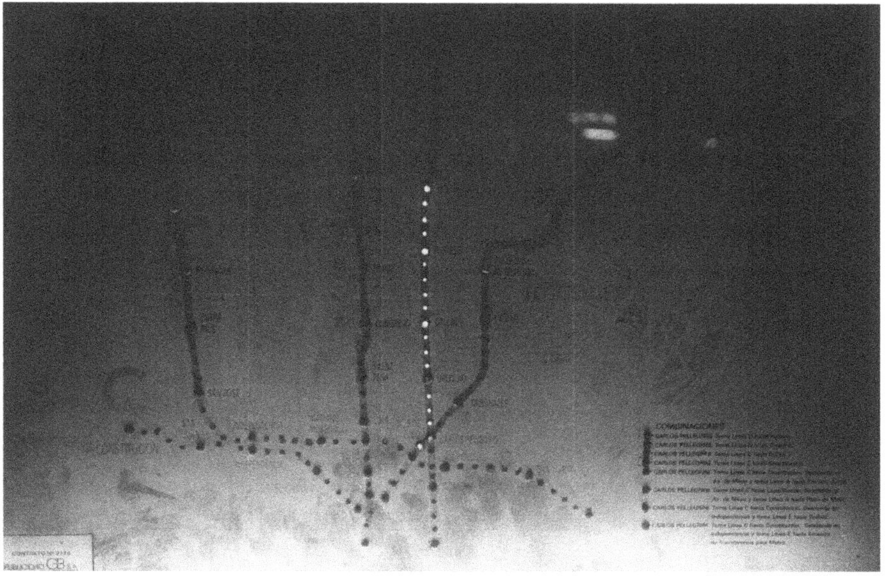

Fig. 2.3 (Gabriel Valansi).

hoods (see Barreda for an interesting series of photographs on the Argentine subway system). Ground zero of the city, on the edge of the old colonial core, is the Casa Rosada, the Argentine Government House; directly to the north extends La City, the financial district. These are the areas served by the original subway system, and the original line (Línea A, which runs under Avenida Rivadavia, the principal avenue of the city) ends beneath and behind the Casa Rosada. There are two more lines (D and E) that branch out from a station close to that terminus, and there is a line (B) that runs parallel to A along Avenida Corrientes. The B line is anchored at Correos, the nineteenth-century palatial main office building of the mail service (Correos is one of the major edifices of the oligarchic liberalism of the late nineteenth century, while the Casa Rosada incorporates the previous seat of the mail service and goes back to the colonial period of the eighteenth century). There is also a perpendicular line (C) that links two of the three main railroad stations (Retiro on the north end — actually a cluster of three stations — and Constitución to the south; the third rail station, Miserere — also known as Once — is an important railway intersection of the A line). Currently, a sixth line (H) is being built west of the city.

When completed, it will be the only line to exist outside the center of real and symbolic power of the city.

Thus, this image too records the organizaton of power in the Fatherland. But there is another dimension to this photograph: Valansi has rescued an information board from the Pasteur station of the Corrientes line (Línea B). This was the station in the heart of the old Jewish quarter of Once just blocks from the seat of the AMIA (Asociación Mutialista Israelí-Argentina), which was bombed by terrorists in July 1994. The death and destruction from that bombing were extensive, and one small trace of the devastation of that blast is the fact that the sign board's contacts were frozen in their indication of the Pasteur station; it was years before the sign board was repaired.

The three photographs I have discussed so far are related to abstract social interpretations that rely on essentially geometric images of the city. However, the photographs that follow in the exhibition are more immediately personalized. Whereas the first images represent overarching questions of economic and political control, the remaining images reflect the actions and circumstances of specific human beings. These agents are not directly recorded by the photographs, but their actions and circumstances are. What we see is the detritus of human lives as they pass through the neoliberal system. I have used the word detritus because these images capture in a metonymic function the processes of an economic system that produces waste, garbage, leftovers, material excrescences, discarded and disposed-of items from daily life as it is affected by the system. Like an archeologist reconstructing the nature and dynamics of a society through its garbage — and so much of what archeologists do dig up is the garbage of the past — Valansi the photographer is analyzing the garbage of present-day Argentina. This detritus appears on the streets at night, as what is replaced each day by the fundamental capitalist principle of programmed obsolescence is discarded to make way for the new, which in this case are the particular fruits of participation in the globalized system of imported goods or, at least, goods that are a step up in some way by comparison to what is being discarded.

In a crowded modern city, this is garbage that appears on the sidewalks at night, to be carted off by the garbage service — although, with the economic debacle currently gripping the nation and the city of

Buenos Aires, there is not only less garbage on the street, but what there is is exhaustively combed by organized networks of garbage pickers (the *cartoneros*), cousins to those who sift through the metropolitan garbage dumps of the world. Garbage is here a metonymy of the system because it is a byproduct of it, both in terms of the nature of what constitutes garbage, and of how garbage is recycled by a society. Finally, since garbage is something that appears at night, in part because much of it is generated by human activity and commerce in the course of the "business hours" of the day, it is in the Porteño night that Valansi must do the analytical work of his photography.[9]

Let us now examine some major exhibits of this work.

One of the most obvious faces of the neoliberalist economy was the enormous number of new businesses that opened. Buenos Aires has always been an intensely commercial city, one that prides itself on the number of its boutiques, bookstores, restaurants, and bars. Buenos Aires has some of the best bar life in the world, with "bar" being understood here in a far broader sense than the usual American use of the word. Perhaps a combination of British pub and French café begins to capture this great Porteño social institution, along with myriad specialty shops. Not only were new businesses opened, which often meant recycling spaces, but some had a measure of elegance. This is the case of the bookstore that opened in one of the old Art Deco movie houses, the Cine Gran Splendid, with the stage area used as a café. Tax credits were available for the modernizing and refurbishing of older locales, which for some habitues meant, regrettably, the loss of the early twentieth-century patina that was their most attractive feature.

As a consequence of all this commercial movement, signs announcing the (re)opening of businesses were common, icons of the attainment of neoliberal nirvana. However, the decline of this business activity is captured in a stack of crumpled APERTURA ("Opening Up") banners: these are probably remaindered magazines (**Fig. 2.4**). *Apertura* was a business publication that was tied to this business activity, and the image of unsold copies can be read in two ways (there is also one banner, in English, that reads TECHNOLOGY and, beneath it, a semitransparent one that seems to read TARGET backwards, also in English; these may also be remaindered magazines). But the APERTURA banners, as crumpled trash, signal the opening of yet one other

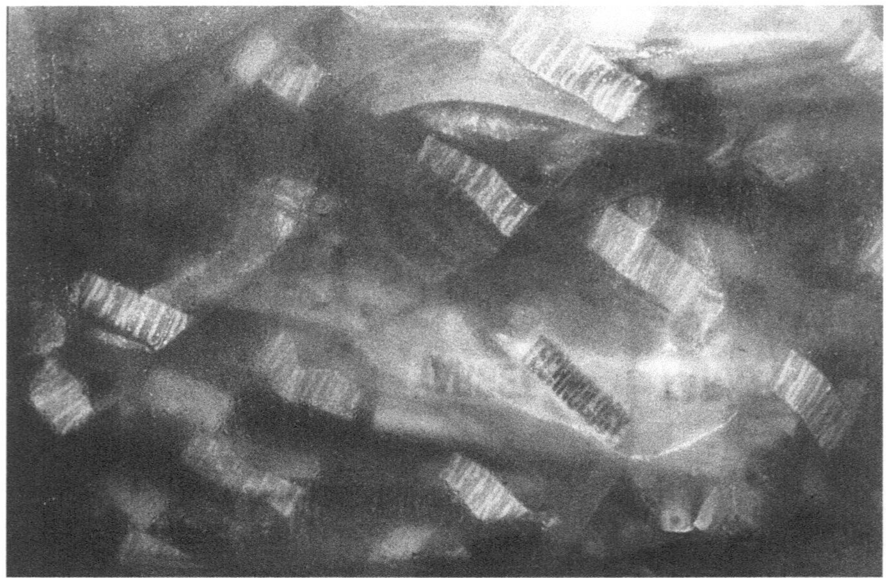

Fig. 2.4 (Gabriel Valansi).

business, one in which TARGET and TECHNOLOGY are somehow involved. Certainly, technology would be, since one of the substantial incursions of new businesses involved those that were technologically based, such as computers and telecommunications, along with a host of others. Every place in town seemed overnight to adopt electronic cash registers in place of longstanding primitive ways of keep track of bills and tabs, including simply the reliance on a serving person's memory.[10]

Yet, there is another way of reading this crumpled heap, and that is in terms of the geometrically increasing number of businesses, especially the trendy ones that came with globalization, that began to go out of business some time before the definitive collapse of neoliberalism at the end of 2001. The decline had been of concern for something like two years, during which the maintenance of parity of the Argentine peso with the U.S. dollar became more and more a science-fiction scenario. Thus, trash is generated in two ways. There is the trash of the establishment of business (which might include the packing of the products that will be offered for sale or, in a previous stage, the debris of the remodelling of a space for the new business). And there is the

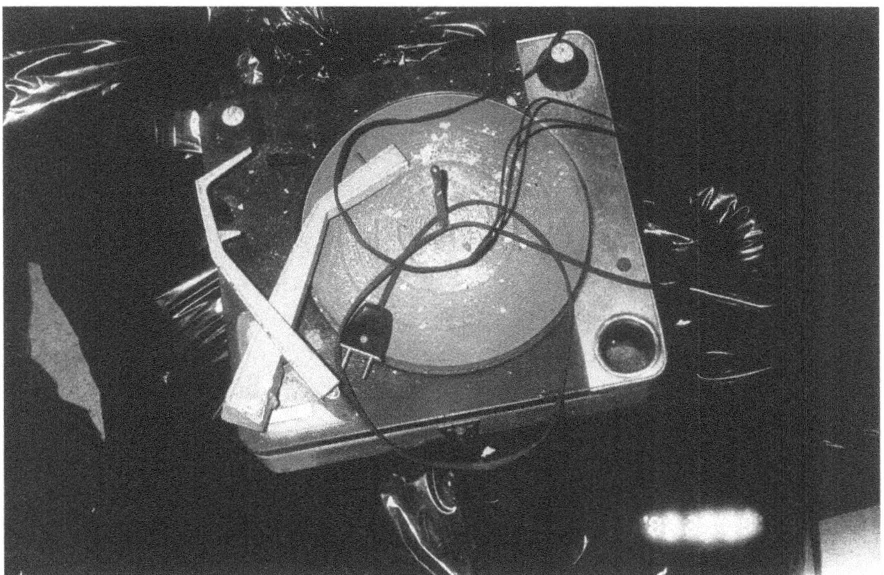

Fig. 2.5 (Gabriel Valansi).

trash of a business that has gone belly up: not the products themselves, but the junked material infrastructure of the business operations.

One of the images I have found most eloquent is of an abandoned record player (**Fig. 2.5**). It looks very much like a Philco-type portable unit from the 1950s or early 1960s, one designed to play a stack of 33⅓ LPs; the cord shows that it was of Argentine manufacture, since the plug consists of the old round prongs that were made for connecting to 220-volt sources. This is certainly an outdated piece of equipment by at least two generations: the replacement of records in general by tape cassettes, and the replacement of tape cassettes by CDs; moreover, the newer equipment is likely to have three-prong plugs (flat ones in a triangular pattern) to permit the incorporation of the ground connection that is especially important at the level of 220 volts. Such equipment was manufactured by Argentine companies, since during the period from which it likely dates, imports were strictly controlled and direct-from-Europe-and-U.S. products were not commonly found, and those that were brought in, at least from the U.S., had to be adapted to the local current or used with clunky power transformers. In recent decades, however, and most assuredly during the 1990s, the market has been flooded by import products, which in the area of electronics has meant particularly Japanese ones, but it is equipment specifically designed for the Argentine user, and there is much to be said about the details concerning marketing of computers and television sets.[11] Suffice it to say that, for the contextualization of this image, the marketing of the latest generation of electronic products in Argentina, including the calculations of planned obsolescence, have rendered absolutely disposable the equipment that reaches back to the period of this phonograph. Not only do the newer products offer the latest technology, but they offer prices that have made it possible for consumers to get rid of the equipment they were holding on to. Such retention was not out of any nostalgic attachment, but because until neoliberalism it was for many simply not possible to replace older equipment and to have economically viable access to newer technologies.

One of the interesting details of this photograph is the disposition of the two mechanical arms that were part of the playing of the record, the stabilizing arm that held the stack of records level and the tone arm that held the stylus that actually read the grooves of the record. The arms are crossed in an X, as though suggesting the annulment of the usefulness/usability of the equipment, while the tone arm is positioned as though uselessly playing the recordless turntable: there are no more records like this to play.

One of the major items discarded during the periods of *la plata dulce* (the sweet money) and neoliberalism were cars. Those who knew Argentina in the 1960s will recall that the city was filled with ancient cars, many of them venerable Mercedes-Benzes that were bought after the war from Germany. There were also cars of excellent quality made by local subsidiaries of American companies and European ones; indeed, the quality and range of automobiles in Argentina during the 1960s was one of the hallmarks of that country's middle-class prosperity. And then there were the tin can–like lower-end Citroëns, jokingly said to lend themselves to disassembly in a matter of minutes with a can-opener; the cars were quite ubiquitous.[12] There were some American imports, but it was generally assumed that they belong to Embassy personnel or someone of their ilk. The tripling-plus of the numbers of cars clogging the streets of the city in the 1990s meant not just increasing the number of cars geometrically, but getting rid of the old cars as unworthy of the new First-World image it was the order of the day to promote.

Valansi's images of a smashed and, apparently, abandoned cans figure this dimension of the new economy. One image is of the seat of a car — one that seems not all that old, because it is possible to discern the female buckle of the seat-belt installation; the seat is covered with the smashed-in glass from one of the windows. Another image shows the open trunk, with some sort of garbage dumped into it. Even if the car(s) in question may not be exactly the ancient ones replaced by the influx of new vehicles in the late 1970s and the past decade, they symbolize the "luxury" of the trashing and abandonment of vehicles in a product-replacement/substitution economy. Cars are the quintessential icon of modernity and of personal and collective prosperity, and the greater the complexity of the modern(ized) economy, the more vital cars are as instruments of the mobility that economy requires for both the production and the consumption of goods.

Finally, one last image, that of a discarded painting (likely to be a reproduction); two halves of the piece of art are piled on top of one another, back-to-back, with half of the image exposed. Tucked between the two torn halves is a newspaper. Newspapers are of the day, to be read and discarded; as the saying goes, there is nothing as dead as yesterday's news. By contrast, art, even that art that is preserved in inexpensive and mass-produced reproductions, is supposed to be eternal; yet here both are consigned to the same rubbish heap. It is as though the actuality of First-World Argentina, which is what the newspaper would be reporting on (whether favorably or critically), brought down to its own level great works of art. This is the theme of the banalization of culture by neoliberalism and the replacement of the self-reflective nature of art by the superficial nowness in which the reporting of mass-society newspapers were all that one needed to know: both newspaper and art work are being discarded, but the newspaper is intact, while it is the painting that is torn asunder.

Valansi's photographs in *Fatherland* are highly effective interpretations of the dark side of recent socio-economic processes in Argentina as viewed through the hardly noticed detritus of the night. Not only does one not customarily scrutinize garbage (except for the aforementioned and highly organized garbage pickers that now make up a booming occupation in Buenos Aires), but it remains essentially unseen. It is dumped in the street or along the sidewalk at night, and the citizen simply assumes that it will be gone by the morning, taken somewhere out of sight, so that no more than a passing notice need ever be taken of machine-produced excrement of modernity.

One closing note. Valansi gives his exposition a title in English. He has claimed, in the interview from which the quote at the beginning of this study is drawn, that the title is taken from a novel (by Robert Harris) dealing with the triumph of Naziism. But the Nazi inflection would suggest the German *Vaterland*. The use of *Fatherland* in English suggests the resonance of American society, since understanding the complicity of, first, the military dictatorships and subsequently the new democratic governments with American financial interests is crucial to an adequate interpretation of current degradation of Argentine national life.[13]

3

La Grande Patria in Lower Case: Eduardo Gil's Photography in *(argentina)*

"Los hombres que están solos ya no esperan"—*Eduardo Gil, (argentina)*

"Argentina es Primer Mundo" (Argentina is in/belongs to the First World) was the oft-repeated phrase, both as an assertion of proud accomplishment and as a parody of presumption, during the 1990s, the period of Carlos Menem's presidency, the parity of the dollar and the peso, the triumphalist installation of a neoliberalist economy, and the virtual pride-engendering pervasive supremacy of corruption.[1] Although Argentina has a long tradition of boastful nationalism,[2] the prosperity generated by what was to turn out to be the failed neoliberalist experiment brought with a sense of euphoria over the belief that Argentina had finally attained the exceptional status it always felt that it was entitled to, but which always seemed to slip elusively from its grasp. Neoliberalism was going to ensure that Argentina was, once and for all, a First-World country meriting a privileged diplomatic tie with the United States and deserving of the same sort of international recognition accorded the Western European societies it always sought to emulate. At least, this has customarily been the official self-image of Argentina — certainly that of a ruling cultural and financial elite — and it was one that most sectors of Argentinian society (or at least, the citizens of the hegemonic urban center, Buenos Aires) seemed to subscribe to during the heyday of the Menem government.[3]

Eduardo Gil's work, particularly the twenty-three images that make up the photographic dossier *(argentina)*, can be examined as one cultural response to the triumphalist attitudes prevalent with respect to Argentina, historically in general and specifically, during the neoliberalist 1990s. Gil notes in a colophon to the dossier that "Este trabajo fue realizado en Buenos Aires, que es donde vivo, entre 1985 y 2000. Intenta ser una metáfora de la Argentina desde la dictadura militar hasta el presente." What is interesting about this statement is that, although Gil, like other photographers — and, certainly, an enormous sector of Argentine cultural producers — has dealt with images of the neofascist dictatorship,[4] these images are focused on the period between Argentina's return to constitutional democracy in 1983 and the neoliberalist experiment of the 1990s.

Gabriela Liffschitz, in her review of *(argentina)* underscores Gil's interest in what one could call in English "lower case Argentina." This is the Argentina that falls outside the purview of the grandiose Argentina touted by the power elite. It is the Argentina that has, since the beginnings of the collapse of the neoliberal system in the mid–1990s, with the final collapse in 2001, fallen from prosperity into poverty, which as of this writing means fully 40% of that country's citizenry. This distribution is strictly an economic one. Yet there are other axes that must be taken into account for a full interpretation of the difference between "Argentina" and "(argentina)." One is geopolitical: it is easy to confuse Argentina with Buenos Aires and vice-versa, since the hegemonic urban center, with fully one-third of the entire population of the country concentrated in the Greater Buenos Aires area, can only exist as such by virtue of the exclusion of enormous sectors of the country from its actual and symbolic wealth and power. The sustainment of Buenos Aires as virtually the only point of reference for Argentina in terms of power and wealth has come at the cost of the increasing impoverishment of the provinces. While it is true that there are pockets of wealth and perhaps even some middle-class prosperity elsewhere in Argentina, the evolution of Buenos Aires into a megalopolitan center, which has taken place since early in the Peronista period (1946–55), has brought with it a cycle of impoverishment.

It is an impoverishment that has been driven in part by the industrialization of the city than began with Perón in the late 1940s. Buenos Aires is no longer just the port city of the farming and cattle-raising wealth of the provinces, but its industry now competes with the cattle and other rural baronies such that Buenos Aires can exist with its back to the rest of the country — i.e., such that Buenos Aires no longer needs to depend on those baronies for its reason to exist. Moreover, this impoverishment becomes a vicious cycle, to the extent that the loss of agricultural and other sources of employment in the provinces means a vast migration of citizens to Buenos Aires seeking employment. Whereas Perón had set out to bring provincials to the city (among other reasons) as a form of cheap labor in his attempts to industrialize the country, now those individuals flood into the capital of their own accord. And whereas the Peronist promise was that the so-called *cabecitas negras* would move into the middle class as a protected work force, today they form a precariously situated lumpen proletariat that provides Buenos Aires with a host of poorly addressed and mostly unresolved social issues.

There is still another geopolitical axis. Buenos Aires attracts the provincial unemployed, a certain portion of which remains destitute in the city, moving from rural poverty to urban poverty. However, Buenos Aires also attracts a similar class from the many surrounding Latin American republics, from Bolivia and Brazil to Chile, from Paraguay and Peru to Uruguay, and one comes upon even those from the noncontiguous republics.[5] In the current rapid transition to generalized impoverishment in Buenos Aires, the ranks of the eternally poor have been swollen by the influx of provincials who either remain unemployed or lose their jobs, by former middle-class individuals who descend into poverty, and by other Latin Americans who have become unemployed (although some, but not all, have ended up returning to their native countries). (Jelin has done extensive sociological work on poverty in Argentina; see, however, *Podría ser yo* because it is accompanied by photographic images of Alicia d'Amico, one of the great names in Argentine photography.)

Other axes also come to mind. The class divisions in Buenos Aires are not driven strictly by economic factors, although these are undoubtedly dominant. It is true that there has been, historically, an incredible social mobility for Argentines when compared to other Latin American republics. And it is also true that it has not always functioned ideally for members of various subaltern classes, such as certain classes of immigrants. Jews, despite a considerable amount of mobility, still suffer from endemic anti–Semitism, and the newer Korean immigrants have yet to acquire much symbolic power, although some may have a measure of economic clout. Women also have enjoyed enviable opportunities in Argentina, but sexism still creates a gender subclass in most venues (hence, the enormous success of Maitena's feminist cartoon art; see the published volumes of *Las alteradas*; see also the critical analysis by Tompkins), and, despite formal constitutional guarantees (per the *Constitución de Buenos Aires* approved in 1996) in categories relating to ageism, sexual orientation, religious beliefs and the like, there remain no effective workplace protections for, for example, lesbians and gays or orthodox Jews.

Gil, moreover, is particularly interested in one other mostly underreported disjunction between "Argentina" and "(argentina)," and that is the intense social marginalization of the mentally infirm. Buenos Aires's sprawling major mental institution, the Hospital Neuropsiquiátrico José T. Borda, has been used in a number of cases as a metaphor for social marginalization in Argentina, such as the photographic work of the two great Argentine feminist photographers Sara d'Amico and Sara Facio, particularly in *Humanario* (1976; see Foster, "Sara Facio") and in Eliseo Subiela's 1986 film *Hombre mirando al sudeste*, one of the most successful films of the redemocratization effort (see Foster, *Contemporary Argentine Filmmaking*, 80–92). The Borda also appears in Marcelo Piñeyro's 1993 *Tango feroz, la leyenda de Tanguito*; the rock singer Tanguito's death in 1972 is often seen as the demise of the Paris-spring optimism of the 1960s in Argentina (Tanguito's birth name was José Alberto Iglesias). The mentally ill are, to all intents and purposes, permanently excluded from the structures of real and symbolic power and their lives constitute something like a permanent locus of radical social exclusion, an Other that confirms the hegemonic social dynamic that excludes them.[6] If there is a transitory poverty (albeit one that can become permanent, or threaten, under current conditions, to become permanent), mental illness, as Foucault has taught us, is so categorically the excluded Other that it becomes an anchor, a ground zero for an exposition of a society set in lower case.

Not surprisingly, easily half of Gil's photographs in *(argentina)* deal explicitly or by a good interpretational guess can be seen to deal with the mentally infirm. Some images are quite straightforward in dealing with this form of social marginalization, while other are less literal, and it is an educated guess on the part of the viewer to see them as also allegories of real and symbolic power in Argentina by virtue of psychiatric subalternity.

One of the emphases of Gil's photography is on individuals who are radically alone: individuals who are abandoned, have been abandoned, by society. To be sure, it is a cliche that the big city engenders alienation and that its streets are filled with "lonely crowds" (the allusion here is to David Riesman's eponymous study). Yet, perhaps it is an illusion that individuals are always lonelier in the metropolitan mass, since it is a basic condition of humanity to experience a sensation of isolation from other persons. The saying "no man is an island" may be less apophantic than it is hortatory, subjunctive and/or jussive: "Oh, let it be that no man is an island." Yet the sensation transmitted by many of Gil's photographs is not of lonely individuals, but of abandoned individuals, who may or may not feel their loneliness or may or may not even be aware of it. Since many are mental patients, photographed singly or in groups, there is less of a psychic question as regards their personal feelings and more an ethical one as it refers to our perception, provoked by the photographer, of them in terms of our own lives and in terms of our treatment of them as institutionalized human beings.

These too are disappeared citizens. They have been confined, if not against their will, more than likely without their informed consent. It may be for their own protection and, perhaps, even for the protection of society, but the effect is always the same: to remove them from public view, to sever them from society, and to restrict their options for being in the world. One may calculate that the majority of viewers of these photographs are acutely aware of the social injustices of the confinement of mental patients, as well as the confinement of any human being, although, certainly, one feels that criminals in large measure deserve their fate. This is because there is the inevitable tendency to compare one's own life to theirs and to feel, as the saying goes in English, "There but for the grace of God go I." Moreover, the recov-

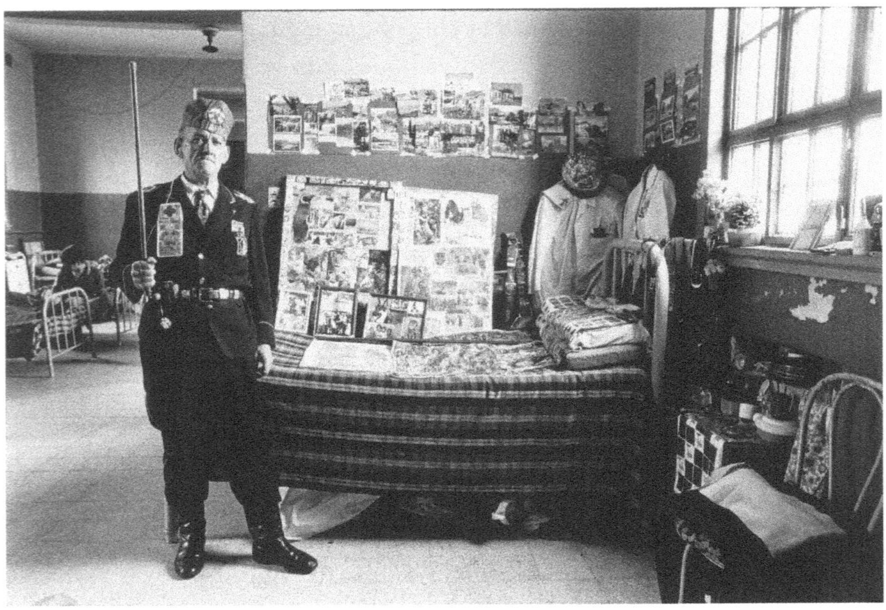

Fig 3.1 (Eduardo Gil).

ery of constitutional democracy in Argentina has meant for many citizens, including their artistic delegates among the producers of culture, a thoroughgoing accounting of the many ways of disappearing in a society, which must necessary embrace the question of the ways in which individuals may continue to disappear. This is why these photographs, whose origins date virtually from the beginning of the return to constitutional democracy, are nevertheless of a whole with Gil's and others' concern over human rights issues that were not put to rest simply by the end of military rule.

One of the most eloquent of the photographs comes early in the dossier (**Fig. 3.1**). It is of a older man decked out in what appears to be his version of full military regalia, which includes lustrously shined boots, a three-quarter length coat with a leather belt, various insignia and/or decorations, and a hat that, although not an example of the typical military beaked heat, is some sort of cap which could be part of a non–Western European tradition or could be a fantasy of the wearer as to what this symbol of authority might look like. He is carrying in his right hand, in stiff and almost perfectly vertical rigidity, a meter-long staff. It looks longer and thicker than the conventional swagger stick of some military traditions, and it has a rubber or plastic tip on it as though it had originated in a walking stick or the leg of a table and had been modified to serve as the symbol of military authority. Its bearer regards the camera in clenched-lip (somewhat sunken because of toothlessness?) determination and, indeed, defiance.

What makes this image particularly interesting is that the man stands beside his bed in an inmate ward. Although he is lucky enough to enjoy a corner and has a large window by his bed, the viewer can see in the left-hand background other beds and another inmate, whose face is turned away from the camera, as though lost in his own world. The beds we can see of the other inmates reveal the customary features of institutional bleakness — the mattresses are thin and swaybacked, covered by identical blankets; there is a simple chest of drawers set against the wall between two of the beds. But the bed of the uniformed man, while it is also somewhat sunken in the middle, is the site of a mosaic of images that involves pictures taped to the wall, numerous framed photographs and images clipped from magazines and newspapers, along with what appears to be several decorated fabrics that are spread out on top of the blanket and wrapped around two pillows at the head of the bed; there are also some images propped up on the window sill. Additionally, there are other military-looking clothes hanging from the wall against which the bed sits, and there are other carefully arranged displays on a small table by the bed and on a wooden chair of the sort found in traditional cafés. There are additional objects under the bed, a collection of belts hanging behind the head of the bed and, next to the framed images, some other object that may or may not be military in nature.

This extensive clutter is undoubtedly the consequence of years of patient collection and arrangement by the man. He has been allowed by the institutional authorities to create this cramped self-contained world that feeds some delusion of military authority. Indeed, he may even be a former military officer who has become a mental patient. The abandonment of this man to some alienated inner realm of which his visible possessions are concrete metonymies is pathetic to the viewer to the extent that it fails to correspond to any socially integrated behavior. And perhaps the pathos is intensified by the image of military authority, whose enforcement of power through violence is represented by the upraised and at-the-ready staff, since that authority has, for a good part of the recent history of Argentina, been an agent in the disappearance of citizens. It is a case of the victim internalizing and assimilating the manner of the victimizer.

I have placed as an epigraph to this essay a verse from a poem of his own, dated 1992, that Gil includes in his dossier. It is a trope of the title of a famous 1931 sociological essay by Raúl Scalabrini Ortiz entitled *El hombre que está solo y espera*. Written at the height of the heady brew in Argentina of socialism, anarchism, and assorted other forms of radical politics, yet published a year after the first, fascist-inspired, military coup in Argentina, Scalabrini Ortiz contemplates as much the Argentine common man (whom he situates at the popular/populist downtown intersection of Corrientes and Esmeralda) who awaits the fulfillment of the promises of social amelioration prevalent in those decades (Argentina was particularly responsive to the 1917 Russian Revolution) as the Argentine who must now wait out the imposition of military rule.

However, in the universe of Gil's photos — quite aside from a climate of political despair in Argentina seventy years after Scalabrini Ortiz's investment in the image of stoic patience — the alienated have nothing to look forward to, nothing to wait for because of the way in which they are now lost to consciousness of social history. Gil concludes his poem with the couplet: "Solo hay una duda. / Qu[é] corbata estrenar en el propio funeral."

There is an image of a line of a dozen and a half men on an area of the grounds of what is probably the Borda (**Fig. 3.2**). This line is in the foreground; in the background there are three other men: one leaning against the thick trunk of a tree; one sitting on the ground, reclining against the trunk; and someone walking away from the tree. The thickness of the trunk of this tree and the mature growth of other trees we can see on the grounds gives this outdoor setting an ageless quality, enhanced also by the thick and vegetation-strewn carpet of grass underfoot. It is though this were a forest primeval through which these men were passing, most in single-file, as though to some unknown human destiny. The irregular human beings are transitory life, within a permanent thicket of natural growth. The mysteriousness of the

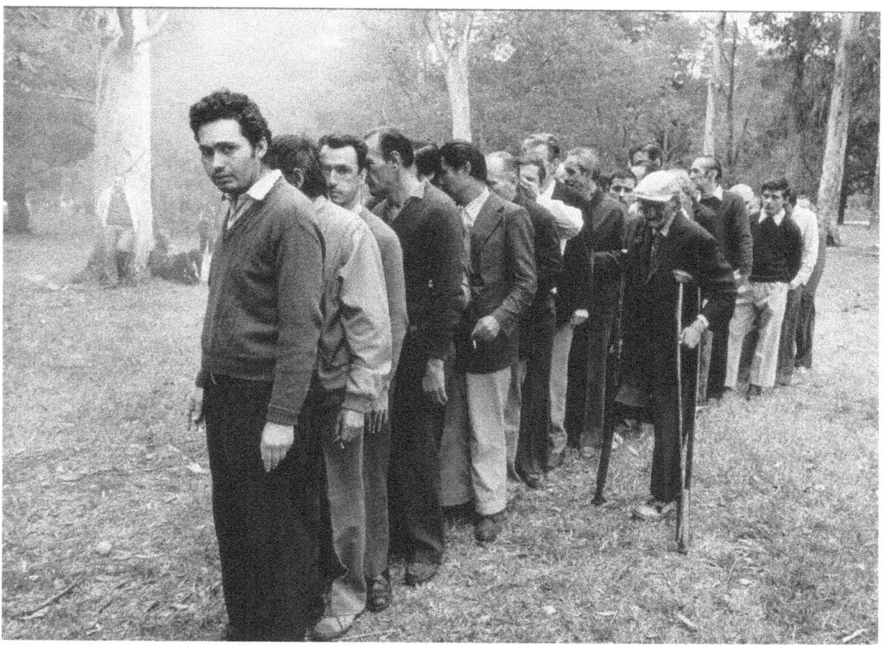

Fig. 3.2 (Eduardo Gil).

assemblage of these men, with the implication of their being formed to march off or be marched off to some unpleasant fate, augments the timeless/transitory disjunction on which the photo is built.

The first and third man in line look toward the camera, as does someone, obscured in part by the others formed around him, a little more than halfway back in the row; in all three cases, their contemplation of the camera is passive, although the third man does seem to have his forehead wrinkled in an inquisitive manner. The men are all fairly nicely dressed and many carry a cigarette, throwing into question whether these are long-term inhabitants of an institution, and suggesting perhaps the context might be another, less threatening one. But the fact that no context is provided — no sign of a goal for the line is seen in front of the first man — adds to the unsettling intensity of the image.

Another image, one that appears on the cover and is included right before the one just commented on, is equally mysterious in capturing the abandonment of human beings (**Fig. 3.3**). By this point, it

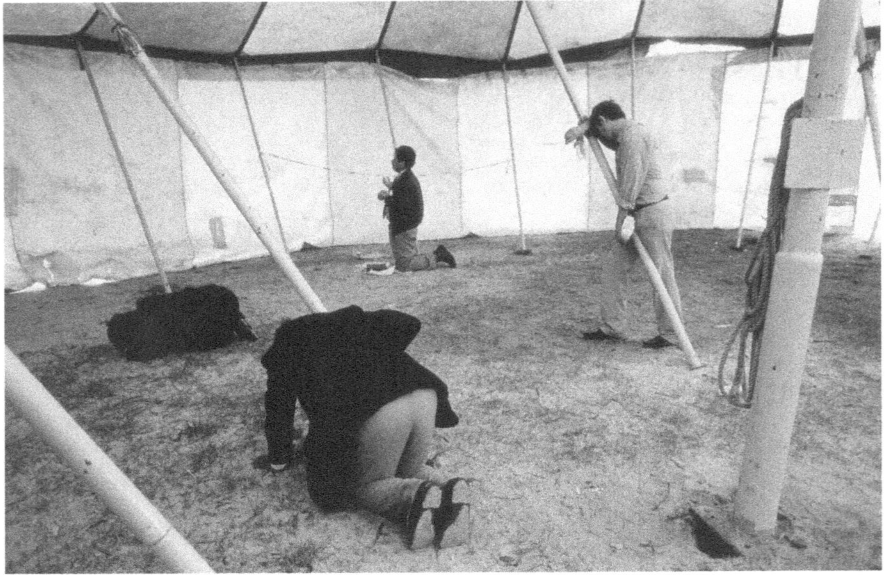

Fig. 3.3 (Eduardo Gil).

should be apparent that Gil has restricted himself as much to mentally alienated men as Facio and d'Amico focused on women in *Humanario*, although it is much less apparent in this photograph that inmates of the Borda are involved. The entire photograph is dominated by a portion of the interior of a circus tent, and the circular wall of the tent, and the roof that stretches off rather irregularly from that wall, make up the top forty percent — i.e., the background — of the image. The central mast of the tent is seen to the right of the photograph, while various other supports are distributed around the portion of the wall that is visible and in the foreground and mid-range of the image; these supports run off at varying angles because of the position of the camera and constitute roof supports. Thus, although there are four men visible in the photograph, it is as though they were caged by these supports, which outnumber them and intersect their bodies.

When I first looked at the photograph, I saw three men and what I took to be a large bundle on the ground. In reality, this bundle is a fourth man, discernible as such because of a barely visible pair of shoes; his body, although he is kneeling, is completely level with the ground. It is an interesting compositional detail that the other three men are in varying degrees of contact with the ground (which is a sandy stretch with some vegetation, such as one finds in the Reserva Ecológica on the southeast side of the city along the banks of the Río de la Plata). One man is leaning against one of the roof supports, and thus the angle of his body follows that of the support. His head is resting on his right forearm, which, in turn, rests on the support. The pose of his body is one of utter exhaustion and/or, perhaps, one of despair and alienation. A second man, in the central background and to the left of the former man, kneels in apparent prayer. His body is completely perpendicular to the ground and the angle of his legs below the knee, and his hands, which extend from his arms held to his side, are raised in supplication. But it is a modest supplication, since it is not the full, upraised-arm supplication of intense pentecostal prayer; like the other bodies, he does not acknowledge the camera's presence, lost also in his own world.

Finally, to his left but most in the foreground, between the man in prayer and the prone man, is a man who is also kneeling. But his left hand is placed flat on the ground and holds his body up so that he is parallel with the ground but not lying on it. His position causes his pants to draw taut across his buttocks, with the bottom portion following the division of the buttocks in the area of the anal fold. This detail is almost obscene, indicating that the man is unaware of what the camera is capturing: conventional Argentine masculinity is no different from that of other Western cultures in proscribing the display of male buttocks which, even when they are covered, implies a (homo) erotic offering that is in violation of heterosexist taboos. Since the context of the photograph as a whole is not (homo)erotic, it is safe to assume that this man, too, is lost in a revery of alienation.

There is a final photograph that I would like to analyze from among the appreciable number that have to do with individuals who are "alone but no longer expectantly"[7]; it precedes the last one analyzed (**Fig. 3.4**). The grounds appear to be those of the Borda, with various installations in the background, including the chimney stacks that dominate the skyline and confirm the institutional nature of the place, despite the modest, almost residential nature of the buildings to be seen. Once again, Gil's photograph is dominated by five men who are standing immobile. Four are irregularly lined up in a shoulder-to-shoulder position; their backs are to us. They hold conventionally mas-

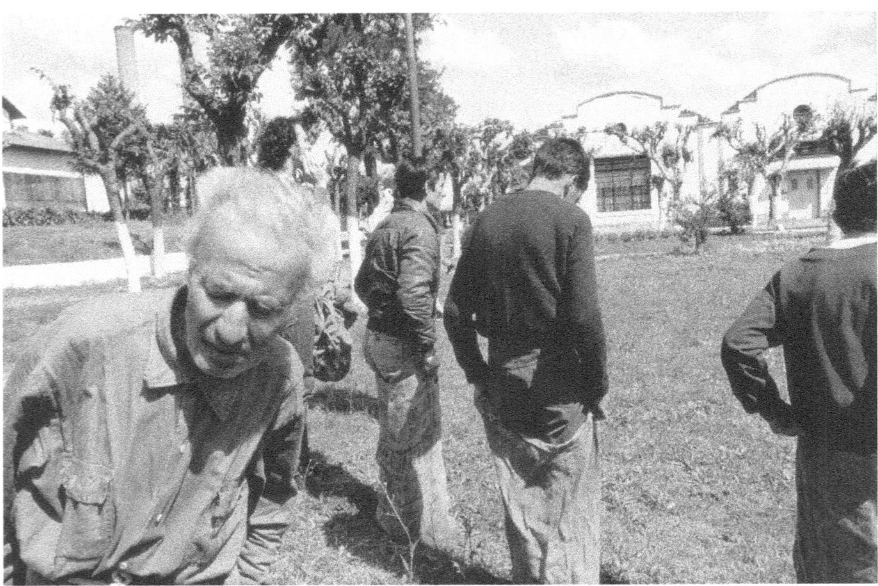

Fig. 3.4 (Eduardo Gil).

culine positions, two with their hands in their pockets, one with his arms akimbo, and one with his chin resting in the palm of his hand. They are in their mid-thirties, and they are all staring off into space, although one has his head lowered so that he is looking at the ground. In the lower left foreground there is a much older, grizzled, and unshaven man. His eyes are closed, and he is slightly inclined toward the camera, but apparently oblivious of its presence. The other four are wearing outer garments, while the old man is wearing only a shirt, as though inured by custom to the cool weather that obliges the other four to wear additional clothing. One could surmise the he is a veteran of the ritual of alienation.

I use the word ritual to evoke Subiela's *Hombre mirando al sudeste*, where the staring off into space (specifically in Rani's case) is a major plot device. No one is certain if Rani is a particularly intelligent mental patient or an alien visitor, whose alienness is confused with the alienation of other inmates of the Borda. Nor do we know whether his standing stock still in the courtyard and staring off into space is just the confirmation of his mental illness or really the pattern of communication with his extraterrestrial masters. The Borda is located in the

southeast corner of Buenos Aires, and the line of sight of someone staring toward the southeast is the vast, open ocean of nothingness, an apt
metaphor for psychotic alienation. In another photograph, while others dance hand-in-hand in a form of ring-around-the-rosy in the common area formed by several multistory buildings that are probably also
part of the Borda, two men stand motionless, one in the mid-range of
the photograph, as though the center of the dance, and one in the
right-hand foreground. The latter is looking off vacantly, with the palm
of his right hand flat over his right ear, either blocking out the noise
the others are making or heeding some inner voice.

The images of mental patients taken at the Borda do not, however,
make up the entire body of work contained in *(argentina)*: the abandoned
are not the only denizens of the homeland written in lower case. Interspersed among these images are photographs taken in various characteristic outdoor venues of the city, such as the street, the Recoleta cemetery,
parks and plazas, a stadium, and outdoor areas of other institutions, such
as a Catholic high school. These images are of "normal" everyday Argentines, but there are some images that one could call transitions between
the latter and those of the inhabitants of the Borda, such as an outdoor,
mass, full-immersion baptism in a soccer stadium, a quirky event by the
everyday standards of Argentine life; an outdoor Catholic confession with
a child's merry-go-round in the background; another image of some sort
of outdoor religious event at the edge of what I believe is the Jardín
Botánico in the elegant Barrio Norte section of the city (the antithesis of
the south side where the Borda is located); and one of a woman — perhaps his mother — holding the hand of a bloated youth, who although
not precisely someone with Down's syndrome, appears to have some mental deficiency. The images of everyday Argentines in public spaces, including those shading off into the quirky, is reminiscent of the Swiss
photographer Robert Frank's groundbreaking 1959 collection of images,
The Americans, on everyday American citizens. Just as Frank's book captured the unheroic citizens of postwar/cold war triumphalist America, Gil
is casting the eye of his camera on the ordinariness of post-dictatorship
Argentina, where dead-end loneliness still prevails. In this sense, then,
there is a continuity between the radically alienated of the Borda and
those who are on the outside but are no less alienated, even if they are
not certifiably insane.

These are pictures, then, of individuals gathered together in a public space; some are motionless and tranquil, while others are visibly agitated. For example, there is an early plate of a group of people vociferating before a low wall topped by a chain-link fence with an overhang of barbed wire, which indicates that it is meant to be impossible to scale either from within or from without. One's first assumption is that it is the wall of a prison, and the people that are gathered there are attempting to communicate with the inmates, who may or may not appear at the windows. This is an arrangement in some prisons where an infrastructure is lacking to permit regularized face-to-face visits with prisoners. The majority of the individuals in the photograph are looking at some objective on the other side of the fence, and are gesticulating; one assumes, in the case of those with their mouths open, that they are shouting. Yet not all are facing the fence. In the case of one couple, the man is, but the woman with him, probably his wife, is facing him, and he is resting a hand flatly on the top of her head as though consoling her for some reason. But what is most disturbing about this enigmatic image — we don't know what exactly is going on or where it is taking place; all we now is that the individuals captured here are emotionally affected by what they are experiencing — is the image in the central foreground of a woman in a wheelchair. She is looking toward the camera and her mouth is open in, perhaps, a silent expression of pain. Her head is tilted back and to the side, and her overall expression is one of intense emotional agitation. A woman with her back to us, in the lower left-hand angle, contemplates her suffering as we do: they are the reflex of something that is going on on the other side of the fence that we cannot see.

All the photographer allows us to see is this one woman's suffering as a synecdoche of the response of the other individuals in the photograph, just as the other woman who looks at her reaction is a stand-in for the viewer's contemplation of the first woman's pain. These individuals are alone in their pain, whatever it is, and we the spectators are powerless to do anything about it, less because we don't know what the origins of that pain are than because it doesn't matter. This is one more image of the enormous sense of social futility in the universe of Gil's photographs, that of human life in the lower-case homeland. In this sense, then, the emotional agitation of the individuals in the photograph is continuous with other motives for suffering, and one is as exemplary as another to capture the condition of their lives.

The photograph is complemented by others that deal with "common Argentines," such as the one of a group of men being held back by security forces. We don't know why they are being held back or what the nature and the motive are for any behavior that would require them to be restrained. The center of the photograph is occupied by the bodies of two young men. One has a diffident look on his face — he is looking directly at the camera — as he is gripped by a security agent in such a way that an open shirt he is wearing over a T-shirt is being pulled back from his shoulder. The other man has more of a look of consternation, and he looks off to the side. He is carrying something that involves a strap over his shoulder, and this may signal he is a student. Other men in the picture — and it is notable that all are men, which suggests perhaps the picture was taken in the male-dominated financial district know as the City — are dressed in suits and ties, while others show the casual dress of the two young men in the center of the picture.

There appear to be at least two security personnel in the photograph. One has his back is to us (he is wearing something like a protective vest) because he is gripping the first of the two young men mentioned, the one whose shirt is being pulled back off his shoulder. The second is somewhat blurred, so it is not clear if he is looking at the camera from his position in the right-hand foreground, although we can see he is wearing an official badge. A third man is gripping the left arm of the first of the two young men, but he is not necessarily a security agent, since we can clearly see the cuff of his suit jacket, the cuff of his dress shirt, and a leather watch band. The picture is taken from the position of what they are watching, but the camera would not seem to be what they are looking at. Nevertheless, we have no way of knowing if they are onlookers being restrained at a crime or accident scene, if they are protestors of a perceived injustice, or perhaps even claimants at the doors of a failed establishment.[8] The point of the photograph is that there is some sort of collective reaction to a socially significant event taking place, and that reaction is being contained on some basis of authority.

Less ambiguous is the following photograph (**Fig. 3.5**). Ranged

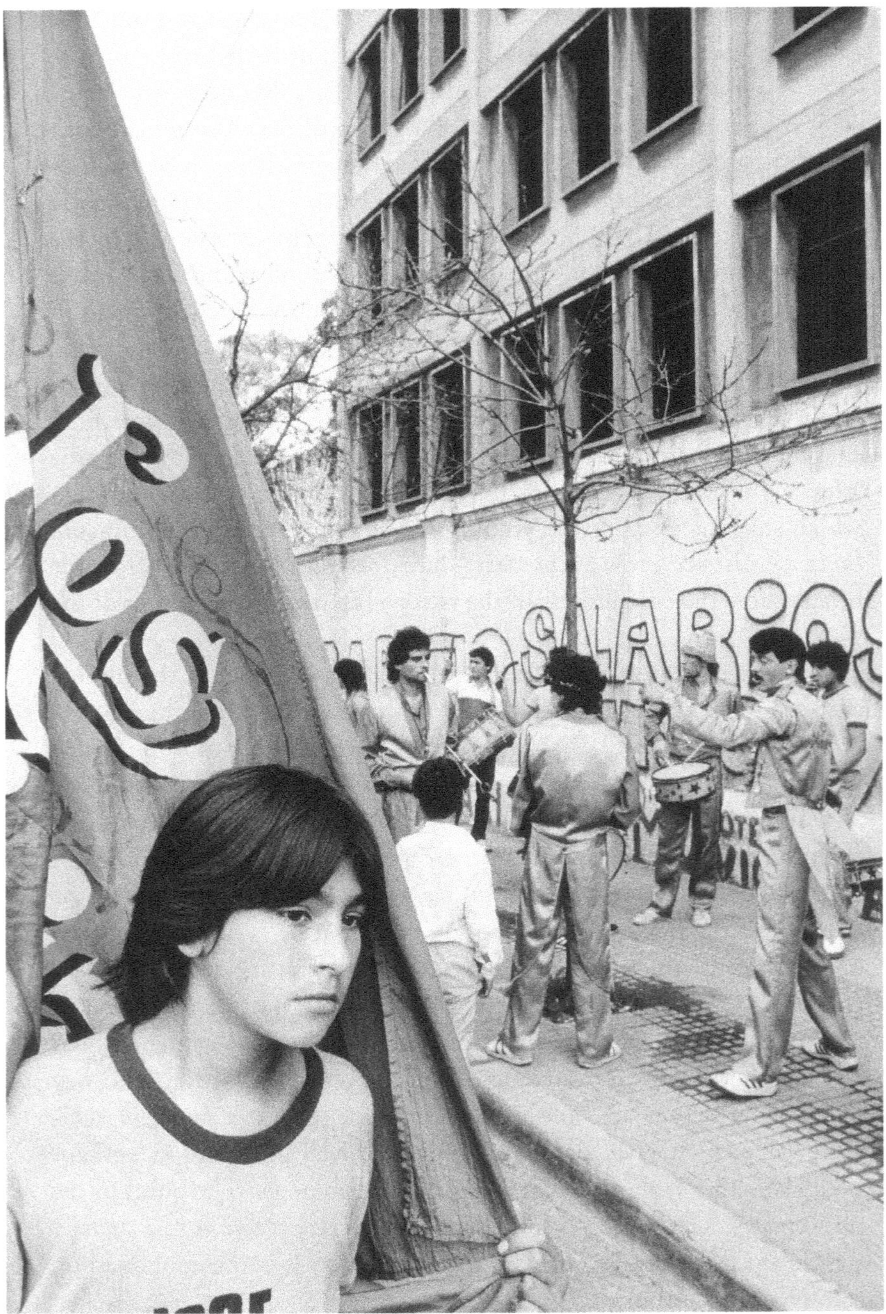

Fig. 3.5 (Eduardo Gil).

against a wall on which a slogan has been painted in large letters in which the word *salarios* (salaries) can be discerned is a ragtag snare drum group. While they are wearing a suggestion of a satin uniform consisting of a jacket and pants, other details of street clothes can be made out. One man has a cigarette dangling from his mouth, while another has on the sort of flat-topped conical cap (we cannot make out the slogans written on it) that is often seen at soccer matches or in similar populist venues. In the left-hand foreground a boy wears a T-shirt whose legend is not completely visible, and he is holding the corner of a flag on which we can see, in fancy lettering, the article *Los*. This may be a group that provides street entertainment, or they may be part of a political protest or political campaign. The latter dual possibility is suggested by the graffiti mentioning salaries (undoubtedly a demand for wage adjustments), below which it is possible to make out the letters *ote*, which unquestionbly belongs to the imperative *vote* (vote for). Whether there is a connection between the campaign slogan, the graffiti referring to salaries, and the ragtag band is unclear, but the context is more specifically political than the last two images I have referred to.

There is one more detail in this photograph that merits commenting on: the slogan and graffiti are painted on a wall that appears, because of its style, to be of a nonrecent vintage. Beyond the wall, a building rises up that is either abandoned or unfinished — more likely the former, since there are no construction traces such as scaffolding or unfinished portions. Buenos Aires is dotted with the combined blight of abandoned buildings and suspended construction sites, the overt signs of disastrous economic fluctuations. In addition to serving as signs of those fluctuations — and of how the promised universality of neoliberalist prosperity was only a chimera — these buildings constitute a social and legal problem, as they are taken over by squatters. Squatters cannot be easily evicted under Argentine law, and they are alleged to bring crime and unsanitary practices with them.

Finally, of particular note in this photograph, in addition to the way in which the ragtag band is standing around without appearing to be engaged in performance, is the vacant look on the part of the boy holding the flag or banner, reinforcing the sense of isolation and abandonment that are the recurring themes of Gil's photographs in this dossier.

While so many of Gil's photographs involve popular classes, there are a number of what one could call upper-class settings. In addition to the images referring to religious contexts, which are interesting insofar as they allow one to speculate on why people have recourse to religion and why, in these images, there is still a sense of isolation and abandonment, there are three consecutive images relating to the Recoleta, the elegant and staggeringly costly final resting place for the rich and powerful in the central area of the city, on the edge of the most elegant residential districts. These images appear to be in the context of a funeral, and all of the individuals pictured are wearing proper, elegant clothes for a funeral; all have the physical aspects of privilege, of the sort that the Recoleta monumentalizes, with the tree-lined streets of this "city of the dead" flanked by mausoleums bearing the best names of the country. The mausoleums themselves are miniature palaces, architectural signs of their inhabitants' class.

Yet, once again, Gil captures the blank expressions on the part of those present, including one woman's half-bewildered, half-defiant stare at the camera in one plate (**Fig. 3.6**), and another woman's vaguely disdainful stare in another. The socially significant occasion of this assemblage is death, and death among the movers and shakers of Argentina. Nevertheless, there is little sense of human communication between those in attendance: except in the case of the first woman, who rests her hand on the back of the neck of a young boy, there is hardly any expression of warmth or community among these individuals. Indeed, in the same photograph in which the woman is touching the young boy, a noticeably patrician young man, dressed so much in the British tradition cultivated still by a sector of Argentina's elite that he is carrying the traditional furled umbrella, stares off into space, sitting quite apart from the woman and the boy and with his head turned away from them. Although his brow is pinched by some sign of consternation, whatever he is thinking or feeling remains unshared with anyone else. If the pictures of popular gatherings are disturbing — and even more disturbing are those involving inmates of the Borda — the sequence of images taken in the Recoleta are frankly depressing: being rich and powerful certainly has nothing to recommend it here.

Gil's photography is profoundly human in its commitments, not because of any element of engagement or commitment in a social and

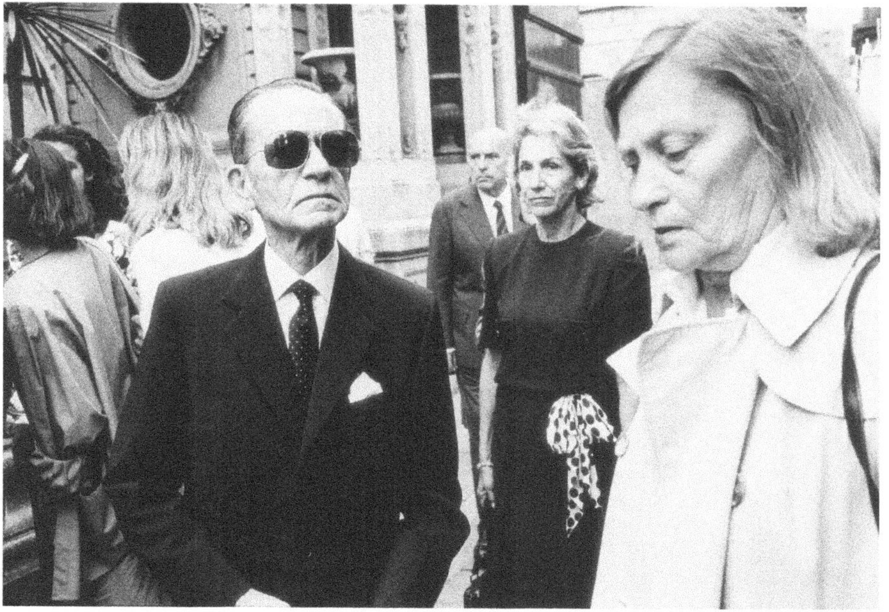

Fig. 3.6 (Eduardo Gil).

political sense. Rather, it is profoundly human precisely in its detachment from the subjects being portrayed. By in many cases abstracting them from the immediate cause of their emotions — or their apparent withdrawal from emotion — his goal is not to discount the importance of what produces those emotions, but rather to portray those emotions as manifestations of a historical condition of Argentines whom he senses to be alone, no matter what their class, with no expectations left.

Gil's most recent work has extended his interest in what I have called Argentina in small letters in two other directions.

One involves the extensive photography of abandoned buildings, such as mills, factories, warehouses, foundries, and the like; also included are the detritus of industrialization (**Fig. 3.7** and **Fig. 3.8**). Although some of these spaces, both those scattered throughout the city and those out in the province, are being recycled as commercial and tourist sites,[9] there are hundreds of decaying and ruined buildings that provide testimony as to both what Argentina once was as a major player on the international economic scene and what it aspired to be as the leading economic power of Latin America.

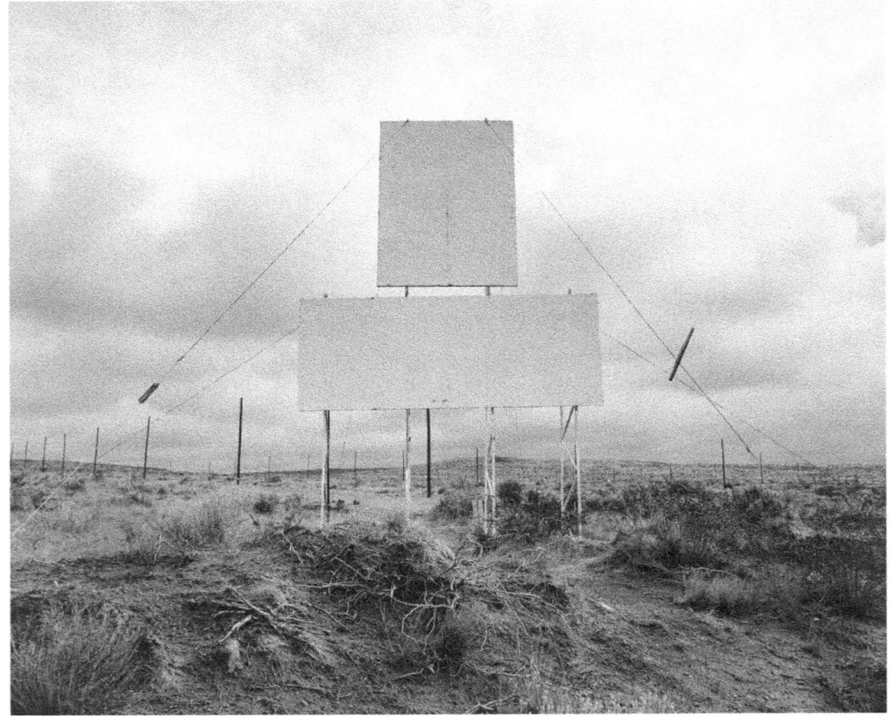

Fig. 3.7 (Eduardo Gil).

Although, as of this writing, the aforementioned images have yet to be mounted as an exhibition, in July 2006, Gil inaugurated, at the Centro Cultural Recoleta, an exhibit called *Paisajes Landscapes*, which consists of thirty-some large color prints of human busts, fairly evenly divided between men and women. These images — for example, **Fig. 3.9** and **Fig. 3.10**— are all characterized by the circumstances that the individuals were photographed with their eyes closed. While the size of the images would tend to give the impression of monumentalizing these individuals, by deflecting the photographic gaze from the eyes, the so-called windows of the soul, Gil underscores the everyman nature of the persons portrayed (most are presumably Argentines, although two are U.S. students who were photographed while visiting Argentina in early 2006 on a cultural tour). Since none of the individuals is identified by name and it is to be assumed that none is a celebrity whom the casual viewer is going to recognize, the overall effect is that of an assemblage

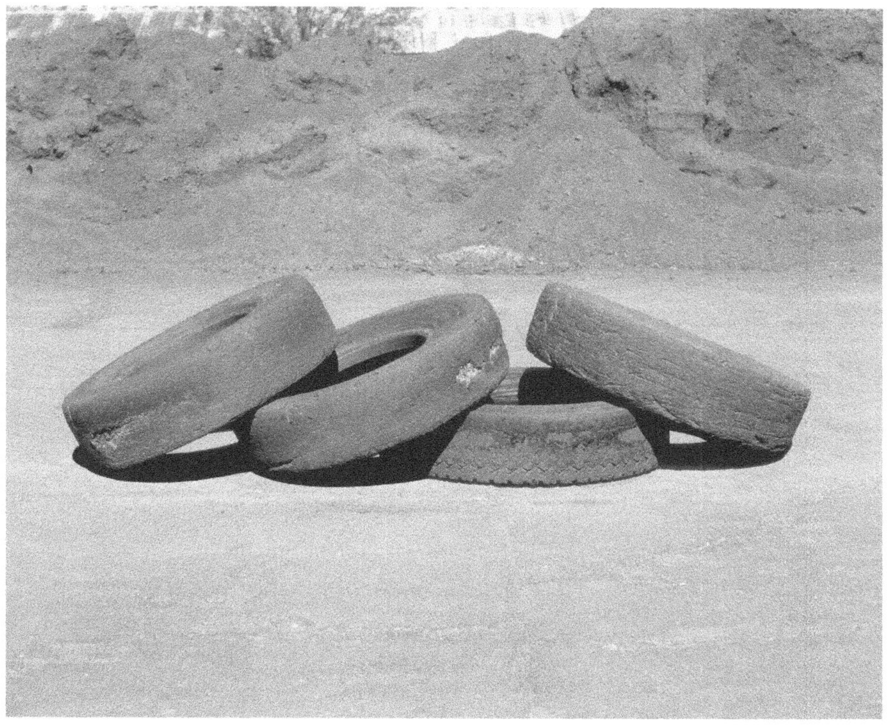

Fig. 3.8 (Eduardo Gil).

of a random sampling of human beings whose one outstanding quality is that they are that and nothing more: human beings. Moreover,
Gil's camera engages in the intense corporeality of precision detail and
intense color resolution, close-up, and minute scrutiny of human flesh.
Since beauty is such a relative concept, it is not here a question of identifying these busts as belonging to particularly beautiful individuals.
Yet the minuteness of their physicality becomes highly seductive, perhaps even erotic, as we scan the texture of their skin, its particular features, regularities, and anomalies.

We are accustomed to studying in detail female nudes, which we
always expect to be full-body and genitally revealing. Gil's busts do
not satisfy that expectation, but they do induce the appreciation of
naked human flesh, if only highly synecdochal in this case. Moreover,
that appreciation, because this is a random selection of both men and
women, invites the spectator to assess equally the physicality of men

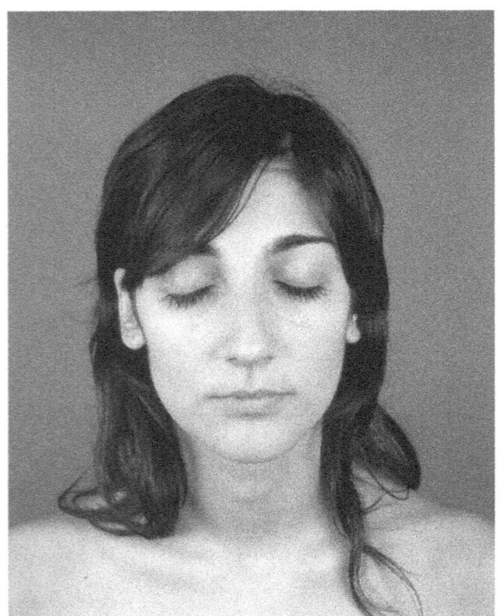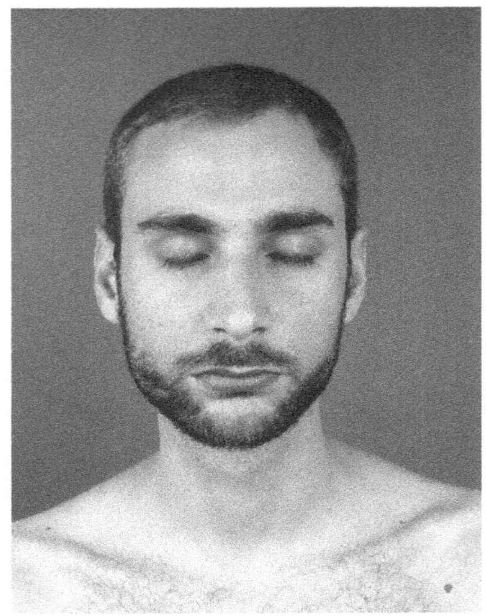

Left: Fig. 3.9. *Right:* Fig. 3.10 (both Eduardo Gil).

and not just that of women. Leaving aside the spectator who may decide to skip the images of one gender to concentrate on those that match the gender of sensual preference, viewers are asked to view all thirty-some of the busts as an equal, as an egalitarian, display of human physical typicality. The collective impression is one of stunning physical attractiveness, and one ought to be hard put to determine which are "prettier," which are "more handsome" than the others.

Gil's *Paisajes* break in other ways with the goal of the portrait, particularly with regard the mouth and body posture: all are rigid with an imposed symmetry of the way in which the head is captured by the photographic frame. This promotes a defamiliarization of the customary codes of portraiture in which mouth, eyes, and body language are presumed to be "in frank and open communication" with the viewer.

4

Gaby Messina's *Grandes mujeres*: Photographing Senior Women

It would probably be inaccurate to identify Argentina as the Latin American country with the greatest concentration of senior citizens: perhaps that attribution would fall to neighboring Uruguay. Yet, there is no question that the many demographic factors at play in Argentina, and especially in the dominant megalopolis of Buenos Aires, serve to make this segment of the population particularly visible. Argentine families are, in the main, small. One or two children per couple is pretty much the norm even in much of the urban working class, and this contributes to the relatively high ratio of older people to youngsters. Health levels and medical attention, while they have slipped noticeably in recent decades, continue in the main above those of most other Latin American countries. Moreover, the continual arrival of new immigrants often means individuals may arrive in Argentina middle-aged if not already seniors. Certain periods see the aging of groups of young immigrants who arrived en masse during a narrow time frame, such as those who came to Argentina at the time of European conflicts between 1930 and 1945, for example. The geriatric home has become an Argentine institution that, between being a good business as the consequence of the frequent difficulty of having older relatives, especially those who are infirm in mind and/or body, in tight living quarters, and more than occasional scandal over mistreatment at the hands of employees and abandonment by their relatives, has become firmly ensconced in the Argentine cultural imaginary, as in the case of Juan José Campanella's 2001 film, *El hijo de la novia* (*The Son of the Bride*), which featured internationally known actors like Norma Aleandro and Ricardo Darín.[1] And too, Argentina, as in the case of other societies, is marked by the greater presence of older women than older men.[2]

It would be possible to develop an extensive bibliography of the representation of seniors in Argentine culture, which would necessarily begin with the old Gaucho in Ricardo Güiraldes's 1926 *Don Segunda Sombra* and would include Roberto Cossa's 1976 *La nona* (*Granny*), Adolfo Bioy Casares's 1973 novel *El diario de la guerra del cerdo* (*Diary of the War of the Pig*), and Alejandro Doria's 1985 film *Esperando la carroza* (*Waiting for the Hearse*), to name only a few of the most important titles.[3] As for the realm of photography, the record fluctuates between the sentimentality-drenched images of Pedro Luis Raota and the unyielding, but nevertheless profoundly touching, ones done by Adriana Lestido, which are examined elsewhere in this book.

The fashion and political photographer Silvio Fabrykant has already held one public showing of his work on *Hombres* (*Argentine Men*) and has another in the planning stages as of this writing (mid–2006); not all of the men are senior, although the bulk are, bringing together socially symbolic power and their years of experience in acquiring it and exercising it (see the discussion of Fabrykant in this book). But it is another photographer whose roots also lie in the world of fashion, Gaby Messina (1971), who, to the best of my knowledge, is the first to put together an important show on Argentine senior women.[4] *Grandes mujeres* (*Great Women*) was hung in the FotoGalería of the Buenos Aires cultural complex known as the Teatro Municipal General San Martín on Avenida Corrientes in the heart of Buenos Aires between March 2 and April 4, 2004.[5] The FotoGalería, which counted as part of its foundation the directorship of the First Lady of Argentine photography, Sara Facio, opens at 11.00 AM and remains open until the end of each day's extensive cultural programming, usually around midnight. Because the San Martín is a major epicenter of Buenos Aires cultural activity, the FotoGalería represents an important initiative, along with the permanent photographic collection at the Museo Nacional de Bellas Artes (also headed up by Sara Facio), in the project to incorporate photography into Argentina's considerable cultural panorama, especially with reference to that production that refers directly or indirectly with the return in 1983 to constitutional democracy.

Messina, whose career in photography began in the realm of advertising — she continues to work for the Mainardi Imágenes agency as an independent photographer — is also interested in painting. *Grandes mujeres* constitutes recognition for Messina in the area of artistic photography (in addition, to be sure, of the artistic dimensions to be found in advertising and fashion photography), and the show has been hung in various other venues since its inauguration at the San Martín.

Grandes mujeres is made up of about fifty images devoted to the foregrounded representation of senior women; on only a few occasions are they accompanied, and in the main they are solitary portraits. All of the images were taken with a high-resolution professional camera such as is used in advertising and all represent a high degree of color saturation, along with the intensity, the sharpness, and the subtleness of detail associated with advertising, images. The result is a series of photographs sustained by rhetorical and ideological premises with respect to the women surveyed by Messina's camera. In the first place, not all of these women are of high socio-economic standing, although the high-fashion photography that constitutes the intertext of this technical level of photography implies such standing. Yet most of them are, in fact, surrounded by the material trappings of the so-called good life, not to mention questions of taste that have to do with personal preferences and generational modes as seen in the type and variety of objects, their marked abundance, and the continuity, especially in terms of saturated color, between the objects and the human subjects they surround, frame, and contextualize. By undertaking portraits of women who appear to be in charge of their own surroundings (I repeat that not all are well-off, but the majority tend to possess a "room of their own" and a life free from concerns with respect to food and medication), Messina underscores feminine independence. Newspaper statistics may tend to refer to the high concentration of women put away in geriatric homes, living on the street, or doomed to precarious abodes, as in the case of many older and rundown — and, in some cases, officially abandoned — buildings in the central core of the city where infrastructure components such as heating and elevators may no longer work, not to mention incidences of public suicides. But Buenos Aires continues to be a city of independent women whose presence is quite evident in the streets, in business establishments, in cafes and restaurants, in galleries and museums, and especially at cultural events, were they may be alone or accompanied by other women (and perhaps by other kinds of consorts).

Along with the representation of senior women who are mistresses of their own space, as much material space (the site at which they are photographed) as symbolic space (their full exercise of life as they make use of their own space for the execution of their personal tastes and interests), Messina attempts to capture the dignity of their being in the world: neither beaten down by life nor reduced by social circumstance, these are women who continue to live life to the fullest and with determination and confidence. Suffice it to say that there are probably hundreds of thousands of women in Buenos Aires who live in unfortunate poverty-stricken circumstances, and their lives deserve photographic representation as fact, and a denunciation of that fact, and as part of a social commitment to their dignity, although one always needs to ask if the mawkish sentimentalism of someone like Raota, for example, effectively fulfills this function, in accordance with the well-known Brechtian proposition that emotion vitiates and purges the horror of intractable sociohistorical reality.

Yet at the same time there is also a social commitment involved in the portrayal of women who to one degree or another continue to exercise control over their lives. Not all of the women photographed by Messina are either real or symbolic embodiments of the great national icon of female socio-economic power, Amelia Lacroze de Fortabat, reputed to be the wealthiest woman in Latin America (Ventura, 82–90). Nevertheless, what is to be gained from these images as a whole is the dignity inherent in being a woman, the dignity inherent in being an older woman, if not specifically an aged one, and the dignity of being able to count on objects and personal tastes and interests that give texture and meaning to that life. By contrast to women warehoused in a geriatric home (no matter how elegant it is, as is the case of the institution where Norma Aleandro is confined in *El hijo de la novia*) or to those who are abandoned in inclement solitude in the parks and plazas of Buenos Aires, the women Messina has photographed have a place to be, enjoy a place of their own in the world and, more than anything else, are able to take advantage of a realm of vitality and relative peace of mind.

The title of Messina's show plays overtly on the double meaning of the Spanish adjective *grande*. Although we usually teach that *grande* belongs to that category of adjectives that change their meaning in accordance with whether they are preposed or postposed to a noun ("great" in the sense of important vs. "large" or "grown-up"), this is in reality a rather inadequate explanation. Just as in any language, Spanish evinces many cases of homonyms (and many historical sources for such homonyms), and from a lexical point of view, it is preferable to identifying them as discrete lexemes, "words" or "word phrases" in more colloquial parlance. Lexemes are units of semantic meaning, although it may be necessary, in turn, to recognize circumstances of synonymity between homonyms: L_1, L_2, L_3, and so on. From this analytical point of view, one can proceed to describe the syntactic distribution (along with the morphological behavior) of each lexeme. Thus one can speak of the lexeme {$grande_1$} (which basically means "important"), {$grande_2$} (which basically means "adult"), and {$grande_3$} (which basically means "large").

The lexeme {$grande_3$} appears not to be at issue here, although there are women who could be described as imposing in size, and reference could be made to their physical presence and their apparent standard of living. In the case of {$grande_1$} and {$grande_2$}, once their semantic difference has been established, it becomes possible to deal with whatever syntactic differentiation might be involved. While it is true that, precisely, the distribution of *grande* in the sense of "important" usually falls in front of the noun that it modifies, and *grande* in the sense of "aged" will usually fall after the modified noun, poetic license, which customarily enjoys the broadest of latitudes in the maximization of the expressive quality of language, can take into account the disruption of this distribution pattern, which looks so easy when one is teaching it as part of basic grammar. The simple fact is that, socio-historically, "important men" (and the sexist note is intentional) are often of an advanced age, as one can easily note in the paradigm of the Pope, of Chinese and indigenous wise men, and the like: as a consequence *grandes hombres grandes*—"great aged men"—would be almost a redundancy.

When Messina extends this sociohistoric detail to the sphere of women and when she undertakes portraits for our contemplation that include as much senior women as women who are important because they are in charge of their own lives, there is an implied redundancy, *grandes mujeres grandes*, which ends up being, in terms of the esteem and consideration that our societies in general accord women of a certain age, somewhat of an oxymoron. For this reason, Messina would appear to privilege the preposed position of the modifying adjective, which is more associated with the meaning of "important": these are without a question *mujeres grandes* (that is, "senior women"), but what is more important is that they be seen as *grandes mujeres*—grand/important women, worthy exemplars of the degree to which it is possible for a woman to be in command of her own life and her own space. Such a command is, to be sure, relative: no one is free of the contingencies of the world. But the point is the evident degree to which these women exude a sense of self-affirming command that, while it may always be under threat by the contingencies of the world, affords them the sense of focus and centeredness that is amply apparent in these images, as much for women of wealth as women of modest means, as much for women of professional accomplishment as housewives, as much for women surrounded by unusual icons of their lives as for those whose material projections are the humdrum, the quotidian, and the kitsch. Messina's use of intensely saturated colors and sharp resolution contribute markedly to a certain sense of the unusual or the unexpected, and this leads the spectator to invest a great deal of attention in them that might not be case if they were more documentary (especially in black and white) or the more washed-out and perhaps even typically drab colors of the everyday universe of images that one is more accustomed to encountering on the street and in the realm of the domestic. In this regard, it is instructive to contrast Messina's images of these "great ladies" with the "Argentine men," all of importance and influence in typically masculinist spheres, portrayed in black and white by Silvio Fabrykant, which are studied elsewhere in this book. One man does not affirm the dignity of all senior men, because each is esteemed for his—usually—recognized individual talents and place in the world.

But this is not true as such for an older woman. This is not discrimination, but the simple social fact that the underprivileged category of women, and the double underprivileging of a woman of a certain age, transforms her, in accordance with a useful principle of a proper feminism, into an icon that does not apply to men. Of course, it is to state the obvious to note that such iconicity applies also to women of color, the handicapped, sexual minorities, and any other category of subalternity that one might choose to mention.

One cannot simply assume that all of these women are widows (indeed, one appears with a man who is likely her husband), although many are likely to be, given the demographic fact that women tend to outlive men, at least in industrialized societies. And it may be that not all subscribe to the assertion that the best condition for women is that of a widow: she did marry legitimately at one time, but her lord and master is no longer around.... What is definitely notable is that these women, from what we can tell from their hands, only rarely sport a wedding band. Some may be wearing some other types of rings, but not the one that signals their condition as a Mrs. Since sociolinguistic practices always assume that an older woman has long since passed through the hoops of lawful marriage, it is customary to use the vocative title "Mrs." with little regard to whether the woman remains married, is a widow (or now in Argentina, is a divorcee), or, with the cruel eloquence of patriarchal and heterosexist principles, never "was deserving" of being a wife. It is undoubtedly important to underscore how these women are portrayed as though their world were not as important as that of a couple, although in several cases there are others present in the photograph. There are two cases of two women in each other's company (**Fig. 4.1**), one case of a woman and a man, a birthday party that includes multiple celebrants, one case of patients in a geriatric ward; I discount the case of a woman with a baby in her arms or the case of a woman with her maidservant standing stiffly at attention. But even in those cases involving women of relatively modest circumstances (including one who is quite impoverished, who is shown working as a street vendor), the general effect afforded by the photographic frame is that these women function as mistresses of their own world. As I have already stated, the world may not really work this way (and who is, after all, wholly in control of her or his own world?), but

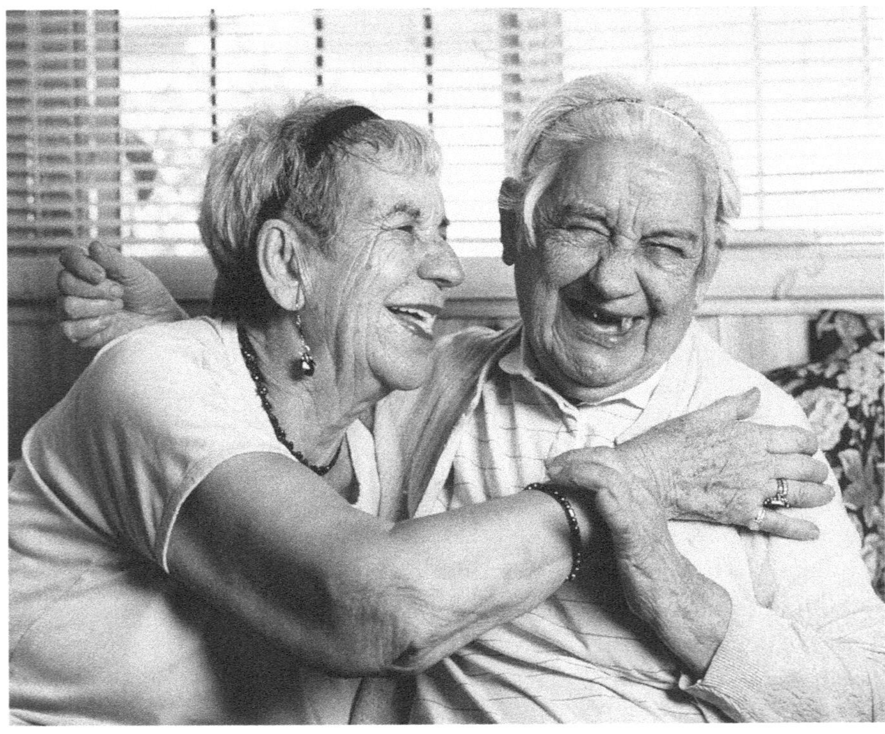

Fig. 4.1 *Ana y Adela* (Galy Messina).

in the main the rhetoric of these photographs would so have us feel it to be the case, and herein reside both their charm and their interest as feminist representation (**Fig. 4.2**).

One of Roland Barthes's most famous declarations about photography is that such images always convey an unmistakable allusion to death. When we scrutinize a photograph, the time at which it was taken is now (often, long) past, the point in time to which it belongs chronologically (9 inter alia). Of course, this is true of any semiotic gesture: it is virtually impossible for the present time of narration to be the present of the moment of its reading. Nevertheless, photography (along with film and the latter's derivative, television) share the quality that they are representative codes that conform more to the outlines of what we identify as lived reality; television, of course, is most able to provide the effect that what one is witnessing is what is (even if it is not) taking place at the very moment of watching the

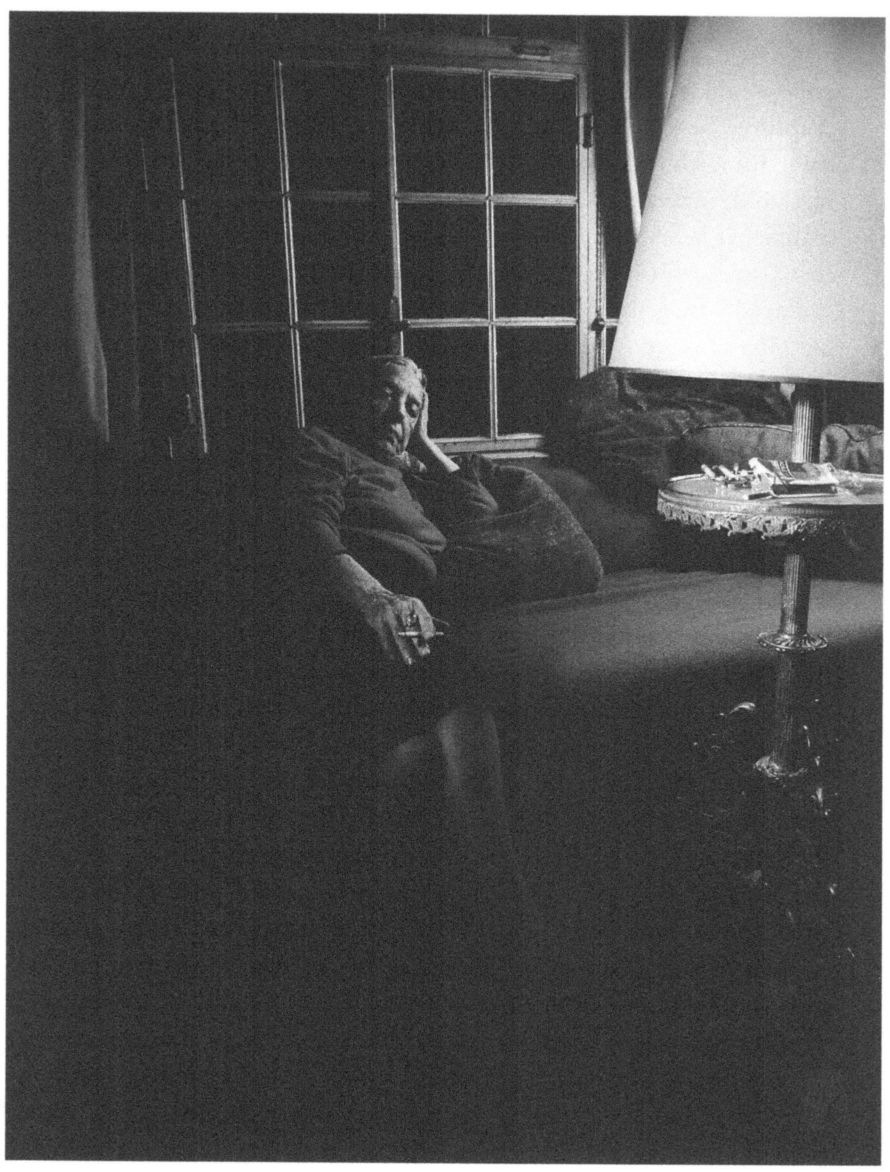

Fig. 4.2 *Chincina* (Galy Messina).

screen. To put it differently, except for the varieties we are likely to call "experimental," photography and its peers are understood as the most accurate transcription of lived reality. Barthes's proposal is that, since this is so, we cannot, as a consequence, avoid comprehending how the instant of lived reality that the photograph captures is now dead and gone — and it would be more appropriate to say "captured" rather than "captures," even when we understand the latter verbal form semantically not as the present tense but an indefinite durative. One could, in fact, and, indeed, one should, take for granted that the photographed reality has been lost, and what is more crucial, that the human beings that populate it have undergone their inexorable transformation into the dead. As in the case of the infirm (e.g., the photographic autobiography of the now deceased cancer patient Gabriela Liffschitz examined elsewhere in this study, or the sick children photographed by Helen Zouk and Gabriel Mistral), there always exists in the case of seniors the possibility that any photograph of them will be the last one, and, in fact, some of the subjects of *Grandes mujeres* have passed on.[6] I do not mean by this that *Grandes mujeres* is an exercise in necrophilia, but quite the opposite: it affords meaning to an account of the life of these women precisely at a time in which they are, in the main, still in the flush of life, a dimension that quickly and definitively affirms itself to the extent that they are photographed in their own universe, surrounded by the (for them) meaningful icons for them of that universe, and carrying on a life that is mostly still active and dynamic. There are some exceptions, of course: the woman surrounded by the celebrants at her birthday party appears to be quite feeble. But the majority stand out for the conviction of their pose and the sharpness of their awareness of the photographic gaze. Obviously, the very studied pose of the ballerina Galina (**Fig. 4.3**), with her dancing tights and holding what appears to be a bouquet of canna lilies, securely ensconced in an elegant armchair in an ostentatious display of her still fine legs, is indicative of a photographic subject interacting fully with the gaze of the camera. If it is true that death always hovers over the camera, Messina holds it at bay by underscoring the life that still remains in these women. That some of them may already be going down the path of irreversible decline and debilitation, nevertheless, only serves to reinforce the vitality of the others.

Since Messina comes from the world of fashion photography, it is legitimate to ask to what extent the saturation of colors and the sharpness of the image does not lead to a certain parody of these women, as though they were professional models, when they are anything but, and the degree to which what is involved here is a parody

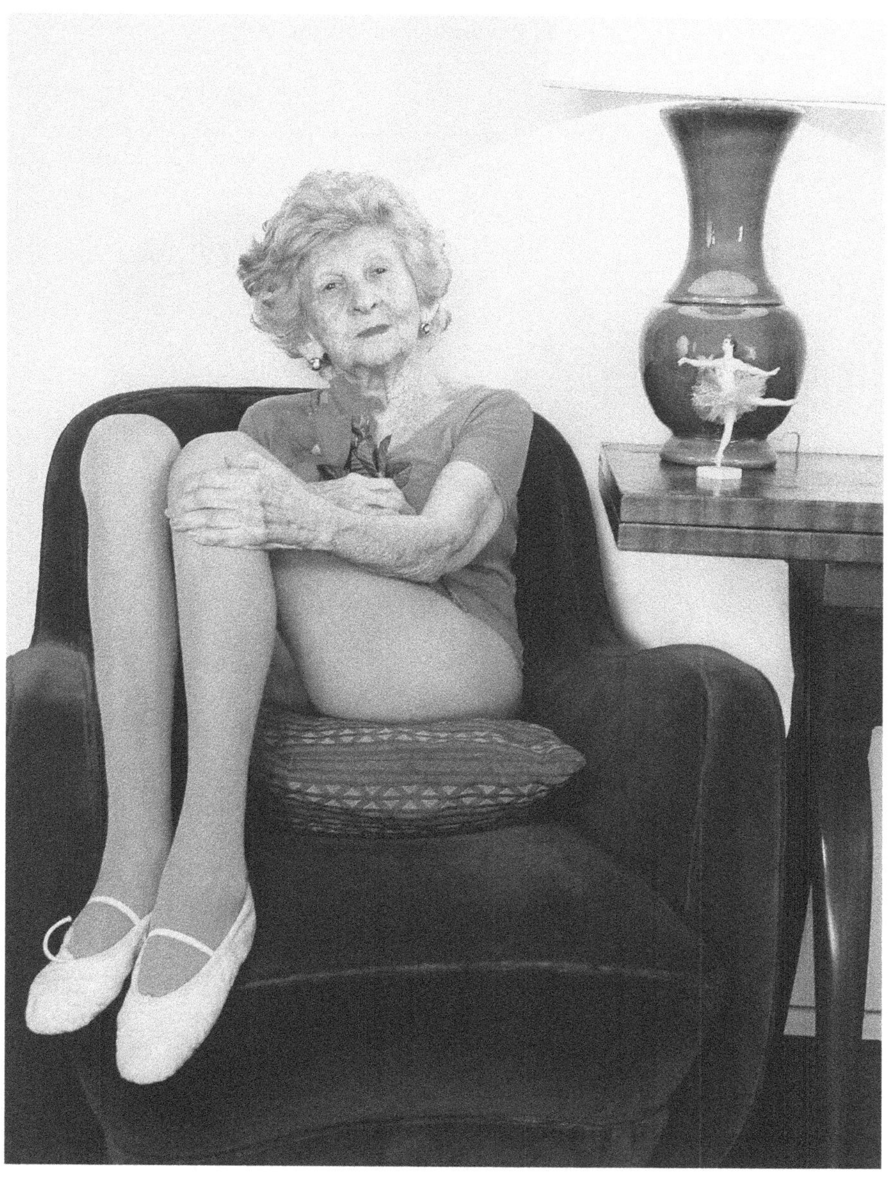

Fig. 4.3 *Galina* (Gaby Messina).

of the fashion model by employing women who are, shall we say, quite far over the hill in terms of the conventional codes of the industry. It is immaterial that fashion magazines may occasionally include older women, at times to produce a generational effect or one of contrast as regards the products being sold; one may also note the mature regal

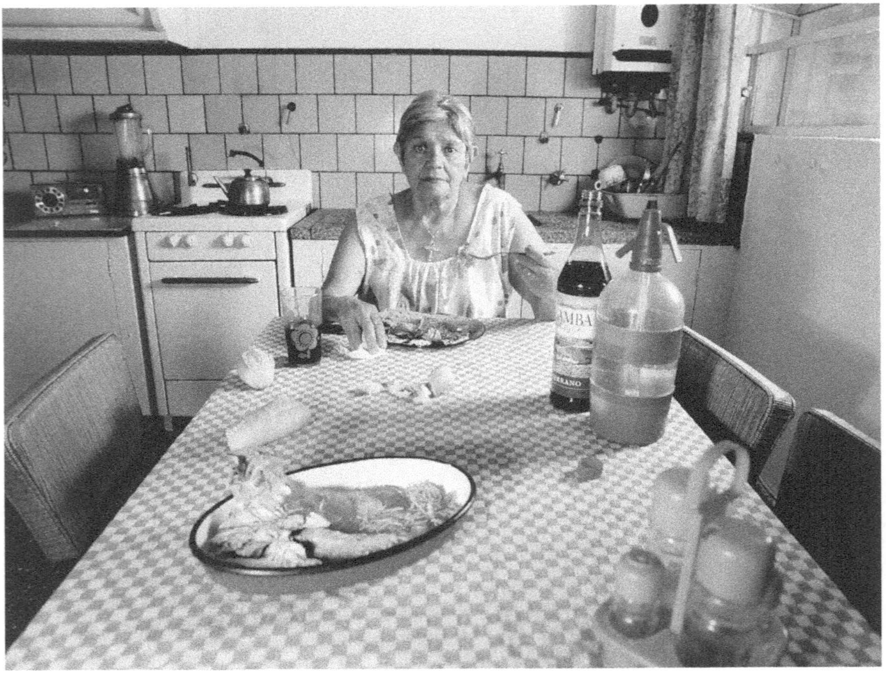

Fig. 4.4 *Haydee* (Gaby Messina).

presence in their advertisements of the women whose names are attached to certain products, such as Helena Rubenstein or Estée Lauder, not to mention, in her day, the Ur-type of Coco Chanel. But there is no evidence of any such intent in the photographs of *Grandes mujeres*. Yet, none of them portrays the least hint of parody or condescension. This is so even when some of the aesthetic decisions of the women being portrayed could be alleged to border on the extravagant, as in the case of the previously mentioned Galina and her ballerina raiment. But this very extravagance, rather than giving way to any ridicule on the part of the photographic gaze, is part of the affirmation of their character and their personal life: there is absolutely no reason why an eighty-year-old former ballerina cannot, should not display the tools of her trade. To suppress them would not mean investing Galina with the dignity of an older woman resigned to conform to the demands of decency of bourgeois normativeness. Rather, it would be to deprive her of the best memories of her life, and this would be an unpardonable repression. We have no way of knowing whether or not dance continues to be the center of the life of this woman, although one of the icons of her accompanying decor is a tiny statuette of a ballerina; along with a porcelain lamp, the statuette rests on a table next to the chair on which Galina is delicately poised, her slight figure almost overwhelmed by the imposing chair. But it is all too evident that such is the identity that she wishes to have the photograph record. In other cases it might be the books of a retired professor; the kitchen utensils of a woman who has always prided herself on her culinary arts (**Fig. 4.4**); the piano with which others may have graced their urban existence, if they did not use it to give lessons to legions of students or play professionally. And in one case, what is involved is the laboratory equipment of a fellow photographer.

These great Argentine women may be long retired from the stress of everyday life, but only one seems truly abandoned among the fel-

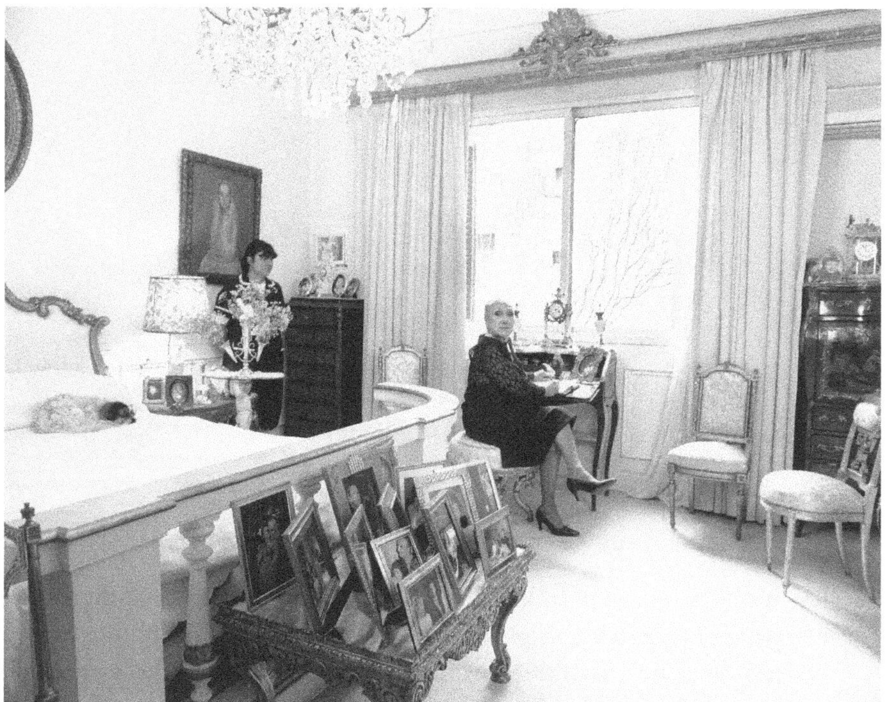

Fig. 4.5. *Nina* (Gaby Messina).

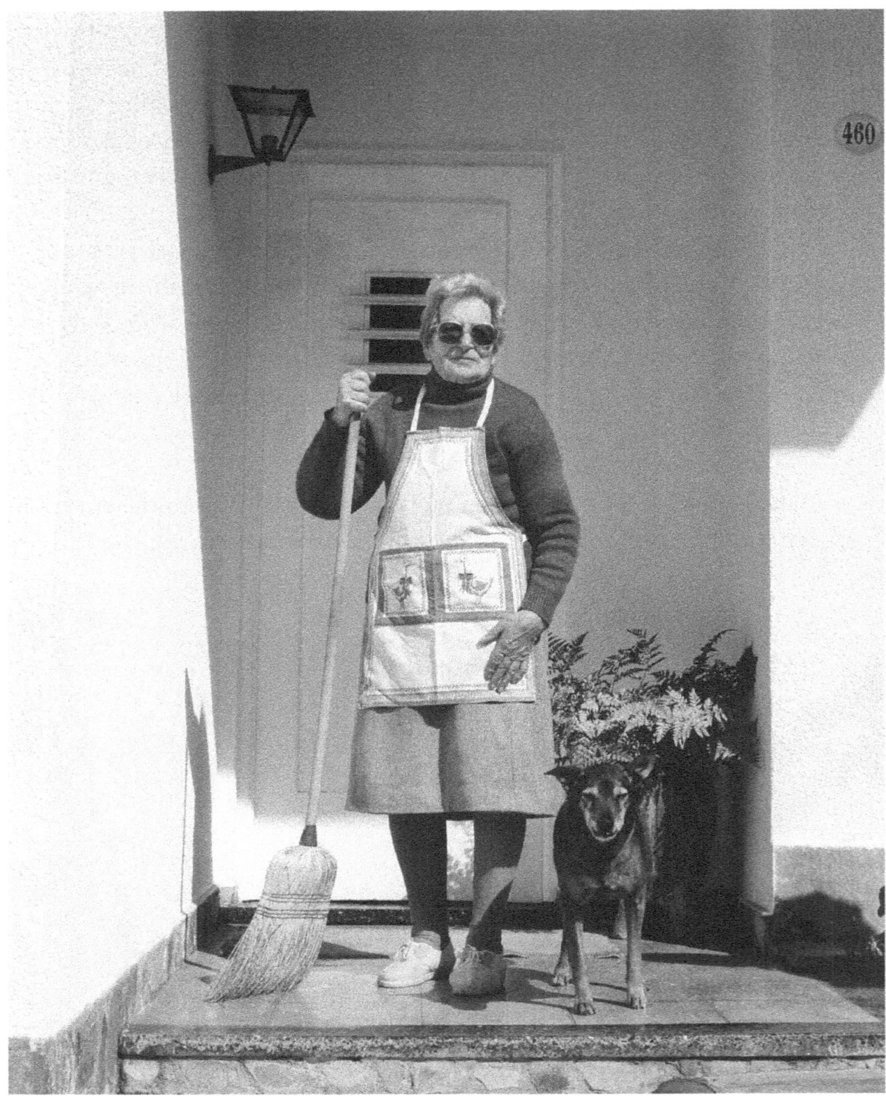

Fig. 4.6 *Elena* (Gaby Messina).

low inmates in an old folks' home, so abandoned that it is difficult to tell which is the woman who is the main object of the photograph. Nor do the majority of these women participate fully in the economic apparatus of society, although the woman who sells little packets of grains and spices is as much a cog in that apparatus as the uptown woman who, seated at her desk, could be signing checks and giving orders to her staff concerning the financial backing of the very plush world she occupies: this is the same woman who has her maid standing attentively at order at her side (**Fig. 4.5**). The overall sensation afforded by Messina's photographs is that of a world of senior women whom we do not ordinarily see on the street, so to speak, even though, as noted above, Argentine women enjoy broad access to public spaces. Nevertheless, these are women whose universe appears to be mostly the domestic realm, and it is in their houses that Messina chose to photograph them and not in the so-called public space of a cafe, business enterprise, bookstore, or theater. Even in the case of the woman left to her own devices in the geriatric institution, we understand that now, regrettably, this is her home. We see the senior women of our lives in their houses, and Messina includes her own grandmothers among these great women. But there are only so many of them, and one is not accustomed to frequenting the chambers of any more than a few of them, those who are part of the family. In this sense, *Grandes mujeres* has the virtue of revealing to us a world that is, in its totality, almost clandestine, and one cannot come away from the contemplation of the assembled images without asking, And where in this vast city of apartments and houses do all these women live? What must the house of the older woman sweeping her front porch who lives down the block look like on the inside? (**Fig. 4.6**) Is she one of these great women? Unquestionably, she is.

5

Women's Society in Prison:
Adriana Lestido's *Mujeres presas*

The theme of women in prison has always exercised a morbid fascination on the Western social imagination, at least on the masculinist one. Not only does the representation of the incarcerated female body reduplicate in an explicit way the many ways in which women are imprisoned — metaphorically, literally, and synecdochally — under the sign of male hegemony, but it also evokes the ways in which the trope of bondage is essential to many heterosexist fantasies regarding both the hygienic and erotic control of the female body.[1] Although popular culture has often dealt with women in prison in terms of women's bodies out of control that are only with physical and psychological violence somewhat brought back under the institutional surveillance of the patriarchy through incarceration — with or without a dimension of lesbian fantasy thrown in as an added proof of their precariousness vis-à-vis the patriarchy — imprisoned women speak also to another dimension of social fantasy: that of women as sacred vessels of morality, motherhood, family, and the civilizing force of the feminine.[2] Women are not only, as are all human beings, children of God in this imagination, but in its Catholic version, they are also daughters of the Virgin Mary, whose virtue they incarnate in their status as mothers (Graziano discusses this logic in his book on the military ideology of the Dirty War).

The degradation of men in prison is, in one interpretation of the social text, an inscription of the degree to which the patriarchy intends to enforce its code, with the concomitant incarceration of women a warning to the effect that this too can befall a woman unwilling to abide by that code. However, a different interpretation of the social text would have it that the incarceration of women is — as all incarceration must ultimately be viewed — scandalous. This is so because it points to how social life is unable to ensure the nondegradation of humanity (see Eduardo Mignogna's film, *La fuga* (2001) for an interesting example of recent Argentine cultural production on the dynamics of incarceration[3]). Imprisonment in Argentina also included the massive extralegal human rights violations whereby the degradation of human beings contemplated by democratic law was reinforced by the degradation attributed to themselves as legitimate by the agents of the authoritarian dictatorship, particularly during the period of neofascist military dictatorship.

The photographic series *Mujeres presas* (2001) by Adriana Lestido (1955–) contains images that were part of the exhibit of eleven contemporary — mostly young — Argentine photographers in a 1999 exhibit at the International Center of Photography in New York. Like several of the other photographers in the exhibit (Gabriel Valansi, Gabriel Díaz, and Eduardo Gil, for example), Lestido works in black and white, providing a texture of "documentalism" that is particularly appropriate for the drab institutional life of her subjects (Lestido is mentioned in passing in Domenech's essay on photography and prisons). Lestido is predominantly interested in the continuity of the family within prison walls, of which there are two points to be made, as contained in ancillary prose texts that accompany the photographs:

En Argentina, las mujeres presas pueden tener consigo a sus hijos hasta los dos años de edad. Luego pierden la patria potestad y es la justicia la que decide el destino de los niños. Algunos siguen junto a sus madres en la cárcel hasta que son liberadas. Otros son entregados a familias, orfanatos o familias adoptivas temporales [no pag.].

En las cárceles de hombres se pueden ver mujeres haciendo cola, a veces desde la noche anterior, para visitarlos. Eso no pasa en las cárceles de mujeres. A las mujeres las dejan más solas [Oficial a cargo de los Tribunales de San Martín, no pag.].

This situation provides for a very idiosyncratic reduplication of the family within the institution of the prison. For, if it is possible for women to keep children at their side until the age of two (an arrangement apparently not meant to extend beyond the period of lactation), the possibility of separation after the age of two constitutes potentially severe psychological trauma for both mother and child. And since women do not know if they will be able to keep their children, the very threat and uncertainty of separation, even when it does not take place, is a form of psychological and disciplinary duress. By the same token, the probability that these women will be abandoned by their men (and many of whose names these women bear inscribed on their body in the form of the extensive tattooing that is evident in the photographs, including tattoos worn by children), by men who are not likely to seek them out in prison, is only a crueler version of the extent to which women are particularly likely to be abandoned by the men they love under the aegis of a patriarchy whereby men are encouraged not to think of women, not to consider their needs. Indeed, in Latin America it may even be considered a form of unacceptable weakness in a man, shading off into queerness, to spend too much time thinking about a woman.[4]

Thus, if there is the initial impression that there is some possibility of reconstructing family life within the prison setting, in terms of permitted visits between prisoners and partners and the possibility of retaining contact with, at least, the youngest child from the family unit, it is devastatingly belied by the information provided by these two statements. It may be possible to speak of a horizontal reconstruction of a semblance of family within prison (rather than the vertical one that reaches beyond the prison walls to include these women's partners and other family members). Such a configuration would involve three different but interrelated axes: the women among themselves, the children among themselves, and the children in relationship to both their mothers and other women. This is a slim volume of material—only nineteen photographs—but all three axes are related, and I will return to them below. What is important to underscore at this point is the way in which a perception of alternative configurations of society for these women within the confines of the prison becomes a necessary matter of speculation, interpretation, and discovery, in the face of the precarious nature of the so-called properly constituted patriarchal and heterosexist family.

However, before focusing on questions of family, I would like to take up issues of social class and ethnic extraction. These photographs derive from the Cárcel No. 8 de Los Hornos, La Plata, Provincia de Buenos Aires (according to the website "Mujeres presas"; the volume contains an image of the prison, but does not identify it). Now, it is a well known fact that, universally, prison life determines to an ever-greater extent the degree to which one goes down the class scale; the same is true along other axes such as ethnicity (people of color) and sexuality as well as regional or national origin. It is quite evident from these photographs that Lestido has not photographed women who represent national fantasies about race and ethnicity. If one looks at the women photographed in the Borda mental asylum by Sara Facio and Alicia D'Amico's *Humanario* (1976; the photographs all date from 1966, however; see Foster, "Sara Facio"), there are some very vivid distinctions to be perceived. The women photographed at the Borda are all European in appearance and many give evidence have having led some sort of life of comfort and even privilege before circumstances of their mental health took them to the Borda; there are no tattoos, for example, perceivable on the bodies of the women photographed by d'Amico and Facio.

By contrast, the women photographed by Lestido appear in the main to fall into the category that Argentine classist, if not racist, discourse would call *cabecitas negras*. I have no way of knowing if these women all exemplify *cabecitas negras* (by their age, they would have to be descendants of those Perón originally brought into Buenos Aires over fifty years ago). But there can be no question that they embody a lumpen that has not enjoyed the special privileges of "white" Buenos Aires.

There is the simple fact that any representative prison population will necessarily include something like a majority of individuals whose entire lives have been lived out on the margins of social integration. I do not, by saying this, mean to invest in any way in a sort of social determinism whereby the children of these women will, in due course, also become prison statistics. I only wish to stress that, at least in a society of the rule of law (no matter how unjustly applied — or, perhaps, because it is unjustly applied), one ends up incarcerated in an institution such as that to be viewed in these photographs as part of an entire life cycle in which social marginalization begets social marginalization, with prison only being an extreme instance of that marginalization.

But beyond that simple, if grim, social fact, the women captured by Lestido in her photographs are as much for a prevailing Buenos Aires social imagination an ethnic other as they are, in the prima facie fact of their imprisonment, a class other. This is evident in their tattoos (and it is important to point out that these are not tattoos as body art, but rather as a sort of badge of identification), in their clothes, in their body language, including the defiant look in the eyes of many who stare down the camera.[5] Individuals whose unremittingly harsh circumstances of life are echoed in some of these external, material features of their bodily presence can be found on the streets of Buenos Aires and in varying degrees of concentration according to the area of the city in which one finds oneself (I am thinking particularly of the Miserere plaza and market area, barely ten blocks from the National Congress — veritably a "Third World" island in the heart of the city). But it is their undiluted concentration in these photographs that most dramatically portrays a social other vis-à-vis guidebook Buenos Aires. In this sense, Lestido's women are a frontal assault on the viewer who would write women like these out of history, either not knowing of their existence or refusing to accord them a meaningful place in the social semiotic of Argentina.

What the camera sees in these women is a combination of abandonment and defiance. One could argue that prison photos, along with any other cultural production related to prisons, necessarily contain, if only implicitly, a dimension of abandonment. Isolation, marginalization, ignorance, and the consideration of the prisoner as effectively dead are part of the terrible logic of incarceration, and it is not for nothing that imprisonment has been described as a "living death." The cover image of Lestido's collection of photos shows a woman with pouty lips and somewhat disheveled hair, who intently avoids looking toward the camera (**Fig. 5.1**). Her eyes are turned as far to the left as is possible, as she holds her infant child in something less than an embrace of tenderness; the child's head is lolled forward in sleep. In the context of the affirmation that these women are mostly unsought by their men, the foregrounded left arm of Rosa (the women's names

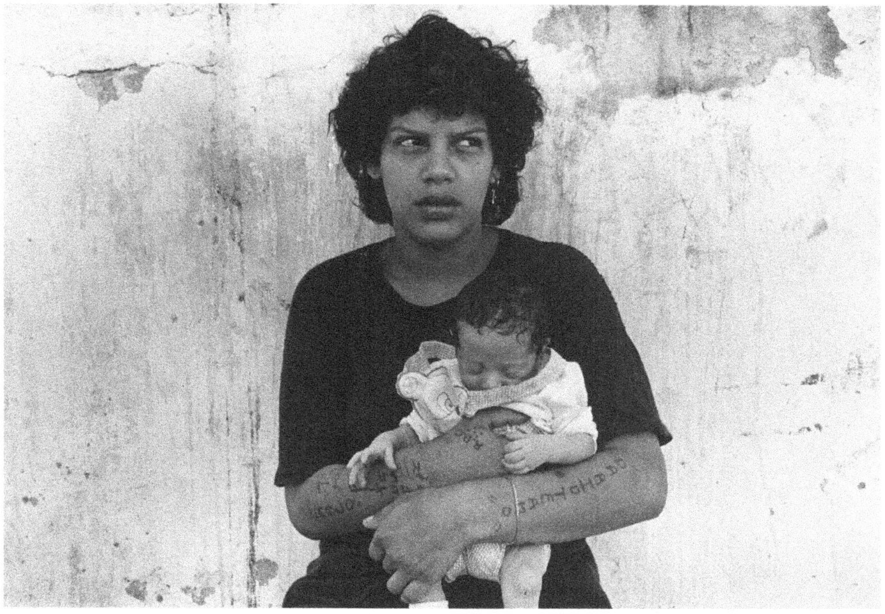

Fig. 5.1 (Adriana Lestido).

are given with the images posted at the "Mujeres presas" web site, but not in the published volume) is noteworthy for the tattoo "DARIO TE AMO." It may not be correct to assume that Darío is the child's father, since we can also make out a tattoo that reads "CARLOS" on her right arm. We can also make out the initials "R.D.C." and five stars (a conventional prison tattoo) on the fleshy part above the web of her right hand; there are other tattoos that are illegible. "R.D.C." may be her own initials. Tattoos in this instance — in addition to other functions such as indicating gang commitments, political affiliations, and initiation processes (the pain of tattooing is often a rite of passage for groups, marginal or otherwise) — are an indelible record of her allegiances. They are also cause for a measure of morbid curiosity on the part of visitors to the International Center of Photography or its Buenos Aires equivalent (i.e., the FotoGalería at the Centro Cultural San Martín) attracts.

Many of the women in Lestido's photographs bear tattoos, and these are notably the traces of the social groups, whether characterized as marginal or not, among/through which they have moved. More-

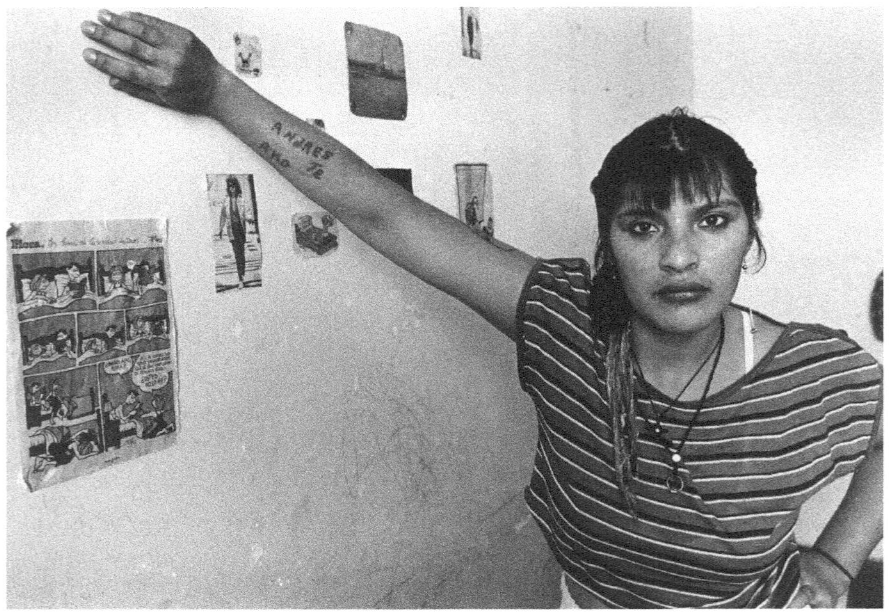

Fig 5.2 (Adriana Lestido).

over, these tattoos also speak to the patriarchal conditions of their lives, since, without exception, they are statements of fealty to men. In one of the photographs, a woman assumes a fiercely defiant — and really quite threatening — pose (**Fig. 5.2**). Her left hand rests on her hip in a time-honored stance of female assertion, while her right arm extends up and out, with the palm planted firmly on the wall above a cartoon and illustrations taken from magazines. The right arm bears the tattoo "ANDRES TE AMO". The use of "amo" rather than "quiero" is worthy of note. Certainly, it may be preferred because it is shorter, requiring less space — and less pain — to transcribe.

Yet the verb "amar" is one of greater formal intensity and emotional subservience than the more colloquial and more semantically generalized verb "querer." In the case of another woman, a woman whose face betrays profound hurt, we can see on her left wrist what appears to be the name "JUSTO," underlined by an arrow whose tailfin is a heart. Her left hand bears what must be the word "MADRE," while her index finger bears an "L": it is impossible to determine if this is part of another name or a common noun, presumably of four letters in either case. What is particularly striking about this photograph is the fact that the woman is wearing a wedding band on her right hand. But what is most striking is the fact that the little girl she holds (she looks to be six or seven, obviously beyond the usual two-year-old age limit) is also tattooed. Running down her left arm is the name "CLAUDIO" and the beginning of another name or word "ABU"—ABUELO or ABUELA, perhaps. One wonders if the Claudio here is her father, although descending intergenerational male-female tattooing is a rare phenomenon. That is, male children may bear a tattoo dedicated to their mother (ascending female-male tattooing), or, as in the case of the previously commented photograph, the ascending female-female tattoo with which the woman prisoner evokes her mother. But the tattoos women wear are typically dedicated to their male lovers, not their fathers.

But no matter who Claudio is in the life of this little girl, one must assume that it is not a tattoo that she freely chose. Hence, one interpretational possibility is that one act of defiance on the part of this woman is to inscribe in large letters the name of the perhaps absent (disappeared? imprisoned? dead?) father on the child's body. There is always the possibility that this is writing on the child's arm and not a tattoo, but for the impact of the photograph in terms of women's relationships to absent men and their stance for the camera, the message is the same whether or not it is an indelible trace of the child's identity: the Name of the Father.

In another photograph, a woman, her face showing distress and perplexity, is holding a large kitchen knife (**Fig. 5.3**). This woman is untattooed and also wears a wedding band, although it is on the left hand. She is wearing a dirty apron, and a wrap-around marble countertop and a tiled wall can be seen in the background, so this is probably a kitchen, and the photograph was likely taken during her shift as a food preparer. Nevertheless, her emotionally charged face and the tense way in which she is holding the heavy knife, which extends straight out from her hand, is unquestionably threatening, the stance of a *mater furiosa*. A strong brew of physical and psychological violence characterizes prison life the world over, especially for individuals of the sort of lower-class strata represented in these photographs, and the inclusion of specific stances of violence only heightens the overall vio-

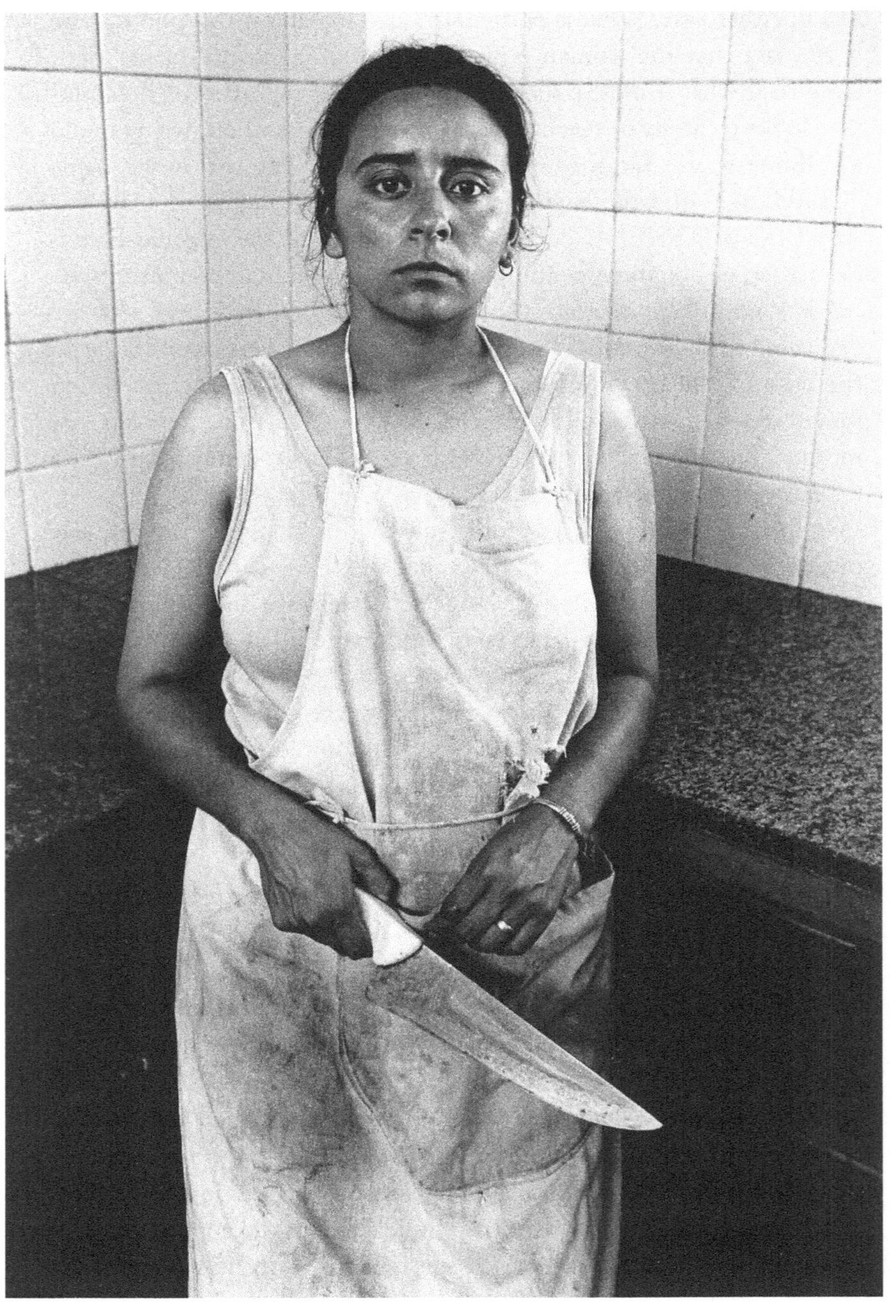

Fig. 5.3 (Adriana Lestido).

lence of this social milieu (in another photograph, a woman, seen from behind bars, raises a clenched fist to the camera, even as she turns her face away from the gaze of the photographer). Lestido's women are not passive victims of their fate. While not all of the women are shown in menacing poses, there is surely the attempt to capture the internalized violence that is part of their lives, a violence that is unquestionably intensified by the circumstances of their incarceration. It is a violence that is transmitted through their entire bodies and it is present in their body language, and it is present in the language inscribed on their bodies, because, whatever it is taken to mean, tattooing is never anything but a painful invasion of the body. The fact that the prison in question shows the signs of disrepair and the complete absence of anything like comfort and amenities — the scrutiny of which is intensified by the unremitting gaze of sharply defined black-and-white photography — only serves to underscore the fundamental misery of these women and the calculus of violence that it drives.

Yet, these are not caged animals, another frequent metaphor of the prison, and there is much to be said about the image of homosocial bonding that takes place between them. Homosocial bonding is not the same as homoerotic bonding, although the latter may develop out of the former, or vice versa. Homosocial bonding does not necessarily contain an erotic charge, but is rather built on emotional feelings, commitment, and a sense of collaboration in the defense of an agenda. Homosocial bonding in the case of men has been, as in the now famous studies of Eve Kosofsky Sedgwick, understood as underpinning and cementing the patriarchy, to the exclusion from power of women and of men identified in numerous ways as "womanlike." However, female homosocial bonding, "sisterhood" (*comadrismo* or *comadrazo*, in Spanish) is more likely to function as a form of defense against the patriarchy, with or without a component of defense against the heteronormativity of the patriarchy. In one register, female homosocial bonding may involve the acceptance of the patriarchy, but there are many contexts involving the need for women to provide each other with mutual support against the problematical dimensions of the patriarchy, such as sexist discrimination, abuse of women's bodies, and the denial of sexual liberty to women, including reproductive decisions. In another register, homosocial bonding between women may become directly confrontational, to one degree or another, with respect to the patriarchy, and may even involve gynocentric imperatives (such as is the case of the Buenos Aires Casa de la Luna, a feminist/lesbian separatist commune in the old Boedo quarter of the city). Finally, homosocial bonding between women may assume dimensions of lesbianism in a sense of the inevitable union of women with each other in rejection of the depredations of the patriarchy. As Adrienne Rich has insisted, lesbianism is first and foremost about women making their lives with other women, and this does not necessarily involve homoerotic attraction, even if some feeling of love, of physical well-being in each other's company, is an inevitable consequence. Women in prison are irretrievably thrust into a same-sex environment, are irretrievably obliged to cohabitate and cooperate with each other, and, irrespective of their heterosexist tattoos, may inevitably forge a greater emotional bond with each other than they ever had with the men who have branded them and for whom they have branded themselves (Brunk). Where/when this becomes lesbian desire is precisely the moment that such a dimension ends up elided from the cultural text and from the interpretation of it.

There are three levels of woman-woman bonding possible in the universe of Lestido's photography. One is not represented, and that is the bonding between the children. But the other two — bonding between mother and child,[6] and bonding between women/mothers — is amply represented. The cover image, which is one of the nineteen images in *Mujeres presas*, is one of several in which women are seen holding their children; I have commented on this image and also on the one of the mother with her older, tattooed daughter (**Fig. 5.4**). There is only one case of a sequence of related images, in the sense of engaging in a narrative, and this concerns a daughter who is being turned over by her mother to adoptive parents. These four images are prefaced by the following text:

> "Recibí carta de la familia adoptiva de mi hija. Está bien, pero se
> asustó cuando le quisieron dar coca cola. Pidió agua." Claudia, una
> semana después de separarse de su hija de dos años [no pag.].

The first image shows the adoptive parents; the second, the mother holding her child, presumably for the last time; the third, the child crying, pacifier in her mouth, as she is apparently being transferred from

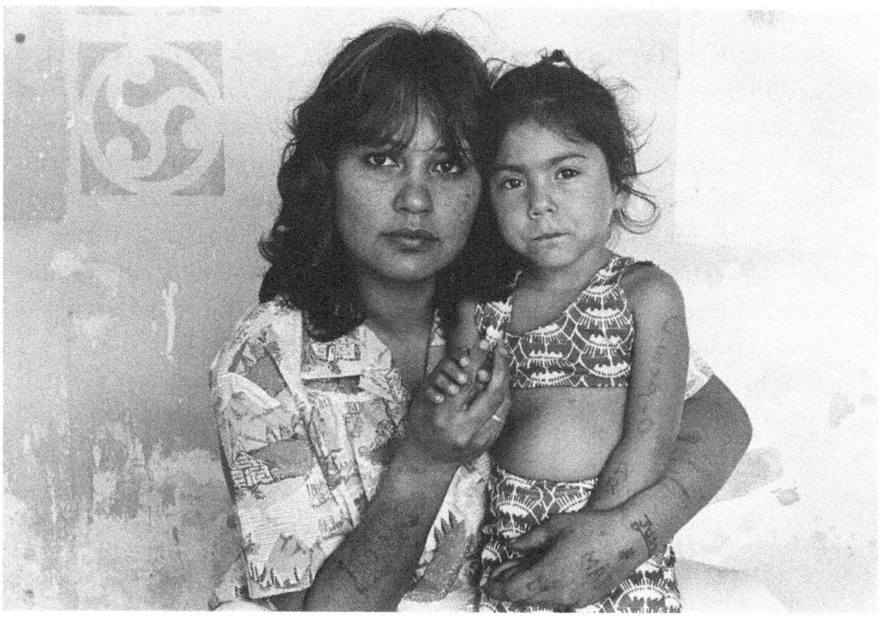

Fig. 5.4 (Adriana Lestido).

biological to adoptive mother; the fourth, the mother being consoled by another inmate.

One is immediately struck, in the first photograph of the sequence, by the relatively middle-class appearance of the adoptive parents. The man is more directly seen; the mother is seen in a foregrounded profile. Both are quite middle-class in appearance, at least by comparison to the general tenor of the imprisoned women. Actually, Claudia is shown as well-kept, and she is shown in all images with her arms covered, so it is impossible to tell whether she has any tattoos. But the point is not that she is disadvantaged in any social category from the adoptive parents (except in her being a prisoner of the state), but the fact that the latter are unquestionably in a position to provide adequately for Claudia's daughter. This is confirmed by the reference to Coca-Cola. The little girl is startled/repulsed by it when it is offered to her: she seems never to have drunk Coca-Cola before. Now, the consumption of Coca-Cola is such a universal feature of Argentine life, cutting across all sorts of social categories and such a staple of lower-class life that it often substitutes for mother's milk, that it is almost astonishing that a two-year-old would never have tasted it. As carefully dressed as the child is, with her hair done up in a cute little top-knot (as seen in the second image in the sequence), and as different as Claudia appears here as compared to her companions (the heavily tattooed two other mothers represented in the volume), the reader is brought up short by this bit of information about the child's experiences with such a generalized drink for Argentines: "Todo va mejor con Coca-Cola" throughout the republic — except in prison, where it apparently is not a staple item in the state's prison budget. In this way, class distinctions and the radical otherness of the prisoners are reaffirmed.

In the second image, Claudia is holding her daughter (who is either eating something like a piece of fruit or sucking on her pacifier). The mother, like other women in the volume, stares fixedly — defiantly, even — at the camera. Here is a woman who is about to lose her daughter, maybe even permanently, and in addition she must deal with the intrusive nature of the camera's eye. It is as though she were being forced to study the camera rather than to focus on her daughter, who is being taken away from her. One also notices that, unlike the other women, Claudia's fingernails — although we only fully see her left thumb — are trimmed and painted. It is worth wondering if this is a gesture toward conventional femininity in the face of the entrance into her world of social decency in the person of the adoptive parents. The point is that Claudia, the sacrificial mother in these photographs, signifies the way in which the state, in a regulated institutional tease, both permits and denies women the right to keep their children at their side, and she is seen as enjoying more of a continuity with those adoptive parents than with the other women in the prison.

All of the pathos of the execution of prison regulations is concentrated in the third image of the sequence in the frightened crying of Claudia's daughter, now in the arms of her adoptive mother. Since she is squirming in her confusion over what is taking place, it is not apparent what she has in her hand. It looks like some sort of cracker sandwich, the sort of bribe adults use with children to get them to do something their instincts tell them they shouldn't do, and the child's tears here are the objective correlative of her knowledge that what is going on is contrary to her well-being — the deprivation of the biological mother. The adoptive mother (with unpainted fingernails) disap-

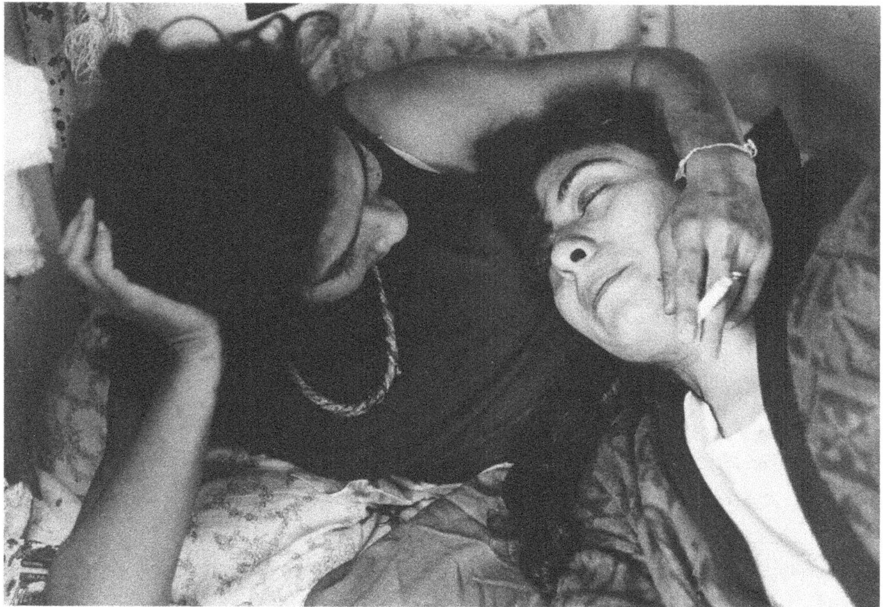

Fig. 5.5 (Adriana Lestido).

pears behind the foreground bulk of the terrified child, who looks off
from the line of focus of the camera, probably seeing her mother with-
drawing (or being withdrawn) from the scene. Unlike the foregoing
image, in which Claudia is conscious of the presence of the camera,
the child here is not: in her anguish in the face of an unforeseeable
change in her life, the camera and the photographer behind it simply
do not count.

The last image of the sequence involves Claudia being consoled
over her loss by one of the other women (**Fig. 5.5**). Now, this image
shifts the narrative away from the relationship between mother and
child to the equally important one of the relationship between the
women themselves. What is striking about this image is the manner in
which Claudia is being consoled. There are many ways to express support for the person who is gripped by grief, so it is not that this image
constitutes a deviation from what we would expect. Moreover, it is
acceptable in Argentina for women to be far more physically demon-
strative toward each other, in the expression of all emotions, than it is
for men (except in the all-male domain of soccer). In this image, Clau-

dia is lying back on a bed, her eyes are closed, and her face is a mask of emotion, although it would be difficult to say whether it is strictly the high emotion of grief over the loss of a loved one. Her head is cradled by the arm of another woman, whose head is propped up by one arm so she can look down on Claudia; her other hand, which holds a cigarette, covers the whole left side of Claudia's face, pressing it into her own body. The hand is disposed in such a way that it is poised to caress Claudia's cheek and neck. I have no interest in reading a homoerotic gesture into this potential caress or into the way the other woman is looking at the closed-eyed Claudia. This gesture is no less intimate, no less an example of the close physical bonding between women that can be an ameliorating force of prison life, for not being necessarily homoerotic in nature.

Surely, for a homophobic viewer, the gesture is either scandalous because it is potentially homoerotic or is innocent because it couldn't possibly be homoerotic: homophobia works industriously both to be outraged by what it suspects to be homoerotic as it does to suppress knowledge of what might potentially be homoerotic. And in the case of women, Queen Victoria's legendary harrumph is pertinent here, to the effect that "Women just don't do things like that." My point is that the viewer needs to be indifferent about whatever the potential homoerotic content of the photograph might be — and to whatever degree it could speak about the vast topic of sexual relations among women in prison. What the viewer might, rather, wish to see emphatically is the way in which the photograph images a woman's gaze of solidarity on two different but equally eloquent levels. In the first place, it is a matter of the solidarity between the imprisoned women themselves, and how they are able to provide moral and emotional support for each other.

The closeness of the two women in the photograph I am describing many involve many emotions and intentions, but, seen in the context of the foregoing three photographs, it is evident that what is going on here is a human closeness that is intended to provide Claudia with consolation. Indeed, this is how the photograph is labeled in the "Mujeres presas" web site, if not in the published book. Significantly, in this image none of the background features of prison life, apparent in other photographs, is seen here: not prison garb, not the stark tiled prison walls, not the metal-reinforced doors with their cramped peephole (there is one troubling image of a woman's distorted face, as she tries to fit it within the confines of the peephole), not the dilapidated furniture of the prisoners' cells. These two closely embraced women could be lying on a bed or divan anywhere, and not just in the confines of a prison.

The other dimension of solidarity is that of the photographer herself. The photographer does not figure herself in any of the photos, and we are only reminded she is there because several of the women stare intently at the camera. And we only know she is a woman because of the name that appears on the published volume. One could well argue for identifying this body of photographs as feminist because of the way in which a woman concerns herself with the history of other women, or simply for the way in which any photographer, male or female, might be concerned with the history of women (see Facio for a commentary on the feminine dimension of Lestido's photography, "Adriana Lestido"). But I would argue for a gesture of feminist solidarity in the way in which the photographer has placed herself in proximity with these women. While some of the defiant looks of these women may register an intrusive camera, the camera in other regards is a participant in the intimacy of these women. This is nowhere more evident than in the physical proximity of the two women in the scene of Claudia's consolation.

Others of Lestido's photographs confirm this fact, as she shares the grief of a woman who has her face covered with both her hands, as though sobbing. She is covered in something that looks like baking flour or ashes or a chemical foam. The very indeterminacy of her grief makes it all the more forceful, as we always want urgently to know why someone is crying, for what reason is she in psychological pain. Another woman lies in bed, the covers drawn up over her head but with her thick hair spread out like an aureole on the pillow. The only other thing we see of her body is an upraised hand sticking out from the sheets as though saluting the photographer. The face scrunched up in the peephole, as well as another face, with eyes closed as though the woman's head were resting on the metal frame of the opening in the door, are examples of photographs that seemed particularly staged for the camera's gaze.

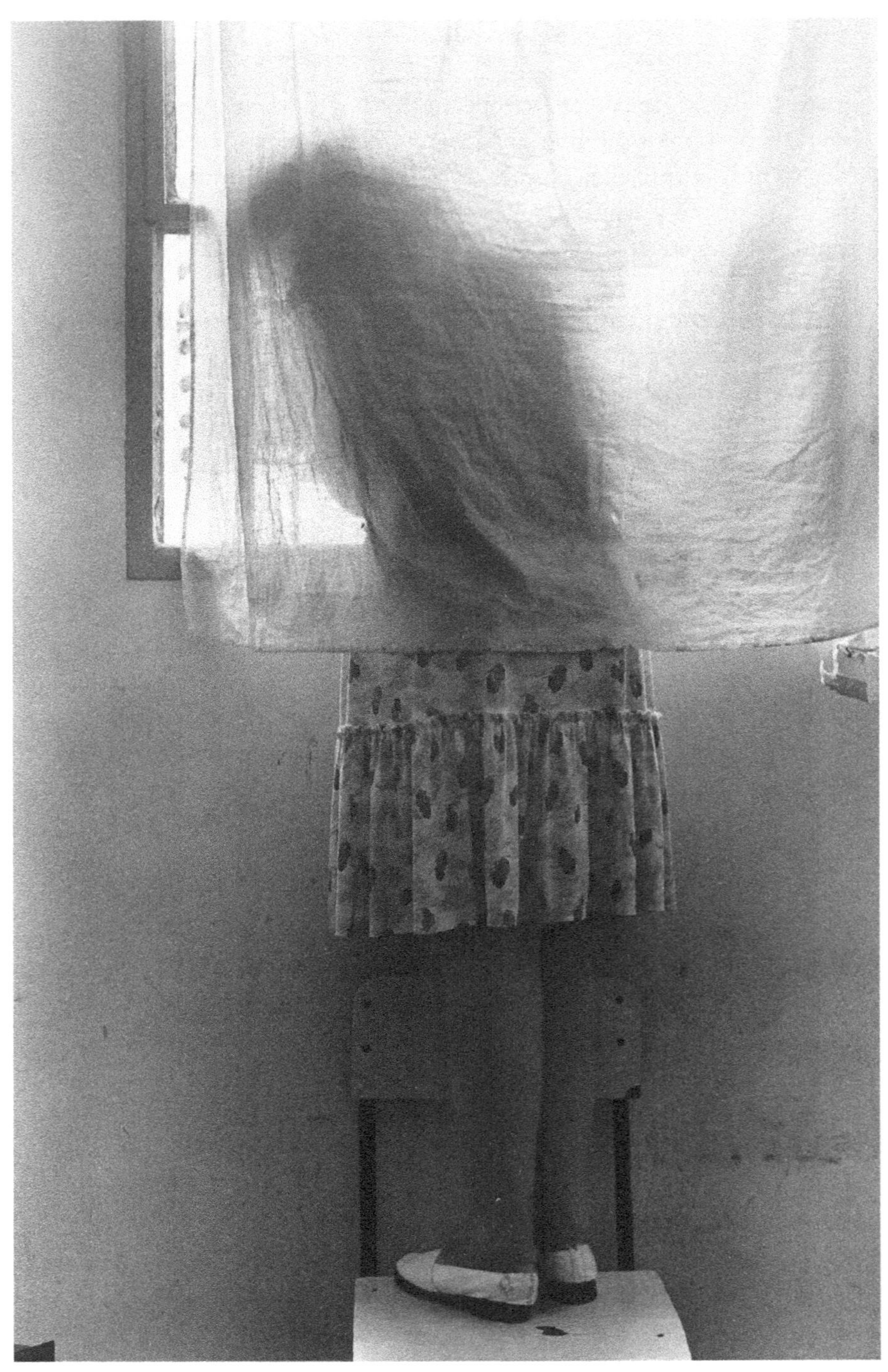

Fig. 5.6 (Adriana Lestido).

The final image is the most eloquent one of all: an apparently older woman stands on a somewhat battered chair, staring out of a window (**Fig. 5.6**). Her modest clothes are complemented by rundown slip-ons, and her upper torso is covered by the cheap curtain of the window so that we can't see what she is seeing outside the window: we are, the camera is, allowed to see her, but not allowed to see what she sees. We don't need to see what she sees, because what she sees is what we are allowed to see all the time: the world outside the prison walls. Here, the viewer of the photograph can only speculate as to whether this woman will ever again be able to see that world on the other side of the window — and the other side of the prison walls that frame it. Lestido's photographs end on this note of pathos, and it is here where the sense of feminist solidarity of her work most surely affirms itself. In a society with a recent terrible history of degrading political persecution, with women as one of three targeted groups (along with Jews and queers),[7] this is no insignificant photographic commitment. Moreover, Lestido's prison photographs wrest, so to speak, these women from the dominion of the State, which could only photograph them as numbered prisoners, thereby rehumanizing them as individuals with personal stories embedded in the details of their body, their clothes, and their deportment.[8]

Lestido has been working for the past few years on a project on mothers and daughters, for which she received funding from the Guggenheim Foundation. In addition to producing a video, she has recently published a new dossier of photos based on this work, *Madres e hijas*. Images from *Madres e hijas* are part of the representation of Argentina in *Mapas abiertos: fotografía latinoamericana 1991–2002* (250–51).

Madres e hijas is a very large dossier, certainly much larger than most of the photographers of her coterie have been able to publish; it was published by Sara Facio's prestigious La Azotea Editorial Fotográfica, and Facio contributes an eloquent introduction. Marta Dillon titles her preface "Amores difíciles," which evokes the by now extensive feminist bibliography and creative inventory on the complicated relationships between mothers and daughters: one thinks, just to mention one recent work of Argentine theater on the subject, of Diana Raznovich's brilliant play *Casa matriz,* which explores a range of Argentine mother-daughter relationships. Although mother–daughter relationships in Argentina, in which the Hispanic model is overlaid by the models of major immigrant groups like the Italians and the Jews, only partially parallel those of Anglo-American tradition, there is nevertheless an enormous amount of sentimentality attached to them, perhaps precisely to cover over the thorny realities of actual lived human experience. When someone gets around to doing an analysis of these images, it will, to refer this time to another genre of graphic art, have to include the ironic performance of daughterhood by Mafalda in Quino's internationally famous comic strip of the same name.

Thus, the first gaze that the viewer may want to bring to Lestido's images is one that includes a question of the pieties — e.g., "Madre hay una sola" — that characterize so much of the cultural production of the subject. And Lestido does not disappoint. It is not that her approach to the subject is demythificational or denunciatory. Rather, it is unwavering and profoundly honest in portraying the physical and emotional interactions between mothers and daughters of widely varying ages, including in some significant cases the lack of physical and emotional interaction.

Many of the photographs have the patina of the domestic snapshot, capturing subjects in the sort of paradigmatic interactions with each other that one might expect: do an inventory of what you might expect to find, and you will find a good share of those moments in *Madres e hijas*, although — I repeat — never with the slightest hint of sentimentality. This is the case of a woman blowing out the candles of her birthday cake: her daughters are shrouded in shadows and the look on the mother's face is more of infinite sadness than celebration.

Many of Lestido's images are deeply troubling because there is a hint of— at least by the petit-bourgeois standards that prevail in Argentina — transgressiveness about them. This involves not only mothers and daughters bathing together, but others in which the mother appears in various states of undress that undoubtedly will strike some viewers as indecent. In one image, a mother is swinging her daughter over the bathtub (it is not immediately apparent that the tub contains water), the daughter's genitals, somewhat spread because of the way she is being held, in full view.

Parts of the dossier include multiple images of one mother-

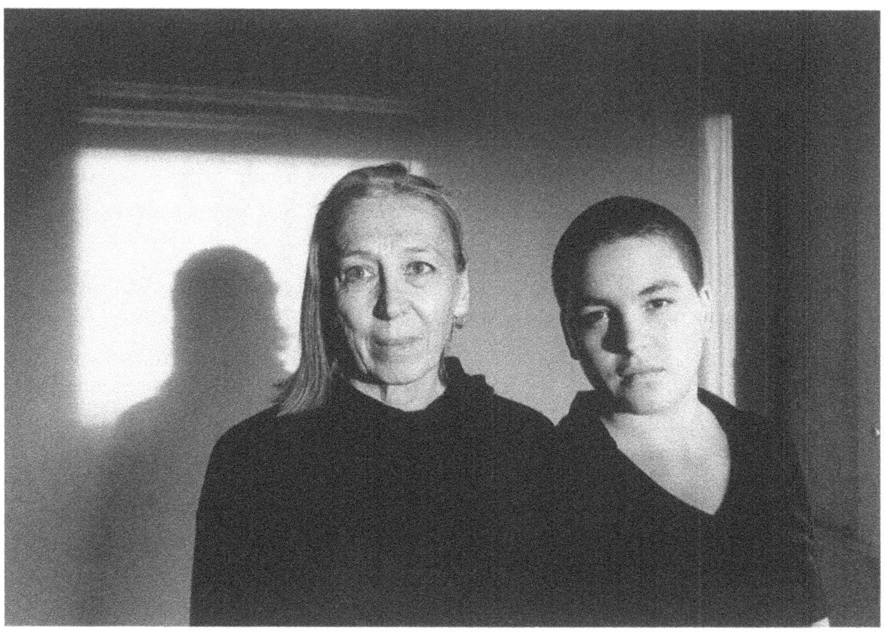

Fig. 5.7 (Adriana Lestido).

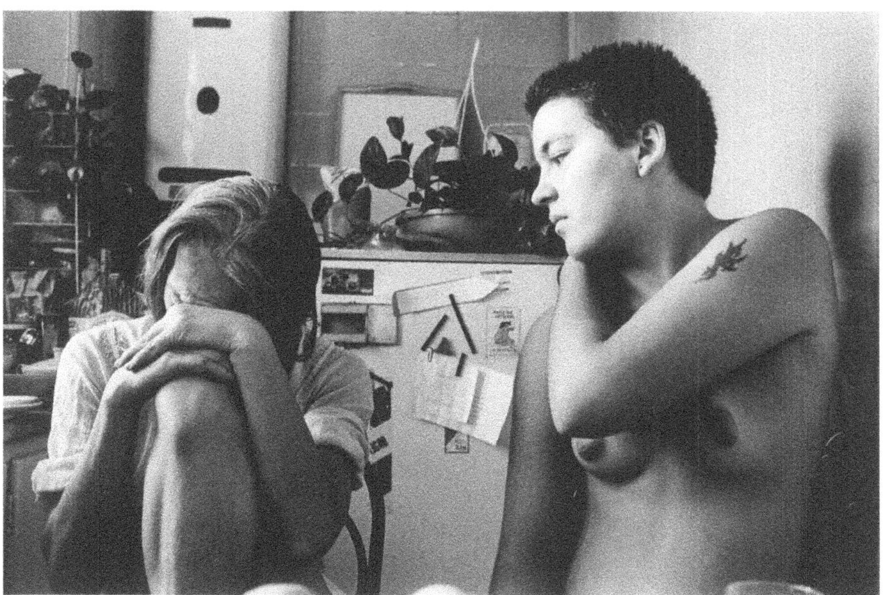

Fig. 5.8 (Adriana Lestido).

daughter relationship. In "Alma y Maura,"for example, photographs of joyous embraces are interspersed with images of the daughter in punk-like (stone cold lesbian?) poses and images of the mother as though mourning, perhaps, her daughter's lost femininity.

Another group of images include daughters alone, clearly lamenting the absent mother as in narratives of death, abandonment, estrangement, and spurning.

By contrast to a more documentary approach to the subject, such as Aperture's 1987 collection *Mothers and Daughters* or Annie Leibovitz's collection, *Women*, where the goal of the photographer, no matter how much artistry is involved, is to present the subject "clearly," one dimension of Lestidos's images involves various degrees of blurring, which I understand to be an objective correlative of the way in which such relationships move in and out of focus as a consequence of all the accidents and contingencies of this particularly intimate dimension of human intercourse.

Lestido is, with *Madres e hijas*, now a major force in contemporary Argentine photography. Personally, it is my hope that this volume will inspire more photographic work in Argentina on gender issues, a category that, with this volume, is now less underrepresented than I would have said before its publication (**Figs. 5.7 and 5.8**).

6

Gabriel Díaz's *Muertes menores*: Buenos Aires Street Children

Let us begin with two social principles. First, in Western society there continues to be an abiding belief in the "innocence" of children. This innocence is often narrowly interpreted in such a way as to have sexual resonances. Children are innocent of the facts of life, of the complications of sexual desire, and of, concomitantly, the exploitation of the individual or the exploitative conduct by the individual that such complications occasion. But childish innocence is, in a broader sense, understood to mean free of an awareness of the terrible features of the struggle for survival, which, indeed, often involves the sexual exploitation of the body. The topic of innocence signifies both that children are putatively by nature innocent (they do not intuitively grasp the terror of survival, although the loss of innocence is understood to mean that they sooner or later will, must, acquire that knowledge) and that children must be guarded in a state of innocence as something like a right of childhood. Whether children cannot or should not understand "the facts of life" amounts to the same thing, and children are viewed as occupying a guarded social space that is usually accepted as outside of a harsh social realm occupied by adults. To be an adult before one's time or to be a childlike adult is to violate the principles of this separation of spheres, to transgress the norms that enforce their separation.

The second principle that I would like to evoke here is that of the status of children as a socio-economic index of a society's well-being. The degree to which the reputed innocence of children is protected and, by extension, the degree to which there are few indicators of the exposure of children to the harsh conditions of the struggle for survival are taken as a barometer of well-being (see the UNICEF *Declaración de los derechos del niño*, illustrated by the Argentine cartoonist Joaquín Salvador Lavado [Quino]). When the suffering of children becomes manifest, either in meeting the circumstances of a problematical survival in general or, specifically, in being exposed to mechanisms of exploitation, it is taken as a sign that the well-being of a society is very much in danger.

There are numerous examples of cultural production in Latin America around these two social principles of children, from Luis Buñuel's ferocious film *Los olvidados* (1950), which challenged the bromides of social amelioration of the still-new post-revolutionary Mexican system; Héctor Babenco's law-of-the-jungle film *Pixote: a lei do mais fraco* (1981); Víctor Gaviria's devastating film on street children, *La vendedora de rosas* (1998); Enrique Medina's novel *Las tumbas* (1973), about reformatories in Argentina, which were touted by the Peronista government as schools of social integration, although they were — and continue to be — breeding grounds for social violence (Foster, "Dirty Realism"); to Sebastião Salgado's internationally acclaimed work on a broad spectrum of social marginalization, including that of children, as exemplified in *An Uncertain Grace* (1990). These are only a few especially notorious examples of what is known as the plight, and the tragedy, of children in Latin America. In all of these cases, there is the implied proposition that the circumstances of these children are the consequence of historical forces, and not just a matter of an expected order of things.

In the case of Argentina, although general prosperity has often meant less visible manifestations of wretched poverty or social misery than one associates with other allegedly Third-World Latin American societies, the failures of the economic system and of specific economic projects have not been hard to find. It became a truism that the neoliberal experiment of the 1990s generated — necessarily — an expanding class of have-nots. And since prosperity, as is almost always the case in Argentina, was concentrated in Buenos Aires, there has been the compounded impoverishment of the provincial underclasses, many of whose members sought relief by migrating to the big city. Yet the definitive collapse of neoliberalism in 2001 brought with it a precipitous descent into impoverishment of individuals and sectors that previously had enjoyed some measure of protection and even privilege within the neoliberal bubble.

The impact on children of the collapse of neoliberalism has been particularly commented on, in part because it is particularly visible. This is especially the case in, for example, the Jewish community which, because of its communitarian infrastructure, historically has seen its members integrated into the mainstream of Argentine society. It is possible to cite examples of immigrant literature like José Rabinovich's *Tercera clase* (1944), about the difficulties of early immigrants. The Jewish community now has something like twenty-five percent of its children living below the poverty level; the situation is equally disastrous, at the other end of the generational spectrum, for the elderly as well. It is therefore inevitable that there be a specific cultural production with reference to children, as a particularly vivid sign of the catastrophic impoverishment in Argentine, both with the implementation of neoliberalism and now with its collapse: these children constitute such a vivid sign because it continues to be possible to appeal to their privileged ideological status and to claim, if only by implication, counting on the efficacy of the way in which cultural representation of children is necessarily heavily ideologized, that their status is what most tellingly reveals the current socio-economic malaise of the country.

Gabriel Díaz's 2000 dossier of sixteen photos is made up of material taken in the greater Buenos Aires area during 1991 and 1992, which places them at the beginning of the neoliberal period. In this sense they can be read as referring retrospectively, from the time at which they were taken, to the inflational-plagued Argentine economic that led to the proposal of neoliberalism as a remedy, as well as retrospectively, from the time at which they were published, as a record of the poverty neoliberalism could not correct and that it, indeed, ended up exacerbating. Díaz's photos are in black and white, which remains the preferred medium of the urban social photographers of the city; a photography in black and white serves to reinforce the continuity between this specific body of work, at the time of the millennium, with the vast body of social photography that has, for over a hundred years, provided a visual record of human lives in the metropolis.

Of crucial importance here is the context of the dramatic shift in the standard of living that neoliberalism was to have brought with it: the radical modernization of the city and what the defenders of neoliberalism claim to be the definitive insertion of Buenos Aires into the "First World." This insertion brought with it the processes of late capitalism, including the massive process of export substitution, whereby the latest products of the international marketplace were to displace the traditional features of national life. The displacement is nowhere more to be seen than in the renovation of the traditional bars and cafes of the city and the development of the American-style shopping center. Seen in these terms, a resistance to the conversion to color photography and the insistence on the continued utilization of black and white are particularly eloquent details of the series to which *Muertes menores* (*Minor Deaths*) belongs.[1]

Díaz's photos are divided into roughly two groups: those that deal with the defiant or sullen stance of the subject in the face of the camera, as though it were intruding on their lives and it were, therefore, legitimate to question the presence of the photographer; and those in which, often as the consequence of an unconsciousness induced perhaps by drugs, the child is unaware or heedless of the presence of the camera. In all cases, the children are late preteens or just barely adolescents: age is an issue here because of the ways in which some of these bodies are sexualized by the camera.

The opening image is a particularly complex example of these parameters (**Fig. 6.1**). It is of a young adolescent who stares into the camera at a fairly close range, and his torso is foregrounded by the camera, as well as emphasized by placing it squarely in the center of the frame, with a string of assembled railroad cars to the child's right (i.e., the frame's left) and a line of railroad track to his right bleeding off around a bend in the background. This is a very geometric, very symmetrical shot, one that emphasizes the symmetry of the boy's body. He stares directly into the camera, which is poised a bit above him, such that he has to raise his eyes from the center of their orbit. The symmetry of his staring eyes is reinforced by the way in which the camera captures the symmetry of his ears (because he faces the camera

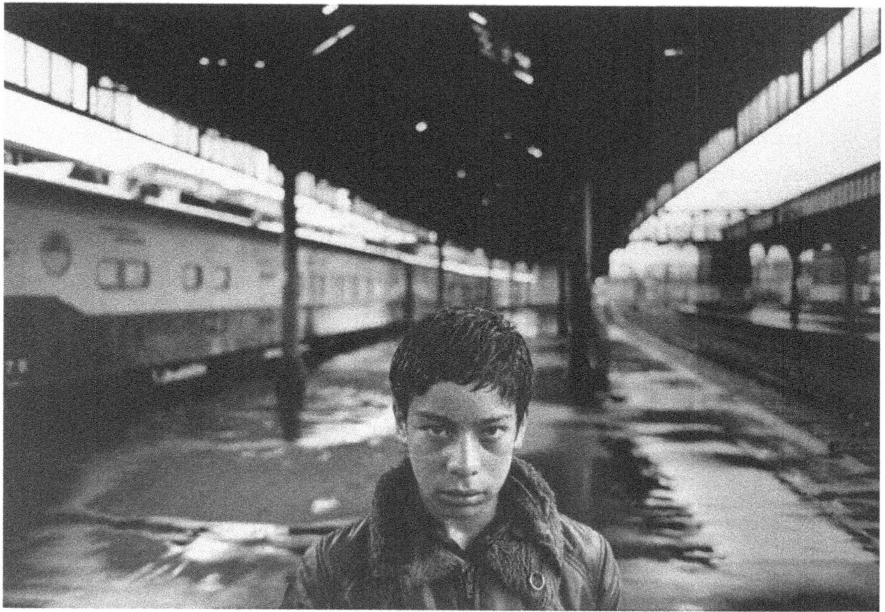

Fig. 6.1 (Gabriel Díaz).

squarely), the symmetry of his nose and mouth (the latter formed into
what can be read as virtually a sensual pout), and the symmetry of his
jacket, broken only by the presence of a fastening ring on one of the
two lapels.

The boy's stare is potentially sexual in that his pubescent body, in
a feral stance reinforced by the heavy leather jacket he is wearing, immediately brings the viewer to the matter of the sexual exploitation of chil-
dren/young people such as this subject, whom one might expect to have
to turn sexual tricks (more than likely also accompanied by acts of
assault and robbery) in order to survive on the street. Their bodies are
these children's only capital (for studies of street children in Argentina,
see Carretero; Maturi; *La bacanal*). Díaz's photograph captures his subject in the context of the railroads. Once a major symbol of Argentine
prosperity — and, with their purchase from England by Perón in the
late 1940s, of Argentine sovereignty — by the early 1990s, many of the
state-owned rail lines, in addition to falling into appalling disrepair,
had become sites of crime and random violence. This rail system was
originally designed to move goods in and out of and through the port

city of Buenos Aires. Incoming they brought the export items that drove Argentine prosperity; outgoing they carried the imported luxury items that fueled the elegant prosperity of the bedroom communities in the greater Buenos Aires area and the villages that served the vast cattle baronies of the ranching provinces (see Scalabrni Ortiz's famous critique of the Anglo-British railway system): the Argentine railway system as it appears in a photograph such is this one is not just a scenic detail, but an integral symbol of Argentina's socio-economic system. In addition to their primary historic role in liberalist import-export capitalism, the railroads have also carried back and forth passengers, individuals from the bedroom communities who work in Buenos Aires and who, thus, realize the commuter circuit common to large American and European cities.

The train system also connects with the Buenos Aires subway system, the first in Latin America, to distribute arriving passengers to locales throughout the city. Just as the train system funnels into Buenos Aires, the subway system funnels into the financial and commercial center of the capital. However, with the impoverishment of outlying areas of greater Buenos Aires, which are interspersed with prosperous bedroom communities, and with the impoverishment of neighborhoods that constitute the inner ring of the periphery of the city of Buenos Aires, the trains degenerated in the periods of economic problems into hotbeds of social marginalization. Although the military governments could control to some extent crime on board the trains and in and around the stations (which are often in the cute British village cottage style), even during the dictatorship the trains were inhabited by tattered vendors hawking all sorts of tacky wares, veritable icons of economic decline. Along with the beggars who also rode the cars (see Fernando Birri's 1960 neorealist documentary *Tire dié* [i.e., "diez centavos"], about the children who would run alongside the trains and beg coins from the passengers; latter they simply invaded the trains), it was not a surprising transition from the vendors and beggars to muggers and thugs, the latter typically soccer hooligans who have often carried their practices of violent rivalry into venues outside the sports stadiums, the trains.

These are some of the socio-cultural issues evoked by the Buenos Aires urban train system, and in this photograph they serve to frame the subject in terms of one of the sites of urban violence. There are several train stations in Buenos Aires that are notorious as places of male-male sexual encounters, including prostitution, and the Constitución station is the one most often cited (Rapisardi and Modarelli, 21–39). Thus, it is not difficult to see in this opening picture of Díaz the sort of youth who is likely to solicit male sexual partners (in rough-trade parlance, the *chongo*, although, in this case, he is not much more than a *chonguito*). In addition to the sexual transaction, which is violent and exploitative in and of itself, there is always the attendant possibility of assault, battery, and robbery between the sexual partners for any of a number of circumstances associated with sexual prostitution (see Carretero, 125–47, on street children and prostitution).

An inventory of all of the details are less important here than the realization that the violence beyond the sexual act itself can move in either direction: abuse of the prostitute by his client, or abuse of the client by the prostitute, often in both cases with the aid of accomplices. One of the most famous treatises on male-male prostitution is that of the Argentine social anthropologist, Néstor Perlongher; although his research relates to São Paulo and was originally published in Portuguese, it is equally applicable to Buenos Aires, and it is important to note that Perlongher himself came from Avellaneda, a tough south-side city, heavily industrialized, served by one of the rail lines attached to the Constitución station. The synergetic consequence of the core of sexual exploitation of young prostitutes (the age of sexual consent in Argentina is sixteen, but many of the children involved in the sex trade are notoriously younger than that) and attendant violence peripheral to the specific monetary or barter transaction have an enormous coarsening effect on these children. This is quite evident in the sullen, defiant, mistrustful, and insolent regard of the boy in Díaz's opening photo. Selling sexual acts in order to survive or bartering sex in exchange for food, clothing or shelter, with the phenomenon of barter involving either sex in order to have something or sex as a consequence of having had something, are facts of life for the street children of Buenos Aires, as they are of any major metropolitan area. It is simply unlikely that any of the children photographed in the contexts of *Muertes menores*, both males and females, are protected in their daily lives from the grim circumstances of sexual commerce.

It is for this reason that the title of Díaz's compilation takes on multiple resonant meanings. In one sense, "muertes menores" refers simply to the mortality of the young as occasioned by the terrible circumstances of life on the streets. Although Díaz's photographs do not deal with dead children, the audience able to understand the circumstances of life depicted by them will necessarily understand, in a process of extrapolation, that many of these children will die from exposure, malnutrition, addiction, disease (including sexual maladies), and the many forms of violent aggression befalling anyone who lives on the streets. "Muertes menores" can also be understood as referring to death in slow motion. While many of these children will die at the hands of aggressors with many possible faces — random aggressors, aggressors who prey specifically on children (including the aforementioned clients of child prostitutes), organized security agents, and even the uniformed police — the majority of them will suffer from the protracted death brought on by their living conditions.

Various of the photos deal with addiction. There is one image of a child smoking, sitting on a spiral staircase in what looks like an inner courtyard or back patio (**Fig. 6.2**). There is another child walking by, his torso bared and what appears to be a towel in his hand, so there is the sense that this is a interior living space, and this latter boy in on his way to or from a bathroom. The overall setting is rundown, with chipped and scarred physical details, and the sort of double door behind the child who is smoking indicates the age of the building and the fact that it is one of the decrepit and decayed buildings these children may have the fortune to inhabit, if not as regular residences, at least as some occasional refuge from the streets.

The child who is smoking also looks defiantly at the camera, with a world-weary expression quite beyond his years. Although his shirt and pants are only somewhat tattered (as opposed to that of children in other images, who wear veritable rags), he looks every bit like an aged derelict whose only occupation is to sit smoking and watch the world go by through jaded eyes. The image of aged derelict I am attributing to this youngster, who looks no more than eight or nine years old, is reinforced by the way which, as his right hand expertly holds a cigarette, his elbow propped on his leg, his left hand holds some sort of staff like the walking stick or the cane of the aged. Díaz

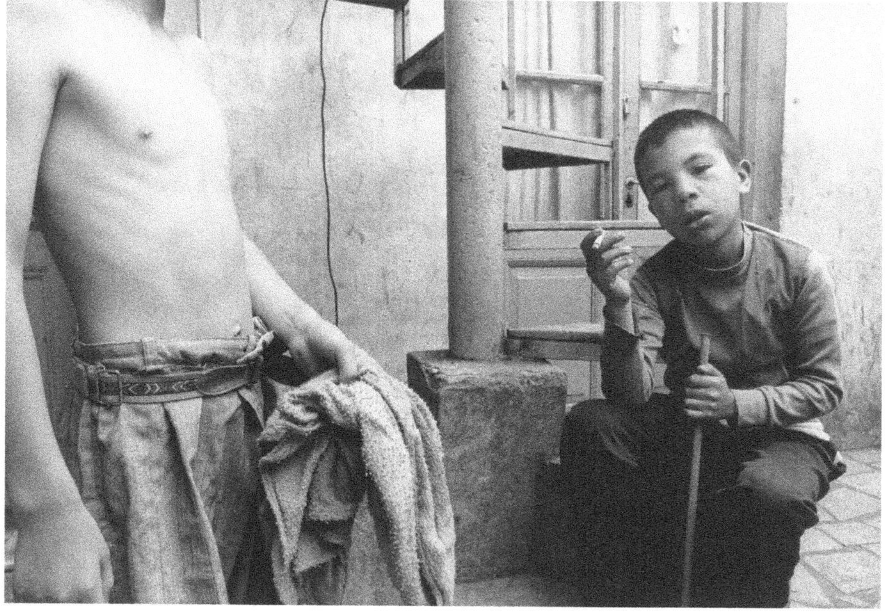

Fig. 6.2 (Gabriel Díaz).

has captured his cocked head in such a way that there are deep shadows in his eyes, and along with his somewhat parted lips and the deep lines on his face, the image is altogether one of unhealthy pallor.

Far more disturbing is the following image, which is almost too staged (**Fig. 6.3**). As part of the enormous European-style development of the city of Buenos Aires at the end of the nineteenth century, the broad Avenida de Mayo was designed, like Washington, D.C.'s Pennsylvania Avenue, to anchor the Casa Rosada, the government house, at one end and the national Congress, built in the style of the U.S. Congress, at the other. Across the street from the Congress, in a park that constitutes the northern terminus of the Avenida de Mayo, there is a huge — one might even say monstrous — monument in the neoclassical allegorical style. Chock-full of national, ancient cultural, historical, and patriotic symbols, this monument has often served as a rallying point for political manifestations. In more recent years, it has served as a favorite spot for kids hanging out, drinking, smoking, taking drugs, and making out with one another (in strictly heterosexual style, since the public display of same-sex affection still has not taken

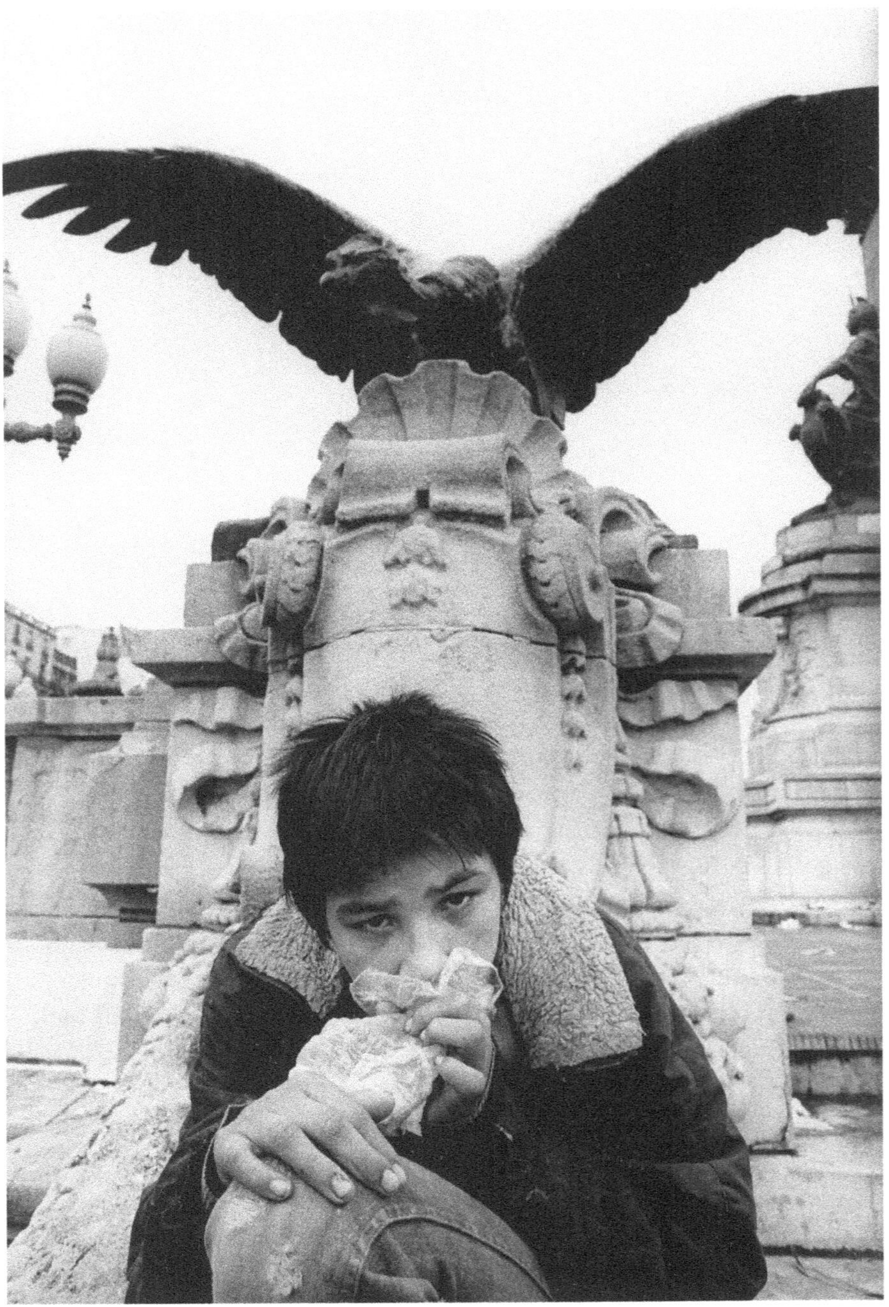

Fig. 6.3 (Gabriel Díaz).

much hold in Buenos Aires). These activities have brought with them the defacement, principally through graffiti, of the monument, and in recent years it has been closed off for public use.

In Díaz's photograph, an adolescent is seated at the base of one part of the monument. He is hunched over, inhaling from a plastic bag; the look on his face indicates that he is drugged out from the glue or other chemical substance he is inhaling (on Buenos Aires street children and drugs, see Carretero, 149–79). Rising up from behind where he is sitting on the monument is a sculpted cement pedestal crowned by a soaring eagle, cast in metal. Unmistakably a symbol of winged human spirit, the eagle, released, as such allegories would have it, from its earthly bonds by the transcendent values of the Republic and its Constitution and laws, represents a promise of individual and collective glory that is, with heavy irony, belied by the sitting boy. Dressed in a heavy winter coat, with a dirty hand resting on the knee of his tattered jeans, the boy is huddled against the winter chill (the humidity of Buenos Aires makes both winters and summers particularly insufferable), and his sniffing may well be a protection against the elements as well as a substitute for food.

One particularly eloquent detail of this composition is the implied disjunction between the child and the allegorical symbol rising up behind him. The congressional monument is a synecdoche for the highly visible trappings of the central government of Argentina in its imposing Buenos Aires base. This monument and the other trappings of that government were originally constructed at a time in which the true rights of the republic, the attributes of full democracy, were restricted to only a few, those that made up what can be summarized as the white, European(ized) oligarchic elite. Although subsequent political projects will extend civic rights to other, and ultimately all, sectors of adult citizens—Peronismo in the 1940s and 1950s being the most ambitious project, noted for giving women the right to vote in 1947—it is, in Argentina as in most other societies, an open question as to the extent to which comprehensive civic rights are actually honored for all citizens. There remains in Argentina very much of a social divide, along many axes, between a white middle class that holds most of the reins of social, political, and economic power, and, at the present moment, an expanding underclass that may have formal but ineffective access to power.

What all this has to do with the image in question is that the young man in the photograph is most likely a *cabecita negra*, which, as I have previously noted, is a metonymy used to refer to a social class in Buenos Aires made up of individuals of immigrant extraction who began to be brought into the European city, mostly from the north, by Perón in the mid–1940s and who have constituted an unstoppable in-migration ever since. While some of these individuals, their children and grandchildren, may go on to accede to the higher reaches of power in Buenos Aires, they are still to a large part both an iconic and a very real manifestation of the underclass of the city. The indigenous factions of the subject of Díaz's photograph and, in particular, his straight and unruly hair, as well as his heavy hands, accentuated by his dirty nails, are all signs of his condition as a *cabecita negra*; it is important to observe that this young man is also staring defiantly into the camera.

I noted that this image is perhaps a bit too staged, as the juxtaposition between the historical resonances of the monument and the socio-economic realities of the world this adolescent inhabits are all too starkly articulated. Nevertheless, it is also a dramatically unsentimentalized image. If Sebastião Salgado's images of marginal social subjects are often tinged with a certain degree of sentimentalism or emotionalism, there is nothing either sentimental or emotional in Díaz's photographs (this photograph is one of the ones chosen to represent Argentina in *Mapas abiertos: fotografía latinoamericana 1991–2002*, 42).

Indeed, the images I have described up to this point involve individuals who are not static, passive recipients of the violence of their situation, but are in some way or another participating in it. Their actions — in each case, highlighted by the defiant regard of the camera by the subject — underscore the fact that they are agents or collaborators of their circumstances. This does not make them any less victims of the social violence in which they are inserted, but only that, because they are interacting with that violence in directly manifest ways, they lose the sort of dazed passivity that is more likely to evoke highly charged pity on the part of the spectator.

There are a number of images in *Muertes menores* that fall into this category, however, and it is noteworthy that they are gender-marked. If various images of young men are characterized by their

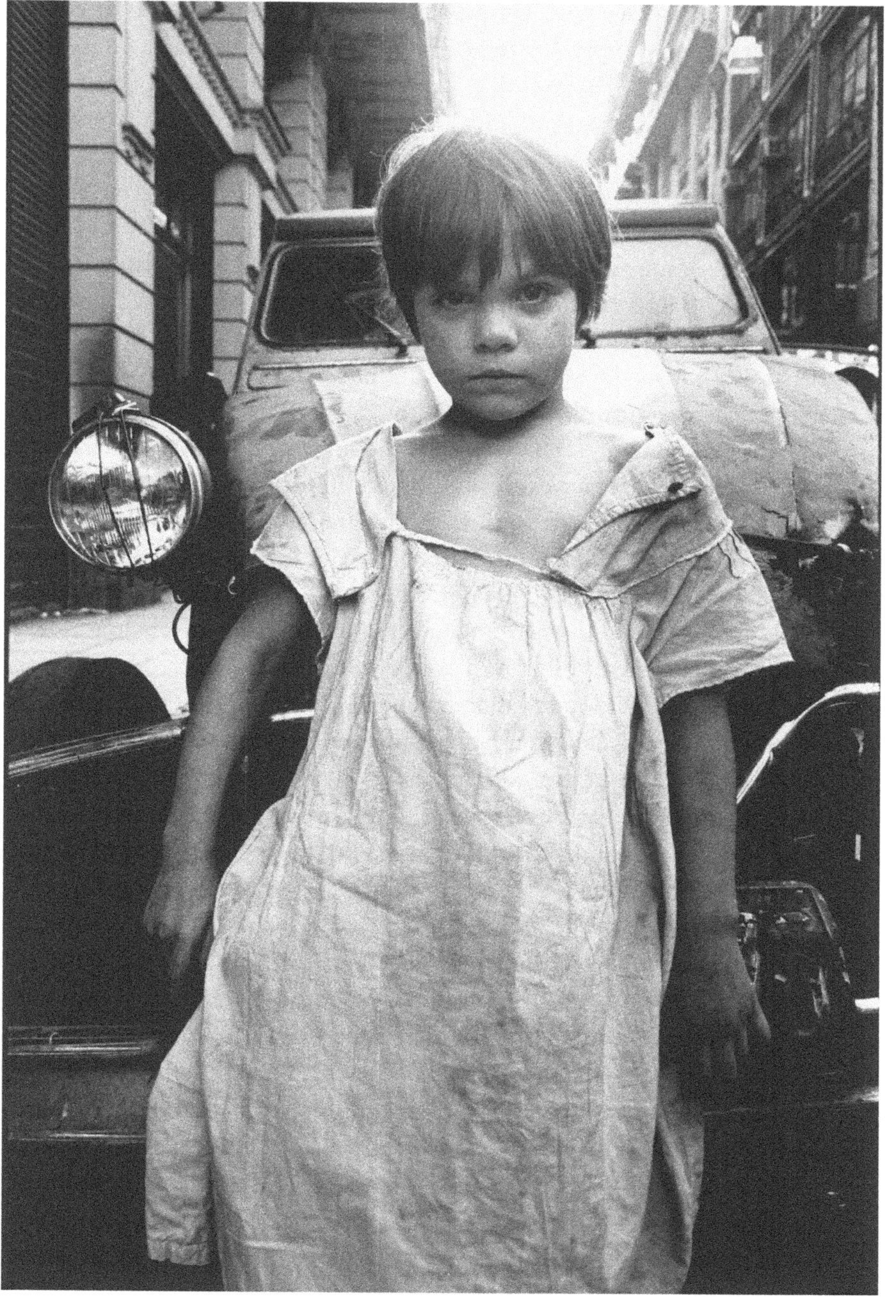

Fig. 6.4 (Gabriel Díaz).

seeming complicity with their marginalization, photographs of young women are more typically stamped with the sort of dazed passivity that evokes sympathy. For example, there is the panel of a girl (**Fig. 6.4**), perhaps six or seven years old, dressed in a simple filthy gown that looks almost institutional, except that a scalloped border around the sleeves and as part of the bodice indicates that it probably started out as a "nice" dress. There is such an adult-like stance to this child that my first reaction was that she was actually an adult, but also a dwarf; indeed, her facial features made me first think of the actress Alejandra Podestá, who plays the part of Carlota/Charlotte in María Luisa Bemberg's 1993 film, *De eso no se habla*, a powerful role about the silencing of sociophysical difference (Foster).

In Díaz's photograph, once again the subject regards the camera with a look of defiance: her eyes are wide open and focused straight ahead, and her mouth is pursed in a pout. Her arms frame her body as she rests on the front grill of what appears to be a battered car (a tin-can Citroën from the 1960s?). As in several other photos, Díaz foregrounds his subject against a context that bleeds off into the background: there is an obvious desire always to place these children in a social milieu with which their poverty and abandonment eloquently interact. The backdrop in the case of this photo is double-layered, consisting of the car and then multistoried office buildings, with the impression that the image is set in the City, the downtown financial core of Buenos Aires (at night and on the weekends, this area, immediately south of the Casa Rosada (Government House) and federal office buildings, is taken over by street people, often groups of children).

There are three symmetrical levels to this photograph: the girl, the car, and the office buildings. The girl's head is perfectly positioned between the two windshield wipers of the car and proportionately placed with regard to the windshield itself. The car is placed a little out of balance in the frame, however, and its right headlight is poised over her shoulder, while the other one is not visible. Also slightly off-center is the girl's head with respect to the V of the vanishing point of the two rows of office buildings that flank her on both sides. In the typical fashion of such buildings in Buenos Aires, there is no space between them, only a shift in styles, which is more apparent on the right-hand margin of the photo.

The effect of this double-layering is to imprison the girl in the frame. In the first place, she is imprisoned by the walls of the financial institutions/commercial enterprises. The symbolism is rather transparent here, in the sense that the capitalist project (in its neoliberal version or in one of the many others Argentina has explored) generates the sort of poverty and social marginalization included this girl and the other children who invade the City during off hours are obliged to live. The poor may always be with us, as the Bible avows, but it is because successive instances of exploitation are always with us as the controlling dynamic of human society. This is all the more evident in the impoverishment that has taken place in Argentina since the time the photos were taken.

In the second place, the battered car the child is resting on (and it is possible once again to refer to a certain staginess about Díaz's photos) is both an icon of capitalism and a sign of its devastations. It is no accident that the number of cars in Buenos Aires more than tripled in the 1990s as a consequence of the frenzy of importation made possible by neoliberalism. At the same time, when prosperity began to decline even before the 2001 collapse, upkeep on cars began to become too costly. In this image, it is as though the child is being threatened by the car behind her, to the extent that the automobile is one of the most imposing outward signs of modern prosperity. Yet, the fact that the car is battered and, indeed, probably dates from before the neoliberalist process would seem to signal that the trappings of prosperity, just like human social subjects like the child, are the "victims" of capitalist depredation. All that is missing is for the financial/commercial buildings themselves, many of which were built in the early twentieth century, to be dilapidated, as they are in some parts of the City. Witness the tremendous eyesore of the old Harrod's building on what was in bygone years the most prosperous segment of Calle Florida; Harrod's of London was once an eloquent, and elegant, symbol of the Argentine period of the *vacas gordas.*

Finally, there is the freeze-frame entrapment of this child by the lens of the photographer. I do not mean to imply that the photographer is part of the process of exploitation. True, it is often asserted that the photographers of the socially marginal are engaged in exploitative slumming, their subjects unwilling, often coerced, collaborators in the

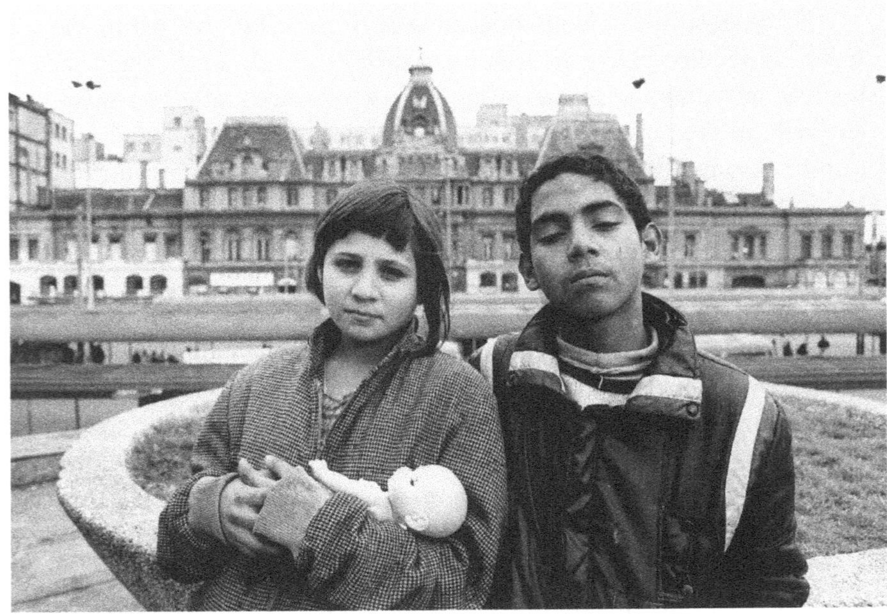

Fig. 6.5 (Gabriel Díaz).

professional success of the socially more powerful wielder of the camera. Rather, I would allege that the function of the camera here is to fix its social subject squarely in terms of the context of her exploitation. The child is entrapped, so to speak, by the critical knowledge of the photographer, who knows, in a way she does not, cannot, what the circumstances of her socio-economic deprivation are.

Another carefully composed image in *Muertes menores* is an ironically constituted Argentine family: a girl-boy couple, with the girl holding their putative child in her arms. But here the child is a cheap doll (**Fig. 6.5**). Both the young man and the young woman are fairly well dressed, especially by comparison with the dirty and torn smock of the child described above; moreover, they seem to be warmly dressed against the gray and damp Buenos Aires winter. The girl's hands, however, are soiled, as is the cuff of her jacket, so in no way can this couple be taken as anywhere near even the lower middle-class. The girl has lovely features, and she faces the camera with something like a "soft" look. Her male companion, however, has all of the sullen cockiness of others of Díaz's subjects, and he stares into the camera through half-closed eyes; his features are very much those of the *cabecitas negras* that make up the Buenos Aires lumpen.

There are three things that are deliberately composed about this image and that converge to reinforce the implication of the social marginalization of this couple. The first is the backdrop, always so important in Díaz's images. It is the Constitución train station, located south of downtown Buenos Aires, a few kilometers due south of Government House (La Casa Rosada) and a few kilometers southeast of the National Congress building featured in the photograph described above. It is one of the several English-style train stations in the downtown corridor that are monuments to the prosperity of the late nineteenth-century Argentine socio-economic aspirations of that period and subsequent generations. In addition to the Constitución station that serves the south side of greater Buenos Aires, there are the three stations that make up the Retiro that serve the north side, while Once and, further west, Lacroze serve the vast west side that fans out beyond the Federal District's political border. These installations are all stations of the cross, so to speak, in the organization of one of the city's major infrastructures, and where they become symbolically relevant for these photographs is not just in the way in which in their origin and superficial iconicity they sign national socio-economic pretensions, but also the way in which, during the post–British period of Juan Domingo Perón's first presidency (1946–52), they were the terminuses of the in-migration into Buenos Aires of the *cabecitas negras* from the outlying provinces of the country. Thus, it is as though this couple had just emerged from one of the trains arriving from the hinterland, although their personal history is more likely that they are grandchildren of the original *cabecitas negras*.

The second notable element of this photograph is the plastic doll the girl carries in her arms, with all of the crossed-arms care appropriate to a real baby and with all of the maternal concern that is supposed to be part of woman's primary inscription in the social fabric. The fact that it isn't a real baby indicates the frustration of this role, with the implication that the young woman will inevitably be propelled to "do it for real." The macho pose of her companion certainly indicates that he grasps fully his masculine prerogatives and the imperative of patriarchal reproduction they bring with them. The fact that the girl is leaning into the man (who does not have his arm around her in any sign of affection) signifies that she knows, if only intuitively, that she is dependent on him and that eventually having a real baby will be an integral part of the narrative of that dependence. In this sense, the doll is only the harbinger of the necessary fulfillment in due course of that narrative.

Finally, the couple is leaning against a piece of stonework that juts out behind the right side of the girl and the left side of the man; it is an untended, or only minimally tended, planter, a vain attempt to landscape the area where they are standing. One cannot help but think of this large stone vessel in terms of a baptismal font. Baptism is part of the symbolic inscription of the newborn into the process of socialization, although in the case of the children of a couple like this, that process of socialization either breaks down and generates the child's social marginalization or, in an alternative view, can be nothing other than the generation of social marginalization, given the circumstances of the child's birth. Of course, the fact that the child may never even be baptized in the first place is, in and of itself, an eloquent testimonial to the breach between the social ideal and the economic realities of these individuals. It is not so much that baptism is understood here as all that important (it is, of course, to a religious believer, but not necessarily to the realm of the photograph). Rather, it is a symbol of the sort of idealized yet bad-faith social incorporation these individuals will not ever really be able to enjoy. And it is, I would insist, only more bad faith to believe that it is best to baptize these children and place them under the protection of a God who will ultimately save their souls in a way in which an exploitative society will always fail to save their bodies. In one way, I am moving here quite a bit beyond the evident signs of Díaz's photography, but the message of the Church in Argentina, always allied with the oligarchy and the capitalist plutocracy, speaks perennially of spiritual redemption because social amelioration is such a dicey affair.

The cover image of *Muertes menores*, which is a slightly enlarged image of one of final photographs of the collection, exemplifies a more surrealist dimension, as the image is blurred and not immediately perceivable. But it turns out, on closer examination than the other photographs require, to be the truncated image of a child, with the torso only partially there and the head cut off above the mouth and right ear, against the backdrop of a corrugated steel curtain of the type that is meant to protect businesses during off hours from burglars — or marauding street children: the synecdoche of the protection of a commercial establishment is more directly focused than the body of the child as social detritus. One other somewhat surrealistic image is that of a boy sitting at the bottom of the numbered steps of a subway escalator; the numbers go in ascending order, so that the farther down the boy is on the movable stairway, the higher the number, as though these were the numbered steps of a descent into a threatening underworld. The steel sides of the stairway are an imprisoning channel for his descent. His face is covered by some sort of filmy substance, either a torn piece of adhering Saran Wrap, a shred of an exploded balloon, or a layer of rubber glue. The impression is that of a death mask. Once again, this is a very carefully composed image, but also a powerful one, since it is as though the boy were being suffocated by the filmy substance, a material of modern industrialization. And his descent into the underworld is facilitated by one of the other icons of Argentine modernity, the Buenos Aires subway system.

Gabriel Díaz's photographs join with those of Adriana Lestido, on women in prison, and with Gabriel Valansi's, on the flotsam and jetsam, the material evidence, of the failures of neoliberalism specifically and capitalism in general in Argentina, to constitute a broad indictment of the illusions of First-World successes so touted by the power brokers of recent Argentine history.

Díaz's most recent work has been both a continuation of his interest in the lost and abandoned young and a project whose principal focus has taken him outside Argentina. Two decades after the Chernobyl disaster, many youngsters still live with the dreadful effects of the explosion which released more than 100 times the amount of radiation as the Hiroshima and Nagasaki bombs combined. Hundreds of these children have been treated at the Hospital Pediátrico Tarara in Havana, Cuba, and Díaz made a number of trips to Cuba between 1995 and 2003 for the purpose of preparing a photographic essay on them, on their bodies and on their physical relationship, given their often significant disabilities, with the world around them. Díaz has named the result exhibit *La herencia de Chernobyl* and a printed volume of the

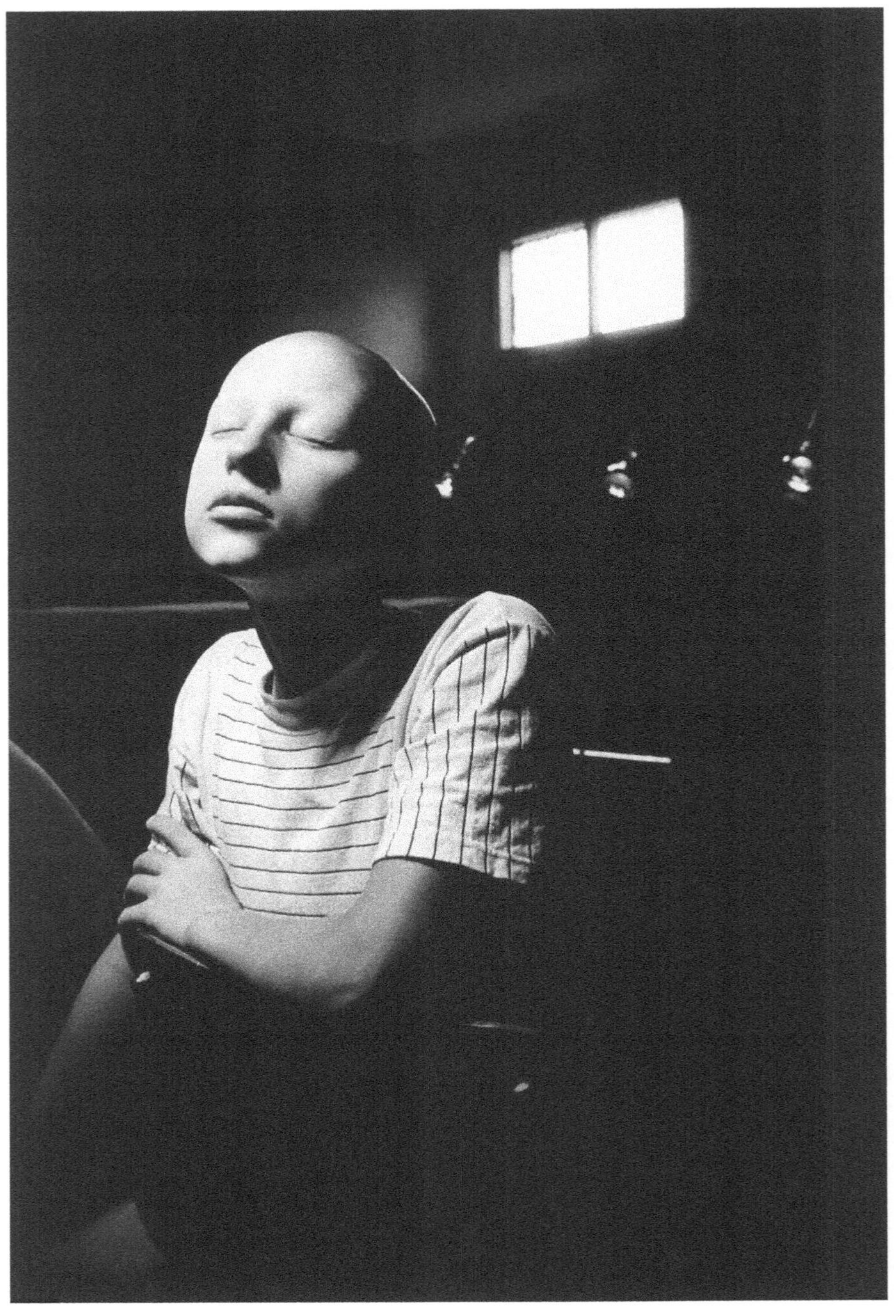

Fig. 6.6 (Gabriel Díaz).

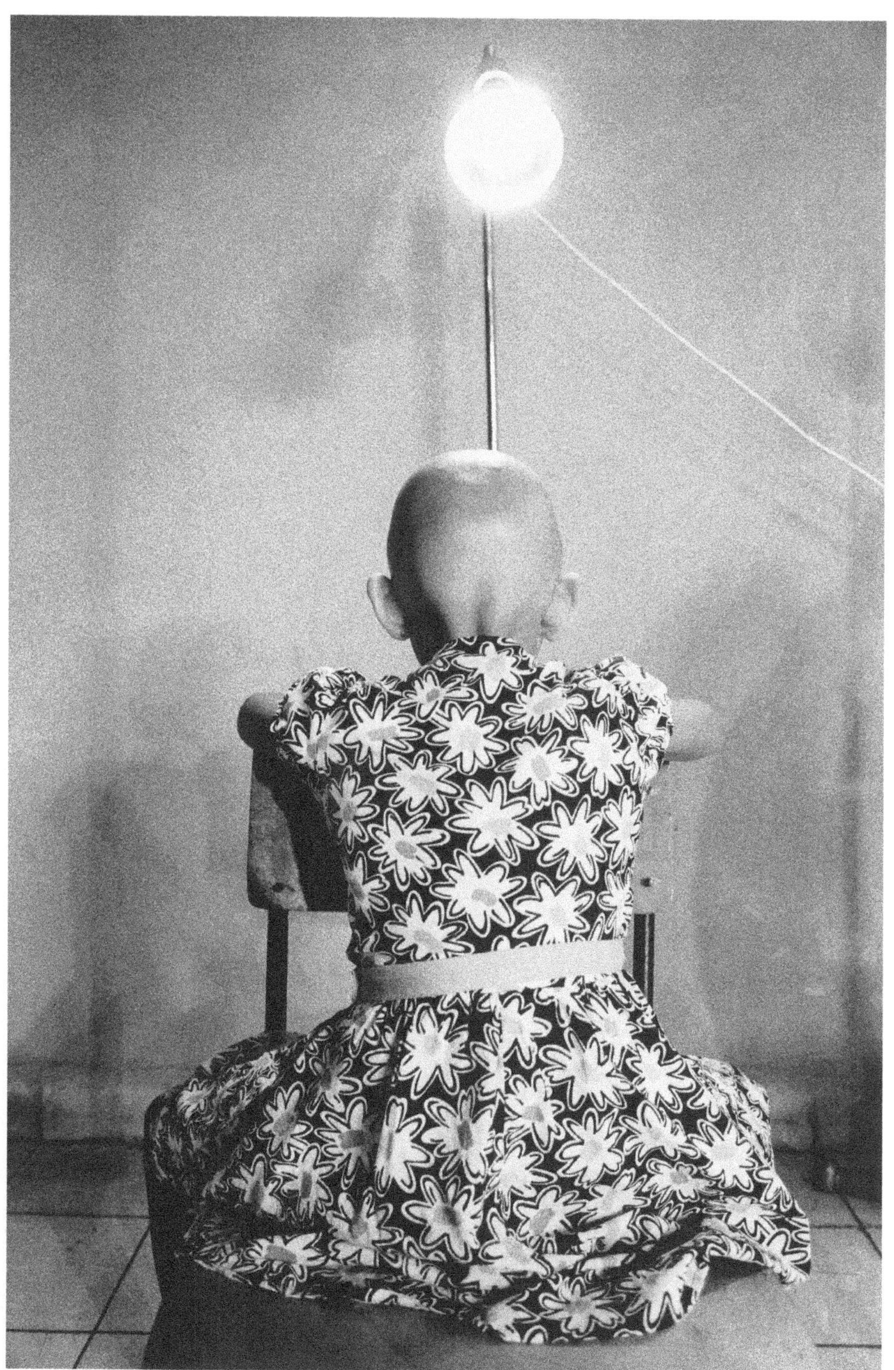

Fig. 6.7 (Gabriel Díaz).

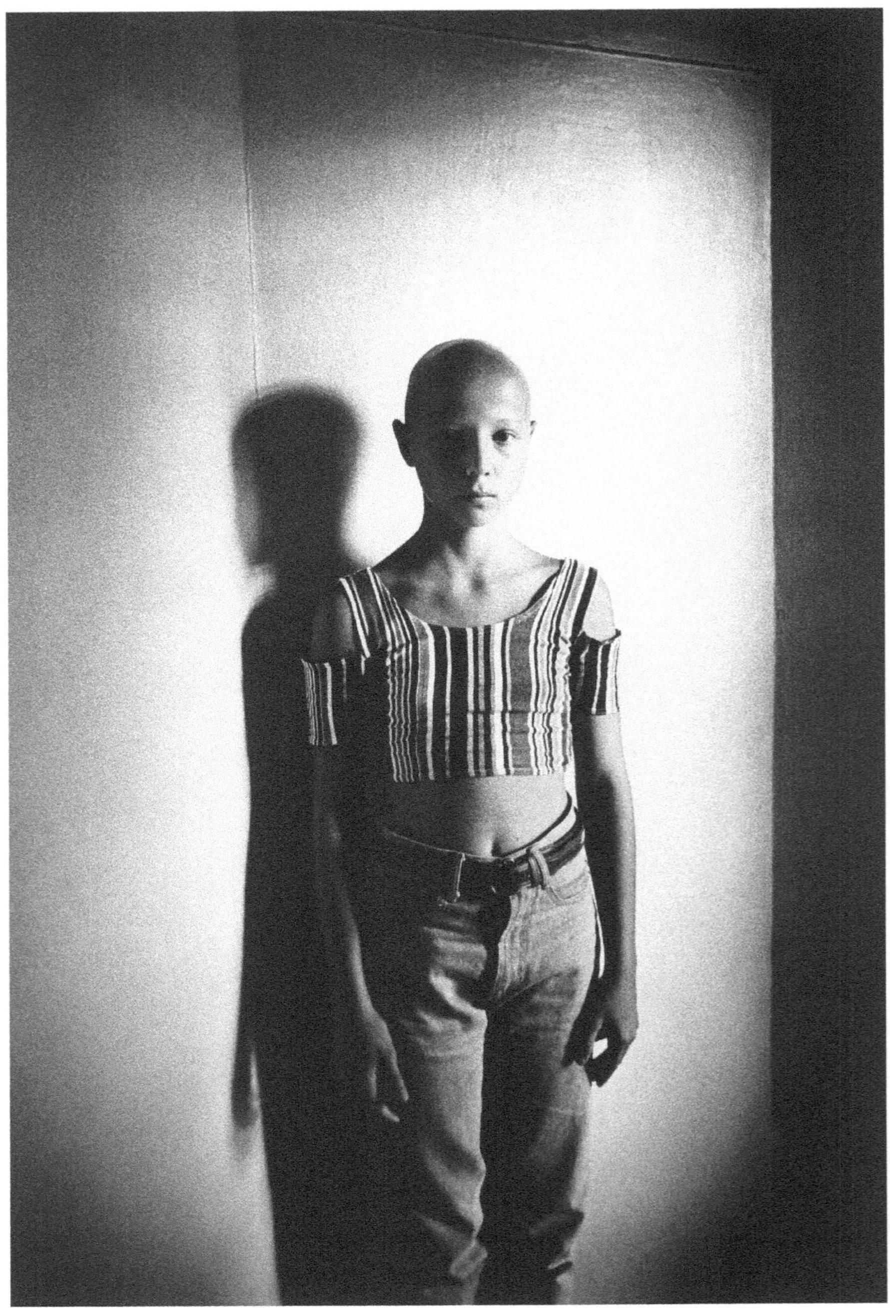

Fig. 6.8 (Gabriel Díaz).

images is planned for 2007 (**Fig. 6.6**, **Fig. 6.7**, and **Fig. 6.8**). Meanwhile, a selection of them may be seen in the Argentine fashion magazine *Brando*, in illustration of an article on Chernobyl by Andrew Matthew. All of the children are between six and fourteen, which means that some of them were born several years after the disaster in what appears now to be an inherited line of genetic defects.

There is something dreadfully ironic about these images (six of the images are black-and-white, while one is in color) appearing in a glossy magazine. What is more, this is the fall-winter fashion issue, featuring not only gorgeous bodies, but an abundance of hair and heavy, elaborate clothing. Since one of the recurring radiation effects from which the children of Chernobyl suffer is baldness, the fashion display of the abundant, lustrous, gorgeous hair on the models, both men and women, is offensively jarring. And since several of the children are shown almost naked, as part of their physical therapy and other treatments, their lack of clothing stands also in brutal contrast to the designer abundance featured in the magazine. To be sure, the photographs were taken in Cuba, where the tropical climate requires far fewer clothes than the chilly midyear climate of Buenos Aires and central Argentina. However, such an explanation based on comparative climate does little to ameliorate the stark contrast between the glossy commercial images of clothing and the simple yet wrenching eloquence of Díaz's photographs. Without going into authorial intention, verifiable or otherwise, Díaz's agreement to have his photographs appear in such a context only serves to underscore quite dramatically the enormous distance between the capitalist modernity of a globalized fashion industry and the Chernobyl disaster, itself one footnote in the human depredations of modernity, whether capitalist or, in this case, socialist.

7

Argentine Kitsch:
The Photography of Marcos López

The debate over the nature of foreign influences in Latin American society is a long and complex one, moving along a scale that sees the destruction of a purportedly authentic autochthonous culture on the one hand, to enthusiastic defenses of the modernizing influence of their incorporation on the other. There are also intermediate points that consider the inevitability of hybridity to the virtues of anthropophagic expropriation (see the theoretical work of García Canclini). These debates have been mediated by various versions of cultural nationalism from both ends of the political spectrum, and they have been inflected by the social, political, and economic consequences of endorsing or rejecting a modernity based on the assimilation of the so-called new as it arrives, apparently, always from somewhere else.

The most positive face one can put on foreign influences (and leaving undertheorized and taken for granted what can be understood by the concept of foreign influences) is that they contribute to the project of modernity. They enhance standards of living, and, if nothing more, make the routine of daily life more interesting by injecting an expanded variety into the usually trivial icons that are the products we live by (see important work for Argentina by Sarlo). The most negative is that such trivial icons disrupt an already richly meaningful existence, although the problem of such appeals to integral cultural purism is how such transcendent meaning is assessed in its prelapsarian state. We have ways of measuring — or, at least, seeming to sense or intuit — when foreign influences have a deleterious effect (e.g., the notorious case involving the scandal of replacing mother's milk with packaged baby formula), but prelapsarianism often remains the unanalyzed signified. What is the "real" culture that has been displaced, corrupted, or replaced by foreign influences?

Latin American societies vary enormously as regards their calculus of foreign influence or even what is to be identified as such and what the sources of that influence are and what agenda — beyond capital gain — may underlie them. The general cry of "American imperialism" may, in fact, be provoked by products that come from any number of national sources and cultures, if they are not simply cases of an underdifferentiated multinationalism. Responses, too, vary, from the traditional outrage of sharply defined nationalistic positions, to attitudes of resignation or indifference from the bulk of the citizenry for whom getting on with one's life may be far more pressing in multiple and complex ways than giving anything more than passing attention to whether the morning's marmalade is now a foreign import and no longer a nationally made product.

To be sure, the matter of foreign influences is more than a question of the brand of marmalade that is the best bargain at the local grocery store. Indeed, one might say, today marmalade and tomorrow one's very own body.[1] Thus, I do not wish to imply that the question of foreign influence is a trivial matter. For example, no one could possibly downplay the impact on Puerto Rican society of the American invasion (on July 25, 1898) and century-long occupation, even if there are reasonable differences of opinion as to whether Puerto Rico would be better off if its history had been other than it has been, whether as a continued colony of Spain, as an independent state, or as some other destiny.

Cultural — as opposed to political — responses to foreign influence have ranged over numerous options. There are those works that provide a fairly transparent image of the models involved (the staggering production in Spanish, as well as translations into Spanish of works written in other languages — most notably English — of texts in the self-help genre that are now routinely bestsellers). There are those works that engage in a denunciation of foreign influences, often by parodying them: the Chilean Enrique Lihn's *Batman in Chile* (1973) was part of numerous works in the period lamenting U.S. involvement in Chile. Of particular interest are fellow Chilean Ariel Dorfman's theoretical and critical writings from the same period: *Para leer al Pato Donald* (1973; with Armando Mattelart); *Superman y sus amigos del alma* (1974; with Manuel Jofré); *The Empire's Old Clothes* (1983). Finally, there are those works which represent the artful accommodation of cultural models that are usually recognized as having a foreign provenance, such as detective fiction, especially the hard-boiled type (although one recalls the parodies of the British intellectual detective genre by the Argentine Honorio Bustos Domecq — the combined pseudonym of Jorge Luis Borges and Adolfo Bioy Casares — in the Isidoro Parodi series), musical theater and film (e.g., Chico Buarque de Hollanda's play *A ópera do Maladro* [1979] and its film version [1985; directed by Ruy Guerra]). Certainly, many television formats are adopted from U.S. models.

One particularly important form of the critical interpretation of foreign influences is through the modality of kitsch. Kitsch is defined by Peter Brooker as

> A cultural object or icon of conspicuously "poor" or no taste (an ornament, a song, picture, verse or cheap paperback) or the self-conscious and provocative preference for such an object in defiance of the conventions of "good taste" or of "high art...." Kitsch values objects that are "so bad they are good" and can be close in this respect to the meaning of camp. It therefore challenges received distinctions between art and mass merchandise, though it is likely to bestow value on one-time popular objects rather than presently mass-produced items, or upon selected, eccentric examples of the latter.... It prizes the eccentric and the aesthetic, therefore, in a world of low-grade disposable junk [125–26].

Kitsch is an effect, and it often arises from the "misuse" of an existing cultural object as it is transformed into one of a different genre and order, such as bed sheets with the design of the American flag or refrigerator magnets that reproduce examples of high art (Brooker mentions the widely recycled image of the Mona Lisa; one can add the image of the Mexican artist Frida Kahlo and her most recognized paintings). Kitsch often is associated with specific sites of cultural production, such as refrigerator magnets, T-shirts, and sundry novelty items like tourist mementos. Kitsch may be simply an inevitable dimension of commercial reproduction, which recycles ad infinitum known and recognizable images, and there is a specific inventory of those that are most familiar to the general consumer, such as the Stars and Stripes or the Mona Lisa.

Kitsch, however, has another dimension, and that is as an instrument of cultural critique, as a modality that can serve to problematize the aesthetic (as Brooker recognizes) and, in increasingly dense ways, to problematize and deconstruct a system of artistic representation. In this way, kitsch may serve productively as a form of metacommentary, in the sense in which Fredric Jameson has used this term: if artistic production is a form of ideological commentary, to what degree does a particular type of production critique an artistic program and the limits, contradictions, discontinuities, and disingenuousness of its ideological commentary? An art that questions and mocks itself is engaged in metacommentary, and kitsch, with its possibilities of descralization, parody, and radical disengagement with the pieties of the aesthetic — especially the bourgeois aesthetic — may be an effective instrument of metacommentary. Several important studies have explored the kitsch in Latin American culture (Olalquiaga; Santos), focusing on precisely its potential effectiveness to engage in ideological critique.

The photographs of Marcos López's *Pop latino* are exercises in creating images of kitsch, or, perhaps more specifically, in capturing the kitsch of daily life by restaging it as a photograph.[2] It might be stretching a point to insist that the images, as a whole, allude to the influence of foreign icons of capitalism, culture, and sociopolitical meaning. Yet there is a unifying quality of the fifty-four images, in terms of their representation of commercial products, of cultural icons that are commercialized and the expropriation not only of foreign products but of a certain type of American advertising technology and popular cultural mentality. As Marcos has said:

> Pop latino: Un shopping center de cartón pintado que tambalea azotado por los vientos patagónicos [*Pop latino*, no pag.].

The popular cultural mentality is particularly evident in the Warholian hyperrealism of López's images, with the sort of foregrounding of the icons in question, the photographic precision of models and products, and the garish colors — often untinted primary and secondary combinations — that are characteristic of popularly oriented advertising, such as billboards, mass distribution magazines, television images, tourist materials, and labels on products themselves. These are far removed from the quasi- or pseudo-artistic and highly elaborated advertising campaigns of publications directed at presumedly sophisticated and self-styled elite audiences. Moreover, in the former case, the products being marketed are relatively inexpensive, and in the latter case large-ticket items are more likely to be the case, justifying the expensive models and the complex details of design and photographic execution.

López's images are *pop latino* less because there is a specific style of pop art that can be unequivocally identified as Latino. Rather, what is more specifically at issue is the insertion of pop art, a style of American and Western European origins, into contexts that are immediately recognized as Latino, whether because of details of language, bits of cultural information, the products themselves, or an intertextuality with images that are recognized as being associated primarily with Latin American — and here, really, mostly Argentine — society or societies.

Let us begin an examination of specific examples of López's kitsch photography/photography of the kitsch with the image from the collection featured on the cover of *Pop latino* (the index identifies the photograph with the title *Carnaval criollo* [1996]), as it illustrates well several of the points I have been making here (**Fig. 7.1**). In the foreground of a large panel (these are 7×11.5 inch photographs), a woman is dressed in a maid's uniform. Although there are several basic colors for such uniforms, in this case it is a palish blue, with faux lace trimming such as one might find on the uniform of the maid or service personnel of an upscale hotel, clinic, sanitorium or the like, establishments where there is the need for individuals who perform menial tasks such as cleaning in public spaces to be marked, nevertheless, as occupying a service category. Their uniform must have some detail that signals the status of the establishment. This is, in itself, a significant detail of kitsch, since the lace fringe serves less as an article of clothing design continuous with the dress to which it is attached and more as an add-on sign, like a detachable name plate or the like, that says something about the workplace of the individual who is obliged to display it.

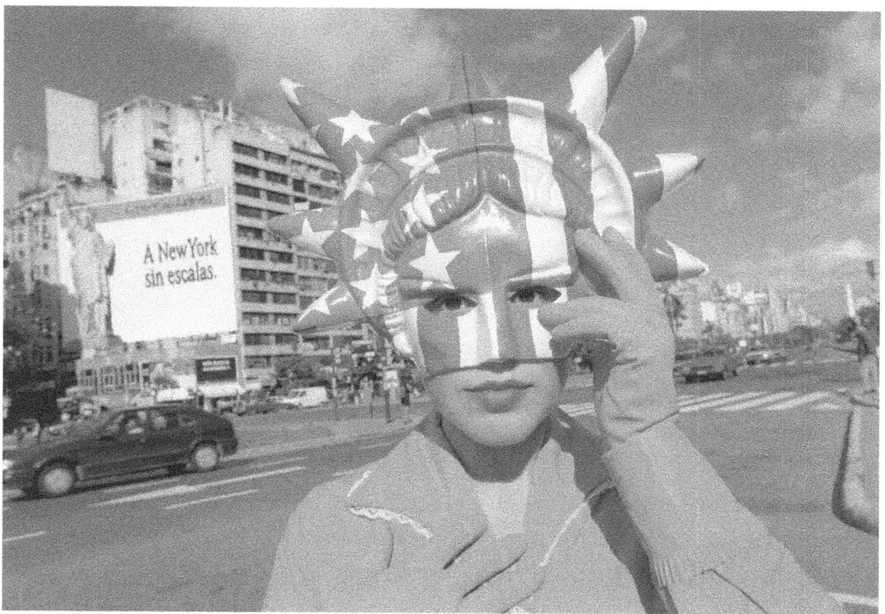

Fig. 7.1 *Carnaval Criollo* (Marcos López).

Confirming her status as a cleaning woman, the model is wearing latex gloves, of the sort used to protect one's hands from harsh chemicals and contamination by unknown/unhealthy substances encountered in the cleaning process. These are not just any rubber gloves, but the top-of-the-line gloves, the ones that are very pliable and mold themselves easily to the hand; the palms are ribbed to enhance their grip even when wet or holding wet objects, and the cuffs are fluted to ensure a snug fit to the wrist and forearm. Such gloves also come in various basic colors, but, in conformance with López's essential utilization of garish colors, these gloves are an intense orange, all the better to clash appallingly with the institutional blue of the uniform the model is wearing.

The main point of the image is the mask that the model/maid holds in front of her face: it is a costume mask imitating the form of the face and crown of the U.S. Statue of Liberty. That this is an American icon is emphasized by the fact that the design stamped on the mask is a fragment of the American flag, with a portion of the white stars on a blue field dominating the right-hand side, with the alternating red and white stripes dominating the left-and side and the portion that fits over the nose and upper lip. The blue picks up the color of the uniform, while the red picks up the lipstick the maid is wearing, and the white the lace detail of her uniform. The maid's left hand holds the mask in front of her face (her mouth, lower cheeks, and chin are left exposed), while her right-hand is pressed against her chest in the typical pose associated with the recitation of the American Pledge of Allegiance.

If we focus solely on the meaning the model is enacting, it is difficult not to see a correlation between the gloves she is wearing and the face mask. The former are a typical American product, either imported or reproduced in Argentina for the local market, while the face mask is indicative of a large number of American cultural icons — in this case, an institutional icon that has become kitsch through its repeated recycling as the myriad objects that cite the U.S. Statue of Liberty — evident in the Argentine marketplace.[3]

Most recently, the American celebration/commercial opportunity of Halloween has joined other festivities that are taken from the American calendar or, if they are already on the Latin American calendar (such as Christmas), are given a focus and an emphasis that resonates with the American business exploitation of those holidays. In the case of this image, the particular/peculiar brand of American patriotism is evoked, to the extent that such masks are part of the paraphernalia of the U.S. Fourth of July and its derivations. While there is no denying the manifestations of Argentine patriotism or that of other Latin American republics, the sort of endlessly inventive kitschification through cheap commercial reproduction is simply not in evidence. Indeed, I would venture to say that an Argentine who might go in for such kitsch is more likely to buy a set of bed sheets with the image of the American flag than to clamor for a set with that of the Argentine flag.[4]

One of the features of López's photographs is that, like a good Baroque painting, the imagery spins almost out of semiotic control. Thus, the image of the model is not enough to underscore the clash of cultural systems represented by the expropriation by Argentina of American motifs. If they are kitsch in the first instance of their existence (as diminished simulacra of institutional or semi-institutional icons), they are even more eloquently kitsch when inserted into the foreign cultural setting, because of the limited resonances of their meaning(s) and/or because of the recontextualizations of such meaning(s).[5] Indeed, one might well ask what meaning accrues to the recontextualized Statue of Liberty mask when it is worn by a fully uniformed Argentine cleaning lady. Is it sufficient that what it probably means is the macro-sememe "United States"?

This would seem to be the case, as we extend our examination of the photograph from the foregrounded human model to the background. The model's backdrop is one of the major Argentine cultural icons, the Avenida 9 de Julio, the reputedly broadest avenue in the word, which cuts a swath from north to south across the city, with close to a dozen lanes in each direction. To the right of this backdrop, and just before the vanishing point of the camera's angle, is the cultural icon that anchors, approximately midway in its trajectory, the 9 de Julio, the obelisk, which commemorates the site of the first raising of the Argentine flag. The obelisk itself is a symbol of the city of Buenos Aires, and its inherent kitschiness (a classic symbol of the sun, it is recycled as a flag memorial, although it is important to note that there is a significant intertextuality in the way in which the Argentine presidential flag contains a sunburst). The official symbology is complemented by popular vulgar references to its phallic meaning and the way in which it is the "great dildo of the nation."

Yet, if the obelisk fades off into the distance, at the other end of the photograph, between the frame of the latter and the foregrounded image of the maid, is a seven-story billboard advertisement for American Airlines. That advertisement is dominated by a symbol and by a text. The symbol is that of the U.S. Statue of Liberty, which thus stands in an inverted semiotic relationship to the Argentine obelisk — the abiding tension between attention to what is Argentine and what is foreign, specifically American — and in a redundant relationship to the impromptu enactment of the Statue of Liberty by the cleaning lady, with her mask and the "patriotic" positioning of her right hand. The Statue of Liberty, to be sure, possesses, as do most public monuments, a plethora of kitschy dimensions, beginning with the by now trite allegories of the figures and symbols they utilize. (I confess a particular attraction to State of Liberty cigarette lighters, an image that I believe the humorist Quino has used in more than one of his cartoon drawings.) These juxtapositions, therefore, are exercises in redundancy and reduplication of a limited number of semantic primes.

The text of the American Airlines billboard reads "A New York sin escalas"; along the top is the name of the airlines — in its traditional red, white, and blue colors, of course. What is noteworthy about this text is the use of "New York" rather than the proper Spanish equivalent of the name of the city: Nueva York. This is an element of linguistic kitsch: the strategic use of a word or phrase of a foreign language rather than what we might call its native equivalent. In so doing, one winks toward the receptor who knows, if not the language in question, strategic lexical items, whose use, rather than their everyday and ordinary Spanish equivalent, conjures up special knowledge of the object or phenomenon, a special relationship, a select meaning.

The process is kitsch because it involves the diminished reduplication of the original in a less valued or less significant context. This is so, because the presumption is that saying "New York" is more elegant or classier than saying "Nueva York," that Spanish, as a language perceived by those who make such linguistic substitutions (at least, in a non-ironic way),[6] is less significant than English, and that Spanish acquires value by such substitutions. The fact that they are token substitutions — a few linguistic signs haphazardly or strategically introduced into the language event — is what underscores their status as kitsch. Such substitutions cannot be said to fulfill any apophantic function and are poetic in only the clumsiest of ways; indeed, they are more probably strictly phatic, signalling the self-attributed status of the speaker rather than contributing to transactional meaning. Therefore, by incorporating a message using "New York" into his photographs, López is underscoring the process of insertion of cultural icons drawn from a foreign culture into Argentine society. Moreover, it is an accession to "New York" and all that city means, with its immense iconicity for the United States, in a fashion that is "sin escalas"— direct and, presumedly, unmediated.[7]

I would like now to consider two paired images. The two images are not included in *Pop latino* side-by-side; moreover, there are two ways of postulating the logical relationship between them. One (**Fig. 7.2**) is that of a waiter holding a formal pose as he offers a bottle of Coca-Cola to the camera in the fashion of a magazine or billboard advertisement (*Mozo* [1996]); the other image functions as though it were a parody of the Coca-Cola ad (**Fig. 7.3**) and involves premodern/nonstylish details surrounding a similar offer of a bottle of Cerveza Santa Fe (*Ciudad de Santa Fe* [1996]). The logical order is relative here. From one point of view, the beer, a national product, could be construed to be something like more authentic, since it is a national product and probably antedates the introduction of Coca-Cola into the Argentine marketplace. Whether this is actually so is irrelevant, since the context of the presentation of the beer is sufficiently premodern (I will explain what I mean by this in a moment) to contrast significantly — and, therefore, to imply a progressive chronology — with the paradigmatic modern drink, which is how Coca-Cola has been traditionally marketed.[8]

Yet, from another point of view, what I am calling the premodern is placed first, as though it were an autochthonous recovery of a national drink, while the Coke image is placed several pages farther along, as though it were secondary to Cerveza Santa Fe and not a displacement of it. To be sure, such products, national and foreign (assuming always that such a rigorous dichotomy is possible and, consequently, meaningful), coexist, occupying different markets and signifying different cultural aspirations as they can be deduced or extrapolated from the preference of clients.[9] Still, these two products do not simply occupy neutrally similar different socially symbolic spaces, because the presentation of one and another is substantially different from the point of view of the semiotics of their respective images and of the respective contexts in which they are inserted.

I have used the term "premodern" to refer to the image of Cerveza Santa Fe (it should be noted that the province of Santa Fe, where this beer is produced and for which it is named, is one of Argentina's most traditional; its capital city is also named Santa Fe). This is not so much because the marketing image of the beer is of long standing and predating more contemporary marketing strategies. Such is indeed true in the case of the image, in the form of a backdrop of the logo of the beer painted in a large format on a brick wall; the paint is worn in several places. Moreover, the logo is distorted at one point by the fact that the wall has a shuttered window, and part of the logo is painted over the shutter, meaning that when the window is open, the unity of the logo

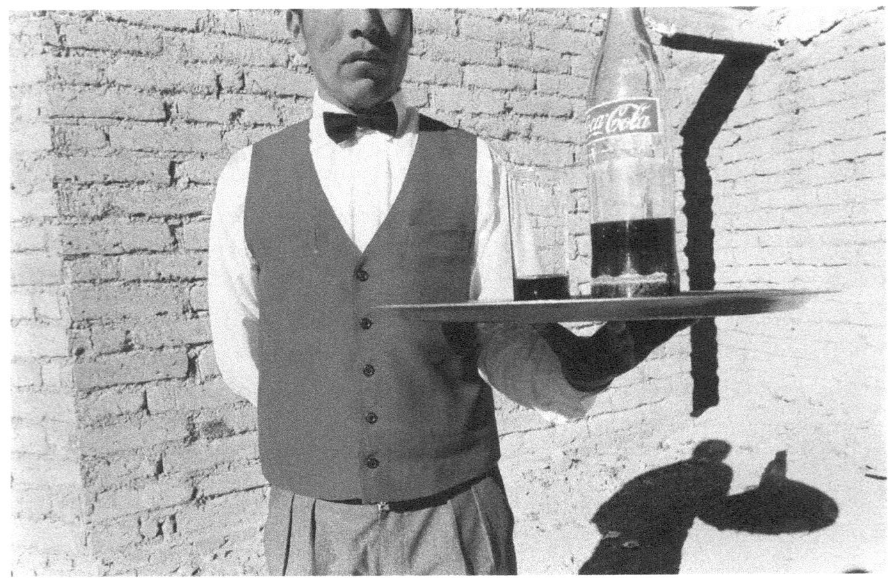

Fig. 7.2 *Asado criollo* (Marcos López).

is disrupted. As it is, it is dispersed to a certain extent because of the change of color, texture, and depth of the image as a result of the material difference between the brick wall and the frame of the window and the shutter itself. The slats of the shutter are particularly at issue in disrupting the surface depth of the logo. By the same token, it should be noted that Coca-Cola goes back to virtually a premodern America, and one can still find in the American countryside vestiges of similar outdoor images of the Coca-Cola logo on the sides of barns, service stations, and rural stores. Indeed, these images, whether still preserved as such or captured in photographic images, are a significant part of the U.S. nostalgia industry, to the extent that Coke is such an American icon and has been associated so much with the development of twentieth-century America, including its role as a major sign of American imperialism throughout the world.[10]

What is premodern about the Cerveza Santa Fe image as captured in the backdrop is reinforced in the foregrounded model, who holds a bottle of the beer, as though offering it to the camera in a canonical advertising format. This involves holding the bottom of the bottle with the finger tips of the right hand, while only two fingers of the other

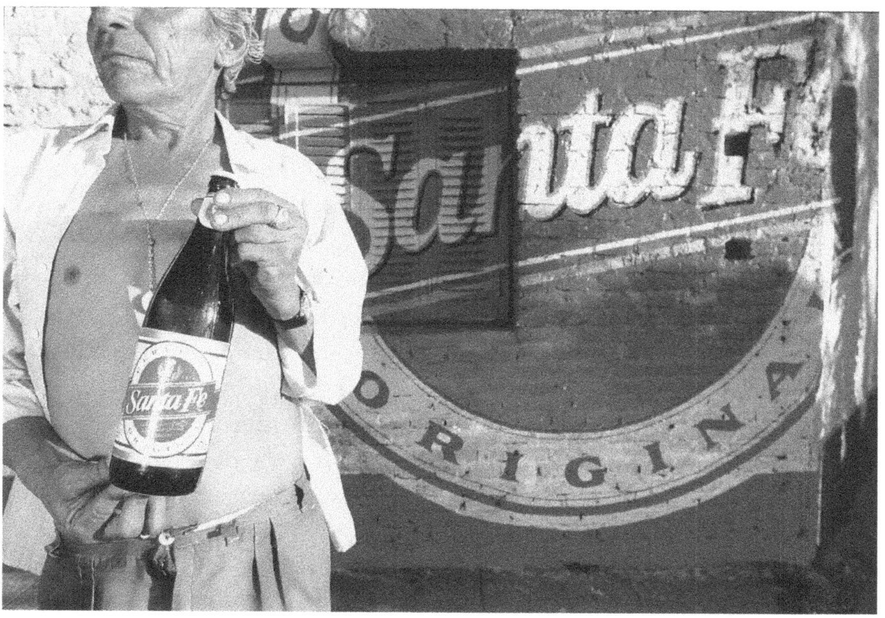

Fig. 7.3 *Ciudad de Santa Fe* (Marcos López).

hand hold the neck of the bottle, thereby providing maximum image exposure of the bottle and its logo to the viewer. The model is, however, what is most notable in this image. The figure is that of an elderly rustic. Although his head is cut off, we can see his longish and unruly hair and his aged skin; moreover, he is looking off outside the frame of the photograph, as though detached from the proceedings, and the upper edge of the photograph bisects his head, such that we cannot see his eyes. As a consequence, another expressive feature of the face, the mouth, is what dominates: his lips are pursed and turned down at the corners, as though this were all a distasteful undertaking. At best, it is not the enticing facial language normally associated with the selling of commercial products.

But what is most striking is his dress. He is wearing some rust-colored and ill-fitting pants that are poorly fastened at the waist; the pants have no belt. Although his white shirt is clean and pressed, it is fully unbuttoned and pulled back, with the sleeves partially turned up, so that what is prominent behind the bottle of beer he is holding is his hairless chest. The bottle hides his navel, but objects outside the frame that provide three different degrees of lighting for his chest highlight what would be for the language of conventional advertising the unappetizing display of his flesh. One must remember that the display of flesh in modern advertising depends on an appeal to a presumed canonical inventory of erotic fetishes,[11] and it is a question of heightening the working of those fetishes while scrupulously avoiding the inclusion of anything that might be construed as antinomous to them: there is only a certain range of male chests that are considered "sexy" in advertising texts, and this model's is not one of them.[12]

López's other image enjoys a significant intertextuality with that of Cerveza Santa Fe. One is immediately struck by the fact that the backdrop of the Coca-Cola image is decidedly non-urbane (**Fig. 7.2**). It, too, is a brick wall, and, moreover, it is a fairly battered brick wall. We see the wall continue to form a corner with a second wall. The floor is made of dirt, and dirt has piled up in the corner formed by the two walls. We can just see a sliver of sky above one of the walls, and the top edge of the wall contributes to the overall effect that the photograph was taken either in an abandoned construction site or in one of those homes that lower middle-class individuals in the poorer sections of Argentina build for themselves and their families, with parts of the construction becoming weathered and worn without the house ever quite being completed, since typically construction stretches out over years, with work only being done on weekends and holidays.

Thus, the backdrop becomes the first, most obvious sign of what I will allow myself to call, in conceptual shorthand, a Third-World setting. This is, to be sure, the locus of the consumption of Coca-Cola as it has spread throughout the world, a world that is not that of the capitalist leader(s). The fact that there is a sociopolitical motif to be evoked here, that of whether Argentina is "First World," the rallying cry of the ultimately failed neoliberal experiment of the Menem 1990s, is also a level of meaning in the photograph. Coca-Cola may be an icon of the so-called First World, but its consumption in Argentina and Latin America does not, except under the conditions of the most delirious wishful thinking, signal these geographic realms as First World.

The presentation of Coca-Cola in this image is, nevertheless, one that is associated with gracious dining in Argentina. A properly attired waiter (neat pants, impeccable white shirt and tie, fully buttoned vest) proffers a large serving tray, perfectly balanced on the tips of the fingers of his left hand, with his right hand and forearm discreetly tucked behind his back. The tray contains a partially emptied large bottle of Coke, alongside a partially served glass of the beverage. Yet the image is not a perfectly First-World one. The fact that the server is standing in the corner of a partially constructed building is echoed in the way in which his pants are worn. Some stitches are missing from the crotch area and the fastener on the waistband seems to have some problem, although we can only partially see it. In a classically dressed server, his pants would, moreover, be black rather than tan — these are almost the same tan as the pants worn by the model in the Cerveza Santa Fe image. The model's face in the Coca-Cola image is also cut off at the eyes; however, from what we can see of the look on his face, it is that of customary obeisance of the professional server. Finally, it is worth noting that the features of the second model are indigenous. While the reputedly finer restaurants of Argentina strive to hire waiters who look more Western European, it is not uncommon for waiters in a high percentage of ordinary restaurants and bars in Buenos Aires to be individuals from the indigenous north of the country that were, as I have noted previously, part of the massive urban immigration that began in the 1940s.[13]

Thus this second image is not simply a supposedly First-World image juxtaposed with a Third-World one. In a very real sense, the first image is more homogeneous in capturing a certain segment of the social reality of Argentina: the marketing and consumption of well-known national products, in contexts that have nothing to do with the (pseudo)modern ones that are promoted in glossy advertising and to which particular segments of the urban population are prone to aspire. By contrast, the second image is decidedly mixed in its cultural anchors. On the one hand, it focuses on the promotion of the icon of American culture, Coca-Cola; on the other hand, it places the promotion of that product in a context that is as equally premodern as that of Cerveza Santa Fe. Moreover — and this is a real clincher as regards what I would call the degradation of the great American cultural icon in its journey downward into everyday Argentine consumption — when one looks closely, the Coca-Cola bottle is well worn, the consequence of the unending, and therefore wearing, recycling of the bottle that is indicative of the economics of consumerism in Argentina. The point is that the image captures the marketing of foreign cultural products, but it also underscores their inevitable degradation as a consequence of the particular pinch-penny way in which they are assimilated into the local economy.[14]

López's images are accompanied by a series of prose texts that basically consist of haiku-like evocations of the Argentine/Latin American material landscape, such as: "Pop Latino: Un shopping center de cartón pintado que tambalea azotado por los vientos patagónicos" (no pag).[15] This characterization casts in a different semiotic code the overall sense of López's photographs: the degraded (or debased or vitiated) foreign sociocultural icon, inevitably and irretrievably subjected to the distorting processes of local sociocultural realities. It is the decontextualization of the former and their recontextualization in the latter that is so productive of the quality of kitsch that López is interested in capturing. One photograph of particularly hilarious eloquence (*Todos por dos pesos* [1995]) involves a model dressed in garish colors, topped off with a pea-green Jim Carrey mask from the latter's 1994 film *The Mask*. Around his neck the model is wearing a collar of Argentine *chorizos*, but he is gesturing toward a billboard hanging from the front of a very traditional Argentine residential facade, advertising a dollar store. Not only is the dollar store a foreign imitation, but this dollar store (actually everything for 1.99) advertises "importación"— that is, all products are foreign imports. One assumes that for those prices, they are mostly cheaply made items from Southeast Asia.

There are several photographs that contain Che Guevara and armed guerrilla images. Some seem to be a commentary on the importation into a country like Argentina of tropical revolutionary movements — that is, the Argentine Che Guevara reprocessed through the very alien culture of Cuba. Against the backdrop of the Argentine Planetarium (one conventional symbol of the Argentine European self-identity, surely), an Argentine dressed in military fatigues is being threatened with a plastic gun by someone wearing a crocodile mask (*Atrapado por las fuerzas del mal* [1993]). The head of a standard-issue guerrilla fighter, in the form of a mask in mostly nonnatural colors, looks gleefully on out of the lower right-hand corner.

In another image (**Fig. 7.4** *La Habana* [1997]), a beefy Argentine

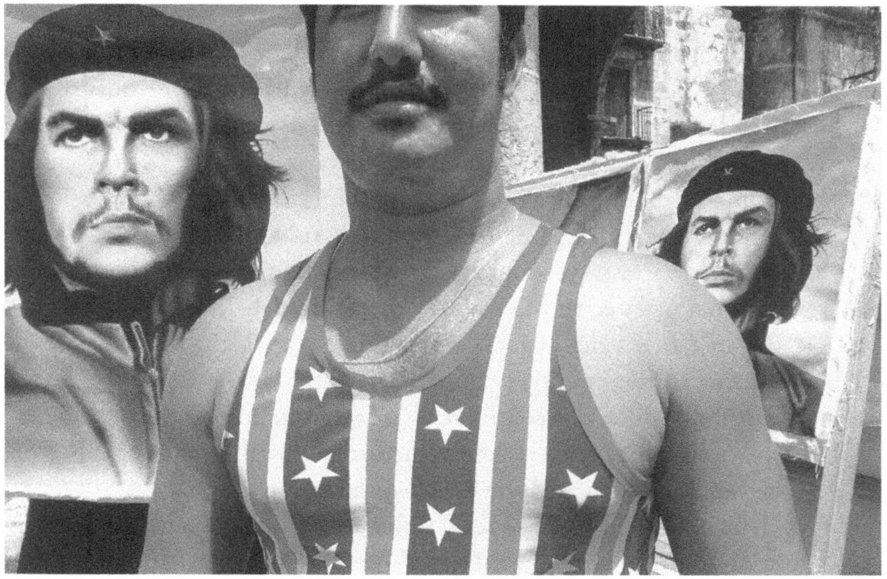

Fig. 7.4 *La Habana*, Havana (Marcos López).

(one presumes), his head also cut off at the eye level, as in the case of the models selling beer and Coke in the images analyzed above (this is unquestionably a technique López uses to disrupt the assumed conventions of the photography of individuals, whereby the head is the most interesting part of the human being), is shown wearing a tight-fitting tank top. The pattern of the top, without actually being the American flag, is that of the stars and stripes in red, white, and blue. The image is flanked by two versions of the same image of Che Guevara, one larger than the other. Che, with the expected icons of his persona, especially his black beret with the single star dead-center front, stares off into the distance, his brow furrowed in the committed determination of revolutionary fervor in a parody of Alberto Korda's famous photo of Che. By contrast, the dress of the model is that of the beachside tourist (concerning the exploitation of Che's image, see Geirola).

Yet let me back away from the implied Americanization of the model's tank top and provide an alternative interpretation, even though one might want to hold onto the Americanness of the tank top as a masculine item of clothing. Alternatively, the model may be read, if not as a postrevolutionary Cuban, as an Argentine tourist in Cuba (his beefiness inclines me toward the likelihood that he is Argentine, since recent Cuban dietary restrictions are not conducive to such male body mass). The fact that the context is probably Cuba is borne out by the detail of the buildings to be seen beyond the Che images, and they look very much like those of old Havana. The tank top may, then, well be based not on the American flag, but on the Cuban flag, which uses the same colors. In this reading of the photography, the quality of kitsch arises from the postrevolutionary transformation that leads from Che's revolutionary stance to the tourism of the model. Moreover, the single star of Che's beret, which is the single star of the Cuban flag, is reproduced in the essentially boundless design of the article of clothing into/onto which it is commercialized (that is, boundless in the sense that the number of stars is determined solely by the geometricality of the design and the size of the article of apparel).

I have emphasized López's universe of images with particular attention to the quality of kitsch of those photographs that involve the presence and juxtaposition of sociocultural icons that intrude, if not on a putatively "authentic" Argentine reality, at least one in which these icons are only precariously — contradictorily, disruptionally — accommodated. López's 2003 collection, which includes the images of *Pop latino* and work subsequent to it, is cleverly titled *Sub-realismo criollo*, another way of capturing his interest in the ironic representation of devalued cultural paradigms. Certainly, from a postmodern point of view, all sociocultural icons are ultimately precarious and problematical as they go about their semiotic work, and even the most naturalized of icons can end up dislodged by paradigm shifts in the structures that give them meaning. Concomitantly, even what appears to be the most outrageously "inappropriate" cultural sign may subsequently undergo a seamless integration into the system of cultural meaning. One of my favorite examples is the way in which the at one point totally alien British derby, a half-century after it is introduced into Bolivia, is as much an integral part of the indigenous costume, especially for women, as is the poncho of the Altiplano.

The particular effect of López's images is based on strategic juxtapositions, such as occurs in the image ("Feliz Navidad" [1997]) of the tinseled American Christmas tree (artificial, of course), which in a very first instance is out of place as a winter symbol in the summer heat of Argentina's late December, is placed alongside a portrait of Eva Perón. In another image an array of sexual ticklers or dildos (there is not likely to be a local industry for these objects) is placed against a seascape, as though, with their "naturalistic" flesh tones, they were sea creatures arising from the foam (*Guardianes del río* [1996]; see also *Antena* [1996], in which a solitary dildo raises up against the desert sky, in consort with the armed cactuses — *sahuaros* in my U.S. Southwest desert setting). These are, in the main, photographs that are simply a pleasure to examine, and it is clear that the models and the photographer spent many hours of fun together producing them. The level of sustained humor that they reveal is, indeed, quite impressive. Yet, it would be a mistake to see these carefully staged images only as humorous collages. There is important work going on in *Pop latino* in terms of ideological interpretation, and Panera Cuevas comments on "The bitterness and clearly insistent subversion that lies beneath [these photographs]" (9). My goal here has been to show how analytical scrutiny is able to demonstrate the careful and calculated artistry of López's images. They contrast significantly with the found images of Gabriel Valansi's nocturnal photographs, but both photographic languages are successful, each in its own way, in commenting profoundly on contemporary Argentine cultural values.

I turn now to the analysis of a specific cluster of Marcos López's kitsch compositions, those that deal with masculinist society and the often prominently displayed homoerotic pulsions that flow, knowingly or otherwise, between the social subjects that are bonded in their privileged all-male (or aspirationally all-male) world. It is questionable whether contemporary Argentina presents a special case of impervious homosociality (it certainly did during the all-male domination of the authoritarian and neofascist military periods mentioned previously); what can, however, be asserted with certainty is that few visual artists have undertaken to critique that privilege, and this is one of the most singular dimensions of López's carefully worked assemblages.

One of López's most internationally recognized images is *Asado criollo*,[16] which is a recasting of Leonardo da Vinci's *The Last Supper* (**Fig. 7.5**). In the place of the sacred Last Supper of Jesus Christ and the Twelve Apostles, the founding event figured in the Holy Mass of the Catholic Church as a commemoration of Christ's sacrifice for the

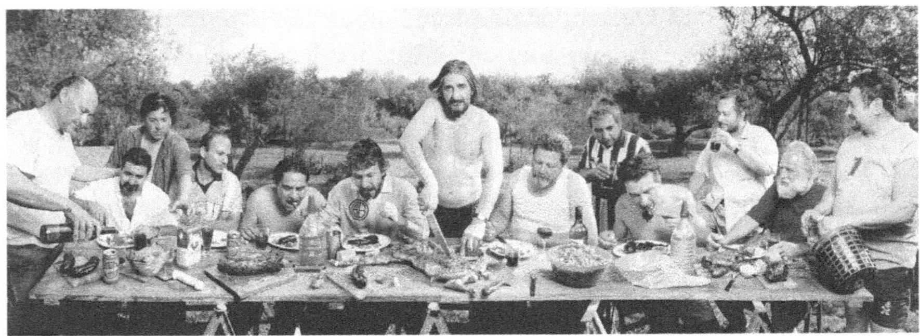

Fig. 7.5 *Asado criollo*, Native Barbecue (Marcos López).

salvation of mankind, we have the virtually sacralized ritual of the Argentine barbecue, where the blood-bathed sacrifice of edible beef is the privileged figure of Argentine communal identity. If wherever Catholics assemble they will celebrate Christ's sacrifice for the salvation of mankind, wherever Argentines assemble they will celebrate the sacrifice of beef for the affirmation of "Argentinity."[17] This is all a pretty hilarious and irreverent network of associations, part of whose resonance is the way in which so many Argentines are not particularly overtly religious, on either a formal or folkloric level — not, at least, in the way in which one associates popular Christianity as so essentially part of the fabric of everyday life in a society like Mexico, for example.

Images like *Asado criollo* (*Carnaval criollo* is another) have contributed to López's growing reputation, and, in addition to Argentina, his work has been shown in Spain, Mexico, and elsewhere in Latin America, and most recently in New York, in a show February 25–March 14, 2005, at the White Box Gallery (www.whiteboxny.org) called *Al sur del realismo/South of Realism*.[18]

Although I have examined above in detail López's use of kitsch in order to critique globalized values through parody, I would like here to address issues of homosocialism, homoeroticism, and their interrelationship in López's images, particular in those that appear in a small portfolio, *López Marcos*, published in Mexico City in 2004.

Let us first define our terms. By "homosocialism" (one could also invest here in the term "homosociality"), one understands the strong and exclusivizing bond between members of the same sex. Such a definition, and its implied or overt sanction — and implied or overt disapproval — by various intersecting social institutions, is predicated on a conception of stable sex identity, such that there is a clear-cut separation between male and female. This is a stability that is maintained, in the main, by both transgendering (the movement from one sexual identity to another) and by transexuality (the anatomical reconfiguration of a body such that it migrates from one sexual identity to another); homosocialism becomes problematical wherever queer theory destablizes binary sexual identity. In Sedgwick's famous formulation, which originally applied only to late nineteenth- and early twentieth-century British literature, but which has been extensively adapted to a wide array of societies by masculinity studies (see Connell for one early survey; Gutman for pertinent research in Latin America), homosocialism is the pact, the so-called gentleman's agreement, whereby power is circulated between men, who are bonded together by a number of social networks and practices: marriage, business, fraternal associations, guilds, societies, shared initiations and acculturations, and the like. Women are both excluded and used by homosocialism as a token or shifter of masculine power in a world characterized by the inviolable company of men. Two typical narratives are the accession to the realm of the boss by marrying his daughter or the use of the sexuality of women as a way of displaying to other men one's legitimating heterosexuality. Such narratives depend on an interaction with women to demonstrate the male's appropriate participation in the hegemonic codes of a male-dominated society.

It is significant to note that, while homosociality may be sustained by an undercurrent of (weak) homoerotic desire, as in the simple comfort of being with other men in an all-male sphere, strong homoerotic desire and the acting upon that desire through the enactment of a number of specifically genital and orgasmic scripts, are taboo and would disrupt the homosocial pact.[19] But there is unquestionably a segue between homosocialism as the approved assembling of men and homoeroticism as what might happen among assembled men under the "right" conditions, such as having had too much to drink or sharing traumatic experiences.[20] To be sure, another dimension of this issue is the question of exactly what constitutes homoeroticism: that is, exactly when is it present and how might we detect it (beyond manifest signs such a penile tumescence or specific acts we can agree to call homoerotic)? This is the problem of what to make of fraternity initiations, especially where practices like often severe and ritualized spanking are involved (see Mattoso's extensive analysis of these phenomena in German, American, and Brazilian university societies), or of the hugging and butt-slapping of team sports, not to mention the display of the male buttocks promoted by tight-fitting uniforms, as in American baseball, and the fetishizing of the legs of soccer players (Manrique); also legendary is the display of the male body in bullfighting (see Afanador's photography, and Foster's study of it, "Toreros de moda") and the way in which the all-male world of bullfighting has always involved a dimension of homoeroticism, as Lorca so eloquently captures it in his famous "Llanto por Ignacio Sancho Mejía" (see other references in my study of Afanador's photography).

Thus, if we reserve the term "homoeroticism" for a series of acts and their accompanying narratives that confirm the possibility of the fulfillment of sexual desire between same-sex partners, it is, nevertheless, evident that the homosocialism that cements the personal relationships between men in the exercise of patriarchal authority may often (perhaps always) contain an undercurrent of the physical, but customarily tabooed and therefore unfulfilled, attraction between male bodies.[21] Such weak homoeroticism can rarely be the subject of overt social discourse, although one does occasionally hear calls for the boys to cut down a bit on the butt-slapping, while homosocialism—"getting together with the fellows"—is an accepted and promoted intercultural norm of modern society.[22]

There is, then, an interesting vein of male homosocial imagery in the recent work of López which has unmistakable homoerotic overtones, even if it is only a weak homoeroticism that the viewer can "strengthen," so to speak, in an attentive contemplation of the insinuations of and the insertions into real-world experience which López's images critique through parody.

Certainly, the homosocial is an issue in López's by now rather legendary *Asado criollo* composition. In the first place, it evokes the founding or grounding homosociality of Leonardo da Vinci's depiction of the Last Supper of Christ with his disciples. Leaving aside the question of whether or not there is a feminine presence in the painting in the person of Mary Magdalene, as touted by Dan Brown in his controversial and transgressive 2003 best-selling novel, *The Da Vinci Code* (which also expounds on Mary Magdalene as the wife of Christ), the assemblage of the thirteen men of Leonardo's painting and the endless reproduction of it which the concept of kitsch helps us to understand confirm a monumental paradigm of homosocialism in Western culture. Now, it is important to stress that López does not simply plug in substitutions for the arrangement, clothes, gestures, and interactions of the participants in the Leonardo painting; this would be rather facile and the essence of noncritical or unreflective kitsch. Rather, he retains the six-against-six balance of the men on each side of the central figure, but has them more in the postures of the consumption of food and drink than in the case of the Leonardo original. Moreover, while the latter is encased in an idealized Renaissance banquet room, López's denizens surround an improvised open-air table, with the unmistakable humid Pampas landscape of central Argentina in the background: that is, where Leonardo da Vinci's image is stylized and dehistoricized, López's photograph evokes a specific sociohistorical reality, that of the gritty texture of the Argentine barbecue.

I use the word "gritty" here advisedly, because the texture of the carefully staged image is that of a casual, real-life weekend convocation of men to eat, drink, and enjoy each other's company. They are all dressed casually, some so casually as to project an offensive image to other, more formal social arbiters, especially given the sacred context evoked by the image. Both the man we can call the Jesus stand-in and two of his "apostles" appear shirtless, one other wears a sleeveless undershirt, while two others wear shirts open to reveal more chest than some would consider decorous. One man, who bleeds off the left margin of the image, appears to be wearing a short-sleeved undershirt, leaving six men whose torsos are respectably clothed. Undoubtedly, a major Argentine cultural referent here are the humorous drawings *Buenos Aires en camiseta*, drawn by Alejandro del Prado (Calé) for Guillermo Divito's popular magazine *Rico tipo* in the late 1950s and early 1960s. Calé, in satirizing broadly the tics of the Argentine petit-bourgeois male, also captured the way in which his habits veered from the rigorous standards of the sartorially perfect English gentleman the national upper middle-class and oligarchy aspired to emulate. Too,

Leonardo's painting represents Jesus and the apostles as impeccably clothed or robed, and López's image subverts as much the decorum of the Renaissance work as it evokes an alleged Argentine careless vulgarity.

Of special note is the way in which the Jesus stand-in does specifically evoke the Savior in ways in which his companions do not merely replicate the apostles (beyond their balanced six-by-six distribution). The stand-in, who hovers imposingly above his companions, has both the long hair and the beard of the Jesus original, just the sort of hirsuteness (paradoxically, given the accompanying allegation of femininity) that the Argentine neofascist guardians of public morals in the late 1960s and again in the 1970s considered a sign of homosexuality. da Vinci's Jesus is seated, with his hands outstretched in the sign of the first offering of his sacrifice, but López's counterimage is masterfully wielding the knife in the central ritual of the *asado*, the cutting and distribution of the cooked meat. Not only is the latter shirtless, but his cutting action emphasizes pectoral muscles, which are complemented by what for some might be the erotic nature of a fleshy belly button and pants that ride just low enough to be right at the nevertheless concealed pubic line. While there is little here that one can call (homo)erotic beyond the possibilities inherent in the unkempt display of the body of the guests at this table and the physicality of dedicated eating and drinking that is crucial to a good *asado*, this assertedly homosocial gathering reminds one that the Ur-homosocial drinking and eating party is Plato's *Convivium*, where one of the crucial topics of conversation is human sexuality, including Plato's character Diotima's intriguing account of the bases and the defense of what we have come to call Greek homosexuality. These convivial Argentines might well discuss the women, the *minas*, but never at the expense of the ritualized shared physicality of their meal.[23]

One detail of the cultural horizons of Leonardo da Vinci's *Last Supper*, so pregnant with meaning as to the founding event of Christian homosociality, is Leonardo's own homosexuality, a detail that the Vatican, and popular art history, would choose emphatically to ignore. Yet no serious art historian can overlook this dimension of the Italian Renaissance artist giant's biography and, therefore, its appearance, if only latently, in his work.[24] Therefore, it would be rather risky, if not outrageous, to suggest that there is a hidden homosexuality about Leonardo's painting, although viewers are always entitled to see what they (want to) see. Since no "protective veil of the sacred" envelops López's photography and since, indeed, one of the licenses of parody is to encourage outrageous meanings, one may feel more comfortable with teasing out the latent homoeroticism of what one might call *Asado criollo*'s "la gran comilona de los muchachos." Boy-men will be boy-men.

The homoerotic is more clearly evident in the cover image of *Marcos López*, where the same model is used for both the carefully groomed hospital aide and his long-haired severely injured patient (the image in turn has a definite intertextuality with Frida Kahlo's signature work *Las dos Fridas*, which need not necessarily evoke Kahlo's well-known bisexuality/lesbianism[25]).

This image (titled *Hospital,* **Fig. 7.6**) would be relatively uninteresting — serving, perhaps at best, as a poster for a national nurses/hospital orderly association — if it weren't for the bonding between the two men that is underscored by their both being enacted by the same model: photography and cinema have a venerable tradition of dual (even multiple) parts being played by the same actor, often around the ages-old motif of the evil twin, as in Bette Davis's 1964 *Dead Ringer* (dir. Paul Henreid) or Jeremy Irons's 1988 reprise of the Davis film, *Dead Ringers* (dir. David Cronenberg).[26] Got up differently — the long-haired, partially nude patient; the soberly neat aide — they are also differentiated by the accompanying details of their role. The patient, of course, has the trappings of his treatment (bandages, the IV connection, the walker to support the traumatized right leg), and the aide his (the simple green cotton scrubs, the stethoscope worn around the neck, the IV drip). The pair is photographed in what appears to be one of the halls of a old hospital from the generation of the Rivadavia or the Ramos Mejía.

But where the expected is disrupted, wherein lies the Barthean punctum that hooks the attentive viewer's gaze, is the fact that the right forearm of the patient is bound to the left forearm of his aide by a tightly wrapped bandage of bloody gauze. There is no indication of why the patient should be wearing such a wrapping, and it is left to the curious speculation of the viewer as to why the patient should be bound to the aide in this fashion. Of course, one could attribute an

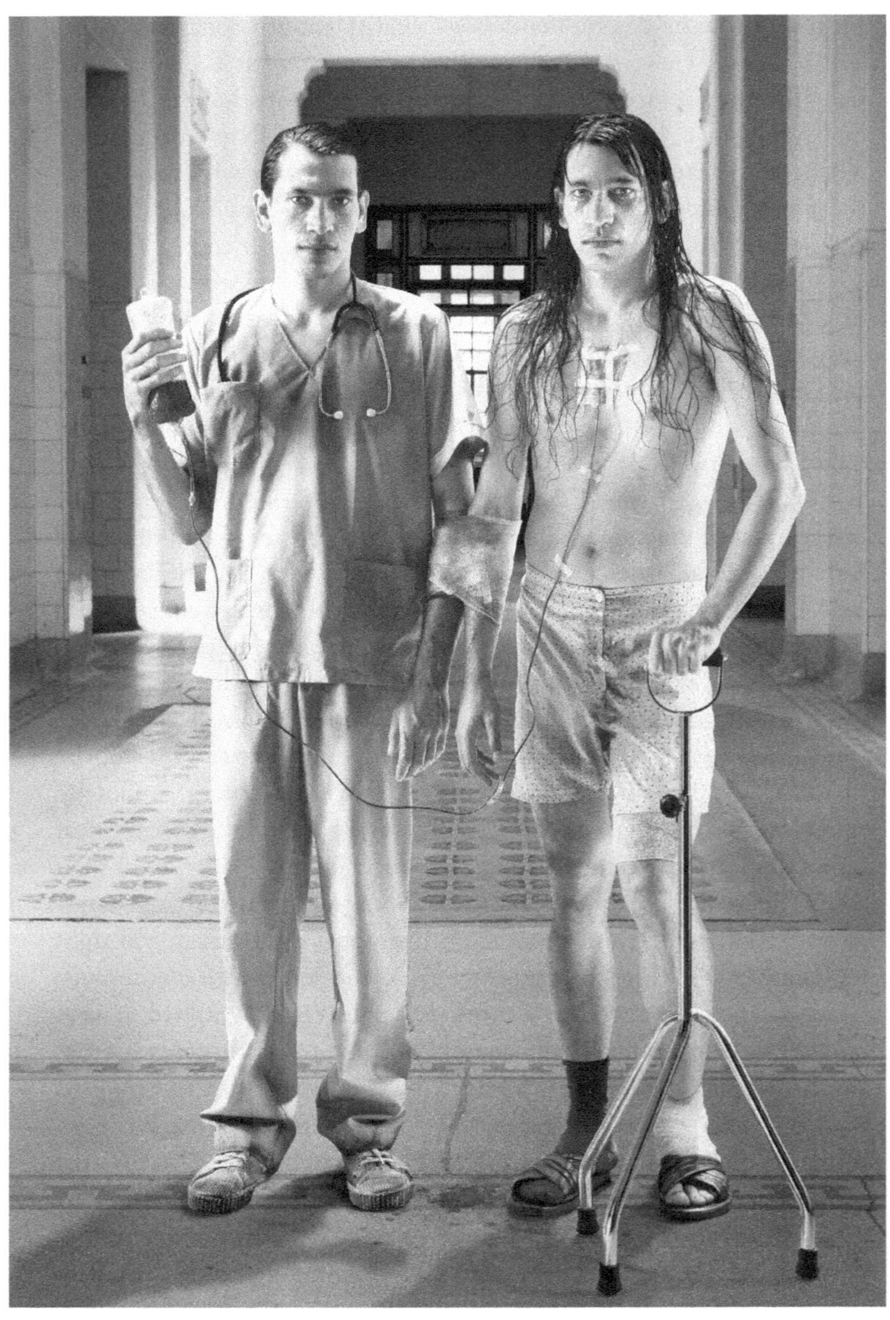

Fig 7.6 *Hospital* (Marcos López).

allegorical function to this detail: the patient needs the assistance of the aide in order to mend or even in order to survive. But that bond is already allegorized by the presence of the IV, which the aide holds (and will subsequently hang from the appropriate suspension apparatus) for the patient, ensuring the continued administration of whatever the bag contains. Again, there is nothing directly erotic about this image, except for the handsomeness of the actor, part of whose body is minimally revealed in the enactment of the patient: much more suggestive would have been an image of the aide dangling an enema bag whose hose is inserted into the patient's rectum, although this would be an unlikely occurrence in the sort of transfer from one place to another that might be the "real-life" circumstance of the event captured by the photo.

Yet, the disruption of the everyday occurrence of a transfer from one place to the next in the modern hospital that comes with the detail of the shared bandage provokes speculation as to the figured relationship between the two. The hospital is the setting for frequent (homo)erotic fantasies, and playing nurse/doctor is one of the ways in which children first discover each other's bodies: nurses and doctors are customarily the first nonparental authority figures who manipulate and invade our bodies in what can be later resemanticized in erotic terms (see the topic of rape by medical instrument as it is developed in the Irons film mentioned above). The intimacy with the body of the patient required in many routine medical procedures, in turn, is one of the reasons, even before the threat of STDs, why some medical personnel are uncomfortable with treating patients they know or suspect to engage in same-sex acts; for others, this will be part of the pleasure of the other's body.[27] Even when the body of the patient is neither manipulated nor invaded (unquestionably where the vagina or the rectum is involved) or metaphorically (the insertion of an IV or even an ear examination), the proximity between the two bodies, the one ministering and the one being ministered to, can be suggestive.[28] The fact that such a proximity is sealed here, one might say, by the bloody bandage cannot, therefore, be dismissed as a quirky disruption of naturally occurring circumstances.

Two other images in the volume equally allow for the displacement from naturally occurring circumstances to the homoerotic. It is

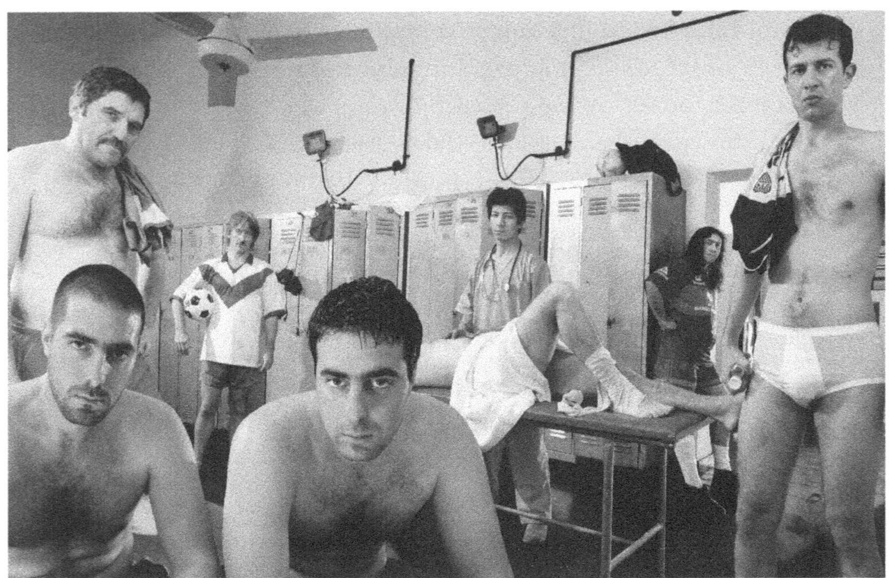

Fig. 7.7 *El vestuario* [The Locker Room] (Marcos López).

questionable to what degree the homosocial is involved in the hospital scene, except for a general policy whereby male patients are tended to by male aides and female patients by female aides. However, one of the most homosocial spaces in modern society is the locker room, which is closely associated with other athletic and gymnasium spaces like the shower, the steam room, the Jacuzzi, the massage room, and the infirmary. The bathhouse/sauna was, before AIDS, one of the great meeting places for gay men, and the fancy gym is, for today's guppy, one major site for same-sex cruising (American university sports centers are notorious in this regard).[29] The homoerotic dimension of sports has long been maintained (Prongher), and it is difficult to forget that the original Olympics were performed in the nude; homoerotic overtones have also long been associated with European soccer, and Bazán recalls the 1995 controversy surrounding the Argentine national team (433–34). The sociologist Juan José Sebreli first broached the subject in print in a book from 1981, *Fútbol y masas*, but develops it as a major theme in his 1998 *La era del fútbol* (see also his "Historia secreta").

In López's image (titled *El vestuario*, **Fig.** 7.7), one is particularly struck by the fact that none of the seven men (athletes and trainers) whose faces can be seen (there is an eighth man stretched out on a massage table, his face hidden by one of the other players) looks anywhere else but directly at the camera: no one peeks out of the closet here at the body of another man.... Moreover, all of the men visible are hypermasculine, confident in their pose before the camera, with marked secondary sexual characteristics well in evidence, such as hairy chest and legs, heavy beard, mustaches, muscular torso and legs, with appropriate tertiary accoutrements such as athletic wear, soccer ball, the ankle bandage and what appears to be a tube or container of ointment that are metonymies of strenuous physical activity. The file of identical lockers against the back wall iconicizes the continuity between these men where the sameness of their macho presence guarantees the easy circulation of the norms of homosociality without any trace of the discrepancy from these norms that would signal the contramasculine, the effeminate, the threat of homosexuality. True, one of the men, to the left of the image, somewhat older than the others, is fleshier than what one associates with a sustained athletic life, while in the right-hand background there is a frankly paunchy individual with long hair (he is, nevertheless, properly uniformed for athletic play). But these are minor discordant notes that only serve to affirm the overall conventional hypermasculinity of the men we see in the foreground. In short, this is a world of men and for men, and if resolute homosociality were ever to segue into homoeroticism, it is not likely to include any sign of the feminine. It is precisely the homoerotic undertones of the hypermasculine universe of soccer that both Bazán and Sebreli speak of, and, while Archetti underscores the way in which soccer — like many all-male sports — serve transculturally to assimilate young men to the codes of masculine homosociality, there is no way of categorically specifying when the frisson of the homoerotic will occur.[30]

One of López's most outrageous compositions is *Tomando sol en la terraza*, which was used for the invitation and publicity for the early 2005 show of his work at the White Box (**Fig. 7.8**). Unlike the images I have discussed up until now, this image and the next one to be discussed involved a single male model; hence, there is no immediate homosocial context, since no explicit interaction with other men is involved. Yet, by contrast, the two images both more readily evoke the homoerotic, which is located here in the display of the partially naked

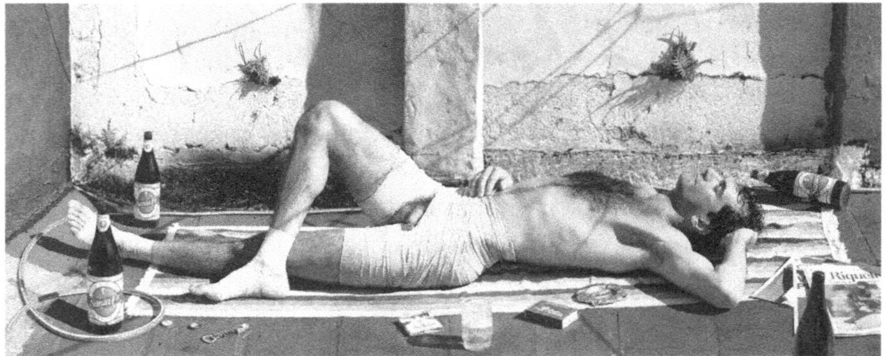

Fig. 7.8 *Tomando sol en la terraza* [Rooftop suntan] (Marcos López).

male body. Although the image of the partially naked male body is legitimated in certain contexts, such as that of the athletic locker room, it does not customarily involve the privileged exposure of the penis.

Tomando sol is constructed around the common occurrence of sunbathing, which in an apartment-dwelling metropolis like Buenos Aires often means stretching out on a towel on the rooftop terrace of one's high-rise building. Certainly, the majority of sunbathers are women, and sports and other physically active undertakings are the most appropriate way for the male body to gain whatever are considered the beneficial aspects of direct exposure to the sun; concomitantly, to lie inert in the sun is a female/womanlike activity. True, López's male sunbather is surrounded by the details of a masculine world: various bottles of beer and a bottle opener, along with a half-consumed glass of brew. There is an ashtray with the butts of two consumed cigarettes, a carton of Malboros (unquestionably a real man's tobacco of choice[31]), and there is a stack of magazines at hand, the top one of which appears to be a sports magazine, as its cover carries a routine soccer image. One rather whimsical detail is the garden hose (often laughingly referred to as a penis substitute), which runs alongside the reclining man and loops its way around one of the beer bottles, as though it were a sunning serpent; its two tones of green partially match the colors of the blanket on which the man lies sunning.

The model here is, in all regards, one of López's by-now familiar hypermasculine bodies: trim and muscular, with firm and hairy legs and a nicely matted chest; his strong facial characteristics are manly in every regard: in sum, a man's man. What is jarring, however, is the way he is dressed and what that dress leaves exposed. Nude sunbathing on a private rooftop may be preferred by some men, although heterosexual men are less likely than women (or homosexual men) to worry about tan lines: indeed, the tan line on a naked male body might be viewed as some as sexy, since it frames the now exposed but usually concealed genitals or buttocks. But the covering of the lower regions of the body means wearing a swimsuit; even underwear might be permissible. However, López's model is swathed in athletic bandages from his midriff to halfway down his thighs, something like an improvised locker-room version of surfing shorts, although tighter and neutral in color, as opposed to the often colorful and baggy original. Moreover, the athletic bandage around the model's middle picks up on the more reasonable presence of the wrapping around both his ankles and insteps, such as one might find on an athlete's foot to prevent or remedy a sprain from action in sports.

But what is specifically transgressive about *Tomando sol* is the way in which the model's penis is exposed. The athletic bandage is wrapped around the man's waist, buttocks, and upper thighs in such a way that, although some minor glimpses of skin are allowed, his genitals are exposed, with his penis (notably uncircumcised from the point of view of a North American viewer) resting on the edge of a strip of the bandage. One does not normally sunbathe the penis without the rest of the lower body being exposed, and, aside from the medical inadvisability of such exposure, one is unaware of any known fetish of the sunbathed (or sunburned) penis. López is known for his over-the-top whimsicalness, and it is amply evident in this composition, with its showcasing of the model's respectably sized penis and the echoes of the strongly masculine phallus in the beer bottles, the cigarettes, and the garden hose. The contemplation of the male body required by this composition, one that underscores the phallic, disrupts the heterosexist homosocial convention whereby the male body is masculine (a condition of the appropriate in the homosocial pact), but it is not erotic: the genitals are assumed to be there, and with acceptable potency, but they can never be the object of confirming scrutiny. Whenever the male body is the occasion for the spectacular gaze, as the female body routinely is, it is placed at the disposal of a homoerotic interest that is inadmissible within the manly homosocial pact.[32] Like so many of Marcos López's photographs, *Tomando sol en la terraza* is parody or trope of a famous image, in this case the Mexican Manuel Álvarez's female figure *La buena fama durmiendo* (1939). The pose between the, first female body and, then, the male body is identical in most details, down to the exposure, despite the bindings or bandages around their waist, of their respective public areas.

I would like to close with what I think is López's most brilliant composition, the *Sireno del Río de la Plata* (**Fig. 7.9**), a revision of one of the tritest motifs associated with the sea. The *sireno* of the title of the composition is the non-occurring (at least in terms of academic Spanish) masculine form of *sirena*, the siren of the sea or, in its more domesticated form, the mermaid.[33] If one may use a queer designation, López's masculine mermaid is very much of a parody of siren of the sea motif.[34]

Whereas standard images of the siren, most commonly evoked in the sculpture that is the symbol of the city of Copenhagen, center on a series of ultrafeminine features — long blond hair, firm and full breasts (but without being bosomy), curvaceous figure, languid pose — López's model is both a refutation of the feminine and an inscription of the hypermasculine. It might be a matter of taste as to whether this male model is grotesque in his masculinity or whether he is the male equivalent of female allure. The model is, without a doubt, as hard and trim as the conventional female figure is delicately curved, and his hairy torso constitutes as definitive a display of sex characteristics as does the former's breasts. But his pose is anything but languid, as he strongly grips part of the stone shelf on which he is seated, his other arm assertively akimbo. His jug-handle ears, unshaven face, almost scowling eyes, and unfriendly line of mouth may, in fact, suggest the way in which the mythological mermaid was actually no friend to those who became seduced by her fateful presence. López's *sireno* suggests the threat implicit in male sexual attraction, whether addressed to a woman or to another man. The fact that the landscape of the masculine mermaid is a crumbling and garbage-strewn beach also undercuts what-

Opposite: **Fig. 7.9** ***Sireno del Río de la Plata*** [River Plate merman] (Marcos López).

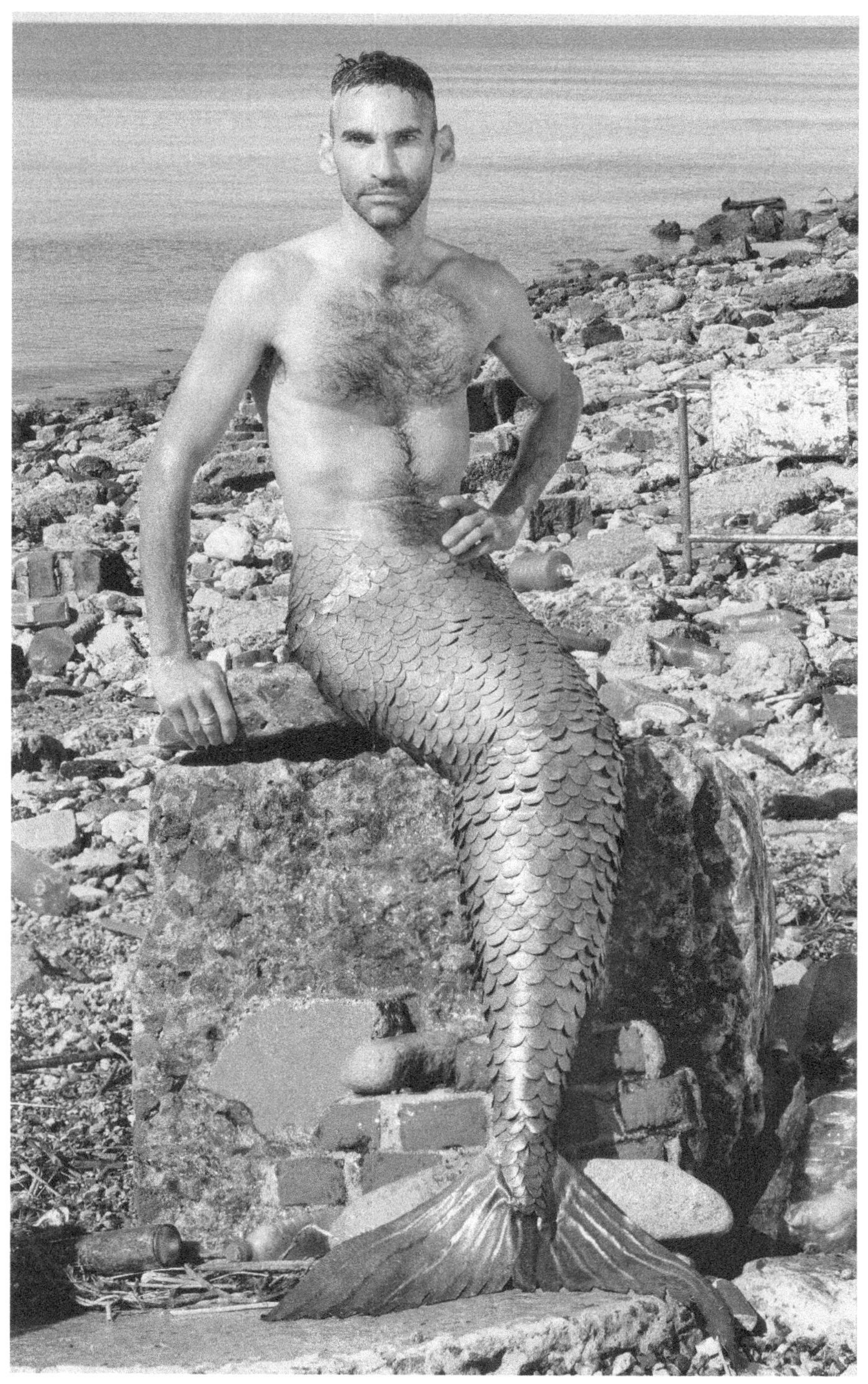

ever conventional artistry there is about Disneyesque depictions of this version of idealized feminine beauty. The effect of coming upon this figure washed ashore is not that of the sensuous swoon, but rather the shock of the radically disruptive of artistic conventions. Of a whole with the men represented in images such as *El vestuario, Tomando sol en la terraza*, and *Asado criollo*— that is, the unquestionably, rigorously masculine body, with nothing of the conventions of the idealized bodies of gay pornographic visual art, such as Ruven Afanador's previously mentioned bullfighters — López's *sireno* both mocks the motif of the mermaid, while offering in its place an aggressively masculine token. But to whom is this *sireno* offered? With its tapering tail replacing the sexual attributes of the lower male torso, the masculine mermaid calls out implicitly to the conventional audience of the siren — men. And the extent to which this male body is not the androgyne of so much of gay male art,[35] López is offering the (homo)erotic gaze of his spectator exactly the sort of image that confirms the all-male universe of the homosocial pact.

8

Argentine Masculinities:
Silvio Fabrykant's *Hombres*

"It is impossible to think of photography without considering the importance of portraiture"—paraphrase of a comment from a lecture by Marcos López, August 7, 2006, at the Alliance Française in Buenos Aires, as part of the Festival de la Luz 2006.

To speak of the construction of masculinity in any culture runs the risk of descending into commonplaces. For example, it is undeniable that the broad majority of human societies, if not all society in general, rests on guiding principles that we might define as varieties of the hierarchical patriarchy, characterized by masculinism (by which one understands the superiority of men in its many guises) and compulsory heterosexuality (the imperative to collaborate with the reproduction of the species through practices that are, whether actually or virtually, exclusively heterosexual), an ideological posture that, in turn, is identified as heterosexism. Such a profile is complemented, at least in the popular imagination that describes Latin America, and as articulated both by Latin Americans and non–Latin Americans, by the adherence to a special affirmation of the patriarchy that is called *machismo*, the hypervisible confirmation (again, either actually or virtually) of compulsory heterosexuality, either in the aggressive seduction of any and all women (and often of any and all men viewed as "feminine/feminized/feminizable") and/or in the confirmation of ways of being a man or being a woman that punishes anything that does not conform to such ways of being. This "ideological package" is so general, nevertheless, that it falls far short of portraying in a sociologically or anthropologically interesting manner any specific society. It is likely an unquestionable fact that there is a continuum of how to be a man from one society to another (notwithstanding the theoretical question of how "man" is defined in any one society and if there is, in fact, a unitary concept of "man"), and that this is true from one historical period to another. But the details, and their manifestation in cultural production that is centered on actual cases involving individuals and groups, are so variable—and, at times, so iffy—that in the end they fail to be very serviceable beyond a completely superficial discussion.

The theme of masculinity begins to be a bit more interesting and to acquire a bit more specific weight in reference to those societies with certain practices, certain institutions, and, as a consequence, a certain consciousness or public mentality that sustain a more measurable focus on questions relating to the concept of masculinity (Latin American masculinities have been studied primarily by feminist scholars; see the work of Piscano and Burin and Meler; in English the basic bibliography begins with the work of Connell). For example, in Latin America, Argentina in the twentieth century was characterized by the bedrock phenomenon of military (coups by the armed forces) and military-styled (the three presidencies of Juan Domingo Perón) governments, the former de facto and the latter (depending on how one assesses constitutional legitimacy) de jure. In addition, this panorama, which comprises virtually the entire second half of the century, is accompanied by the imperative, articulated as much by officialist sectors as by non-government or independent ones, to address intensively the matter of masculinity as it is portrayed in cultural production. This becomes openly evident after 1983 with the return to constitutional democracy, which brought with it the analysis of the "authoritarian mind," which was mostly defined by the armed forces and their allies in solidly masculine/masculinist enterprises such as the Church, the professions of law and medicine, business, and commerce. One could also maintain that a "contestatory" production, as much one that was relatively open as one that was clandestine, as well as that which was exercised from the safe haven of political exile, had already undertaken this process from the time of the first military tyrannies. What is more, it would be difficult to maintain that the ways in which masculinity was addressed from a post-masculinist and post-authoritarian point of view ceased to be important at any one specific point in time. Quite the contrary, as one would do well to examine how such a point of view has become a constant in Argentine society as part of the efforts to sustain a democratic society and impede, ever again,[1] the armed forces from taking over the national government.

If the first fascist-inspired coup occurs in Argentina in 1930, which leads to the constitutional government of General Juan Domingo Perón in 1946, the military coup against him in 1955 inaugurates a sequence of de facto governments that evolve with increasing clarity into progressively more neofascist regimes of unyielding corporatist violence, only to be displaced in 1983 by the return to democracy, although not without many and profound institutional problems, which continue to the present day (see Graziano on the mystification of violence by Argentine neofascism; Bergero and Reati are responsible for a compilation of key studies on the period as interpreted by cultural production; Ramírez brings together the best work of plastic artists on the period of military repression). The return of Perón in 1973, as part of a reinstitutionalization that failed to prosper and that soon vanished in 1976 along with profound social disruption, merely served to make it obvious that Argentina was in no condition to pursue a democratic society. The almost complete dismantling of the armed forces after 1983 (which took into account the evidence of their professional ineptitude in the disastrous invasion in 1982 of the Islas Malvinas/Falkland Islands) has been one way of attempting to ensure that they will be unable to stage another military coup, although one might well wonder if such a crippling of resources denies the opportunity to see if Argentina is or is not in any condition to pursue a completely democratic society: if anyone were to assert, as was the wont in days before past coups, that "what this society needs is a strong hand" and to demand that "they put things in order," there is no longer much of a "they" to turn to.

What all of the above means is that there has been, and continues to be, profound revision as regards how to understand the institutions of masculinist and patriarchal power. Without there having been the slightest change in those institutions (an affirmation that is likely to be refuted energetically by those who hold greater confidence in certain "cosmetic" arrangements than some of us are capable of: one only needs contemplate recent debates over new appointments, especially women, to the Supreme Court of the nation and the limitations on any meaningful debate over abortion to share such skepticism), it is undeniable that there are extensive, manifest, and at times quite vigorous voices that have emerged in the project of investigating those who both essentially and in a contingent manner have been the powers responsible for social and institutional violence. Only the naive could contemplate a unique and singular mold for this violence, and the enormous display of proposals and interpretations with respect to interpreting it confirm the rich complexity of such a project. Those who attended the 2004 production of Griselda Gambaro's *La señora Macbeth* (*Lady Macbeth*) were able to appreciate once again the application of Gambaro's considerable theatrical talent to the task of understanding how any consideration of the dynamics of violence must take into account all sectors of society: in this case it is the hypocritical woman who prides herself on her benevolent femininity, while at the same time showing herself to be the phallic woman who exercises the power of the patriarchy in her defense of the latter.

It is in this overall context that a photographic exhibit on important masculine figures of Argentine society cannot just be an exhibit on important masculine figures of Argentine society. I am referring to Silvio Fabrikant's *Hombres*, which was shown at the Centro Cultural Recoleta in May 2001. Under no circumstances do I wish to imply that any of these men were in any way accomplices of the military tyranny. Maybe some of them were, if only in their hearts for pragmatic reasons or personal conviction. But the simple fact that the majority have enjoyed highly reputable public profiles during the twenty years since the return to democracy argues for our seeing them as leading names in the post-military period. Needless to say that many of them, from political, social, or cultural forums, are major spokespersons of an open and democratic society. Having said this, it becomes necessary to recognize, by the same token, that the sole fact of being "men" places them squarely at the core of the dynamics of patriarchal masculinity, with all that that means with respect to a hierarchy of sociopolitical values in Argentina, especially as regards gender and sexual identity.

Certainly, as we will see below, some are known for their resistance, openly or implicitly, to what they consider to be the deleterious effects of masculinity as it is commonly understood. Yet at the same time it is necessary to recognize that no individual is in complete and sustained harmony with the various social elements used to identify someone and with which someone chooses (or feels compelled) to identify. No one is ever completely and fissurelessly a man,[2] just as no one ever unwaveringly matches the ideological criteria of his bases of (self) identity. From a theoretical perspective on the identities imposed on and subscribed to by the individual—language, race, class, nationality, religion, gender, sexuality, profession, regionality, and so on—one always enters into a very fluid relationship with them (sometimes some of them more than others), which allows for one to affirm one and another at any given moment in more or less emphatic ways, with greater or lesser conformance with reigning norms. To be sure, the norms that control one's diverse identities undergo a constant process of transformation, modification, and adaptation to diverse historical circumstances, as can be observed in a very evident fashion by examining the changes in social norms with reference, for example, to Argentine Spanish during the past twenty years (for example, more specifically, in the encroachment of the second-person singular pronoun and verb forms of so-called familiar address on spheres that were formally dominated by so-called formal address).

Such a context explains the importance of Silvio Fabrykant's show at the Centro Cultural Recoleta, an arts complex run by the government of the city of Buenos Aires and that has figured prominently in the promotion of democratic culture.[3] In the program that was distributed as part of the exposition, Guillermo Saavedra places emphasis on the egalitarian quality of such a show:

> Just as before the law, all men are equal before the camera. All have a body of which they are proud or of which they are ashamed and a manner of being that is the result of having been trained in the task of showing to the world how they think of themselves, while at the same time hiding some crucial weakness....

Saavedra underlines how this show is basically a self-revealing act for the photographer, in the sense that he shows himself in what he chooses to show. As a professional portrait photographer with an extensive career behind him, what Fabrykant does here is, as should be evident, reveal his personal photographic codes as regards the exposition of the human character in others. These are undoubtedly the codes of a professional photographer, professional to the extent that Fabrykant lives from his camera. Therefore, his images must be executed in conformance with the acquiescence, comfort, and collaboration of his clients, and we would not be likely to encounter in them an unguarded or transgressive gaze that captures what the others might think or feel without their permission: they exercise the right to reject the product that does not exist in the subjects captured, say, by Eduardo Gil in his *(argentina)*, examined elsewhere in this study. The exact point is that, if Gil's subjects are citizens of the country (and not the masculinist root) as it is written with a capital letter, Fabrykant's constitute in their totality those who lead the pack, so to speak: men whose influence is, not to put too fine a point on it, articulate and reproduce the norms with which society knows and recognizes itself in its daily existence.

Saavedra speaks of how, in a show like this, the photographer is the one who is most on display because of how he demonstrates a certain way of working with photography and a certain way of working with his subjects, who are far removed from the anonymous subjects of Eduardo Gil. At least no Argentine spectator is going to err in recognizing, without any need for an identifying tag, the image of the musician Astor Piazzola, the actor Leonardo Favio, the novelist Adolfo Bioy Casares, or the actor Ulises Dumont, not to mention the former Argentine President Raúl Alfonsín. All of these images are portraits, which means that they constitute the bust of the individual, with little more than the insinuation of the rest of the body in the form of the occasional inclusion of hands and arms, but never the full torso or the body in its entirety. Adhering to the old adage that the eyes are the windows of the soul, the portrait photographer focuses primarily on the gaze of the subject directed at the camera, which is, in turn, a gaze directed at the spectator. It is for this reason that the primordial quality of these photographs lies in the control that the subject exercises — or aspires to exercise — as he faces the photographer, which means determining the specific dimensions of the gaze and adjusting the contours of the face in conformance with the image he wishes to project. Much of this is negotiated with the photographer, but the intent can be assumed to be in large measure controlled by the subject. Thus, it is superfluous to say that the mouth is a crucial detail of the subject's face, and many of them can be said to live by their mouths, either because they are politicians, actors, or announcers, or because they live by the written word, which in Western culture is the displaced representation of the articulated word, because they are writers, intellectuals, and journalists.

But photography, and even more so when it is a question of portraiture, is an art of the studied gaze: the camera studies the subject as the latter studies the photographer and the camera, while the spectator studies the camera's study of the studying subject. There is an intense semiotic of the studied gaze throughout Fabrykant's *Hombres* that depends on something like a magnetic field in which the three participants in the signifying process (subject, photographer, spectator) end up being held. Perhaps one can be excused for insisting once again on what is the guiding phenomenon of portraiture photography: the subject acquires a crucial agency because he is the one who has commissioned the photographic act and, in large measure, approves the final product. And even when the person whose portrait is being done does not commission the photograph, he never ceases to be an accomplice in the semiotic field that is established, by virtue of the simple fact of having agreed to participate in the process of producing the meaning that will be generated, in the final instance, by the image that we contemplate. In Eduardo Gil's documentary photography, the semiotic process involves only two agents: the photographer and the spectator, whose interpretive circuit flows through a subject that often does not even know that s/he is being photographed (note the return here to gender inclusiveness). And even if s/he did, only minimal control of the semiotic object is at issue. This set-up is, to be sure, what is fundamentally at issue in journalism. But like the "authorized biography" of the historian, the formal portrait, executed in a study equipped with all the instruments of the profession, what is accomplished is a triangulation of the signifying process, even though it is subsequently possible to debate the relative power inherent in each one of the constituent elements.

It is this relativization of the role of each one of the three agentive constituents that results in the phenomenon of the portrait (and, if it is not apparent, by "portrait" I understand here what is always a pose that is commissioned and assessed by the individual concerned). What we see is, one can reasonably suppose, always the most highly regarded of the multiple images that, inevitably, are produced during the period of the studio sitting, and this is what comes to constitute the relative critical interest of these images. That is to say, they are interesting not simply because they are, in the main, photographs of important and influential public figures who are, also in the main, mostly well-to-do. They are interesting because one approaches them with the possibility in mind — the hope — of encountering the *punctum* of which Roland Barthes speaks: that detail of the *studium* of which the image as a whole is composed that enables us to question the very process of photography, toward a meditation on the purposes of such and such a pose. The search for the *punctum* also enables us to occupy ourselves in finding and appreciating the moment in which the seamless and consolidated surface of the photograph gives way to the questioning and deconstructive gaze of the spectator.

All of this becomes appreciably more fascinating when what is involved is a phenomenon of such ideological resonance as masculinity. If these, for example, were photographs of female high-school students, it might be possible to concern oneself with questions regarding the social concept of youth, the consequences of being a young lady (or the moment of ceasing to be one, as in the case of Martín Rubiani's work on the *quinceañera*, the coming-out party celebrated when a woman turns fifteen), along with the array of considerations of class relating to even the possibility of being a female high-school student in contemporary Argentina: what are the attributes and the accompanying details of being a female high-school student at that moment in the country or in the dominant urban sector of the country? The context of being a man, and in most cases here, of being a senior man, are very different, owing to the simple fact of the hierarchical and socially symbolic position they enjoy in a patriarchal society such as Argentina and the privilege that derives from being a social subject identified/identifiable as a "man." No one can be surprised upon encountering in this gallery of some thirty images a former president of the nation, a soccer star, a number of prominent actors and authors, musicians and other artists.

Not only is this an inventory of masculine professions as such (one is hard-put to think of a female soccer star or women musicians of equivalent stature).[4] On the other hand, the cluster of masculine enterprise of the three dozen men brought together in Fabrykant's show is unmistakable: even when the enterprise of a semiologist (Oscar Steimberg, brother of the Municipal Prize-winning novelist, Alicia Steimberg[5]) might sound a bit out of place among the triumph of being an actor or politician, the

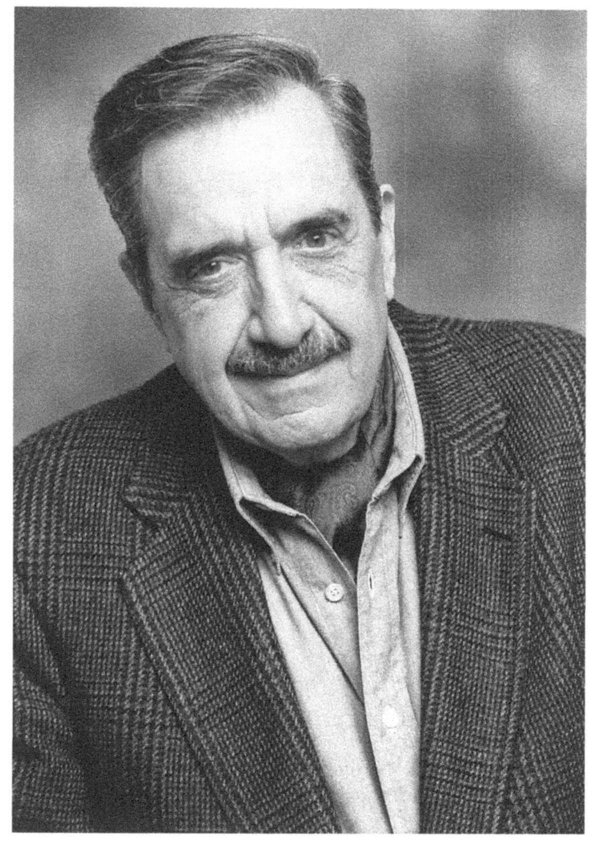

Fig. 8.1 *Raúl Alfonsín* (Silvio Fabrykant).

ranks of men's names among those who dedicate themselves to primary-school teaching is noticeably thin, not to mention manicurists and receptionists. Undoubtedly, in the democratic Argentina of the post-dictatorship, there are many women in the professions originally reserved entirely for men (in fact, by "profession" one historically understood an exclusively masculine agency), while it is also historically true that there have been women in the so-called liberal professions in Argentina long before in the United States. Also, the economic situation of Argentina has meant that many men occupy positions that were formerly considered to be the province of women only, which is why, although their ranks are thin, one can find men teaching grade school, not to mention how men, transgressing the codes of gender, can be found in professions that continue to be understood as basically feminine, such as that of hairstylist, manicurist, or domestic servant.[6]

The consequence of all this is that, within this show of "men," a fundamental detail such as the profession (not just job) associated with each one of them, references a very traditional masculine universe. This enhances, I would venture to say, even more the attempt of the critic to find a relevant *punctum* in these photographs, in order to begin to detail the deployment of the underlying codes of masculinity.

It is inevitable to being with the image of the former President Raúl Alfonsín, who figures as number twenty-four in the ordering of the images (**Fig. 8.1**). This position is neither that of the privileged closing spot nor is it that of the inaugural one, but something like a random ordering, as though, as a human being, his place among others in a gallery of notable citizens is unimportant. (Of course, the ordering might represent the chronology of their execution; there are five deceased participants among them, including, as a matter of fact, the man who figures in first place, Alberto Fischerman. The individuals photographed are distributed into two groups: those who enjoy a more formal pose and those whose pose is more relaxed (not to mention other possible divisions, such as politicians vs. non-politicians, cultural producers vs. those who are not, the living vs. the dead). The formality of the pose is particularly important in the context of traditional Argentine society, where adherence to a British norm of visibility for men meant, until well into the last few decades of the twentieth century, a rigorous compliance with irreproachable sartorial criteria that included fabric color and cut and the imperative presence of jacket and tie, even when the jacket is casual wear. Many of these criteria have weakened in recent years, first with the parameters of informality that began in the sixties and had to do with complex questions regarding transcending social class and the deconstruction of social hierarchies. In Argentina especially, the return to democracy meant the attendant repudiation of the severity of military tyranny.[7] By contrast to the public image of Mexican presidents (whose guayabera is virtually their uniform) or the unchanging military uniform that Fidel Castro sports, the well-cut English suit of the Argentine presidents, and of the entire masculine hierarchy that flows in the country from this guiding symbol, is nothing more than the identifying marker of national masculinity.

There is of course no surprise that Dr. Alfonsín might appear dressed in an alternative manner: who other than former presidents could allow themselves some slight modification in the protocols of their office? Noblesse oblige, but at the same time it accords permission and legitimacy and, in fact, allows room for a so-called different touch that humanizes the subject who occupies such an august place in national symbology. Fabykant has enjoyed the privilege of executing portraits for some of the most important and famous politicians of Argentina. These are images that make up part of the visual record of their political campaigns and of the image that they wish instill in the collective conscious of the nation. When Fabrykant photographs Alfonsín in an "alternative fashion" (i.e., outside of customary presidential dress), he is providing something like a supplement to his social meaning, and it is difficult to see this photograph without comparing it to the many others in which the subjects are dressed in an "appropriate fashion." The open grandfatherly smile Alfonsín displays, accentuated by the lines produced around mouth and eyes by this and many other acts of smiling — here a smile is only insinuated, but it is no less significant — is complemented by the angle of his body in the photographic frame that corresponds not so much to the imposing and assertive pose of an image that would be strictly proportional within the available visual field as to a gesture of amiability and reaching out to the spectator. Formality insists on standing and sitting straight, but Alfonsín here holds his body at a side angle and gives the impression of leaning toward the camera in a frank greeting of friendship. Such an informal geometry of the body is matched by the clothes he is wearing: an unquestionably expensive jacket of rich English fabric, with a shirt of fine cloth (Polo, perhaps), and a loosely tied silk paisley scarf (likely Italian). If the President of the Argentines synthesizes the apex of masculine power in the country (and there is no greater symbol of traditional masculinity than the full moustache he sports), the breaking with the strict formality of his office that tradition would have him respect long after the end of his term, is unmistakable, since once elected, one exercises the symbolic meaning of the office *sub specie aeterna.*

The fact is that the large majority of the figures appearing in Fabrykant's show under the heading of "men" are characterized by a certain degree of informality in their carriage and presence, thereby underscoring, if only implicitly, the slow backing away from the severe norms of masculinity that the period of the military dictatorship served to affirm tyrannically[8] and the newer norms of masculine "informality."[9] One image that serves to capture what is for many the still longed-for rigor of yesteryear is that of Antonio Carrizo, who figures in second place and who is identified as a "journalist for cultural radio" (**Fig. 8.2**). Carrizo, who was born in 1921, goes way back to the era of some of the most venerable traditional forms and he would appear to be quite content with them, with this dark suit, discreet striped shirt, and tie. Even if it is not all strictly British garb, it is more than appropriate. Carefully shaven and combed, he looks out at the camera from an angle with an expression of utmost seriousness.

Although Carrizo also does not fill the photographic frame in a fully squared fashion, the posture of his body is perfectly balanced along an oblique line that runs from the upper right-hand corner to the lower left-hand one. His fine lips are slightly pressed, and his gaze is as though he were subjecting the viewer to a test. What most calls attention in this photograph — what would be for me its *punctum* — is the fact that Carrizo is a radio personality and, therefore, little "seen" in terms of a public presence. Here the photograph gives a bodily presence to someone who makes his living with his voice, a voice that, for the public, does not emanate from his body (or, at least, this is an inconsequential detail), but from the artefact of the radio, thanks to which all voices are different, characterized by multiple dynamic colorings, but their origin is like a series of robots that all look alike physically rather than flesh-and-blood human beings. That is, what one "sees" is a voice (or the suggestion of a voice) and not a corporeal presence.

Quite strikingly different in terms of the collection of *Hombres* as a whole is the photography of the radio and television personality, Hugo Guerrero Marthineitz (**Fig. 8.3**). Guerrero Marthineitz is the man who most breaks here with the outlines of a continuum of Argentine masculinity, beginning with the fact that he is Peruvian, although he has lived and worked for many years in Argentina. This in itself would not be a significant detail, except perhaps for an ultranationalist of strictly Creole principles, who might feel offended by the presence in the show of types who are of doubtful immigrant condition, such as, one might note, the photographer himself.[10] But what is noteworthy is the overall presence Guerrero Marthineitz displays in the show: the Peruvian is the only one who appears, to all intents and purposes, as entirely naked.[11] One supposes that only the torso is involved, but yet that is enough to break drastically with any concept of clothing appropriate to a public presence. Although identified only as an "announcer," Guerrero

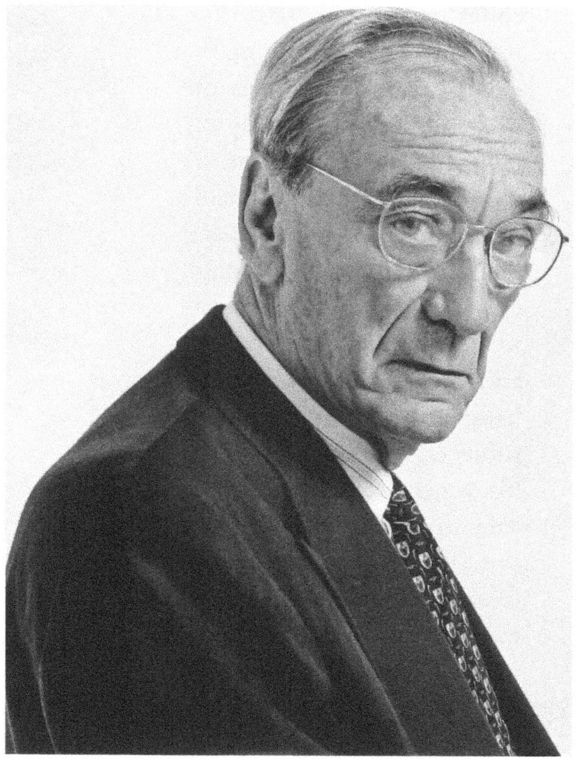

Fig. 8.2 *Antonio Carrizo* (Silvio Fabrykant).

Marthineitz has worked in both television and radio, and as a consequence he enjoys high name recognition out on the street, as it were. His hair closely cropped, Guerrero Marthineitz stares intently at the spectator as he was wont to do with the guests of his television program. His gaze corresponds to that of an investigative reporter who is decidedly not going to be taken in, and by supporting his face on his clenched fist, partially covering his closed mouth, he gives the impression that this is a man who concentrates on listening to what his interviewee has to say, intervening only when necessary to move along what the other is saying, even when that takes the form of a challenging question or a provocative assertion.

But if Guerrero Marthineitz prided himself on stripping naked his interviewees, he strips himself naked for the spectator of the photograph to a degree that would be impossible within the broadcasting codes of a serious television program — at least during the heyday of his success in the mid–1980s. The closely cropped hair, with the indentations of an incipient baldness, underscores the general aspect of the naked, although one supposes that the spectator, accustomed to the ties and jackets and shirts and handkerchiefs of the other subjects, cannot easily draw his or her gaze away from the smooth skin of this subject's shoulders, chest, neck, and forearm, from the evident carnality of his muscular frame, which is especially to be seen

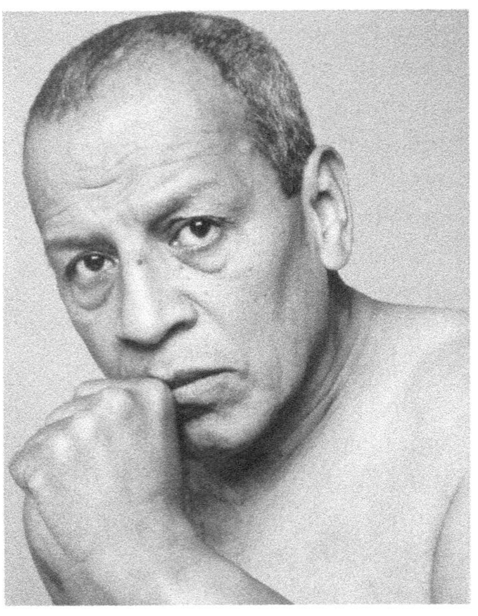

Fig. 8.3 *Hugo Guerrero Marthineitz* (Silvio Fabrykant).

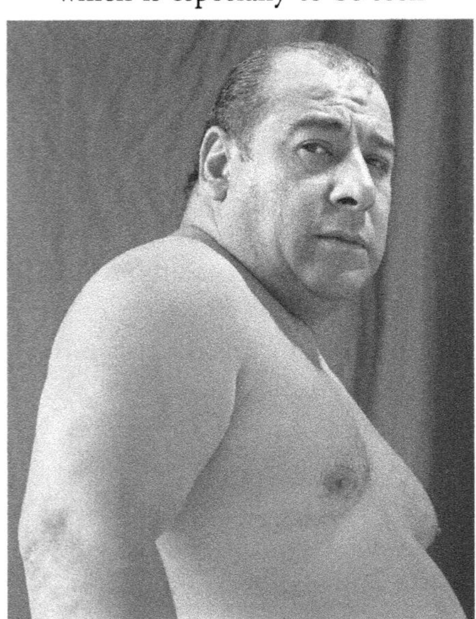

Fig. 8.4 *Roly Serrano* (Silvio Fabrykant).

from the lower right-hand side, where the fold produced between the upper part of his arm and his chest reveals the curve of developed muscle. Going with the implicit affirmation by Saavedra that one is stripped naked before the eye of the camera, which supposedly means in terms of one's inner being, the subject here is literally naked, which cannot help but induce in the spectator the question of what it would have been like for all of these men to be portrayed in the same fashion.[12]

I do not wish to suggest that one can draw momentous conclusions of a socio-anthropological nature from Fabrykant's images. The spheres of masculine being and doing are multiple, whether we are talking about limited social sectors or about society in general, and it would be incorrect to hypostatize the ways of being a man in contemporary Argentina were one to use as a basis only these thirty-

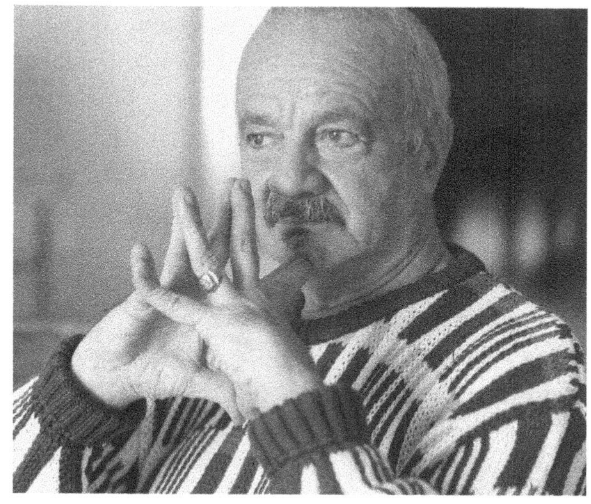

Fig. 8.5 *Astor Piazzola* (Silvio Fabrykant).

some photographs. Nevertheless, no cultural producer is innocent and no cultural production exists in a socio-economic vacuum: no cultural product is "just what it is." We read the photographs, like we read any

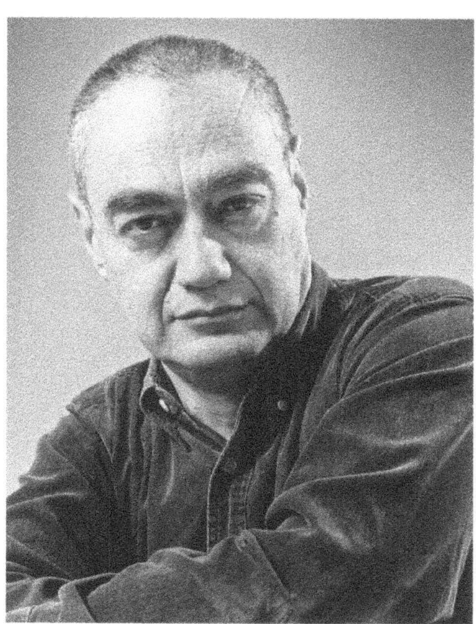

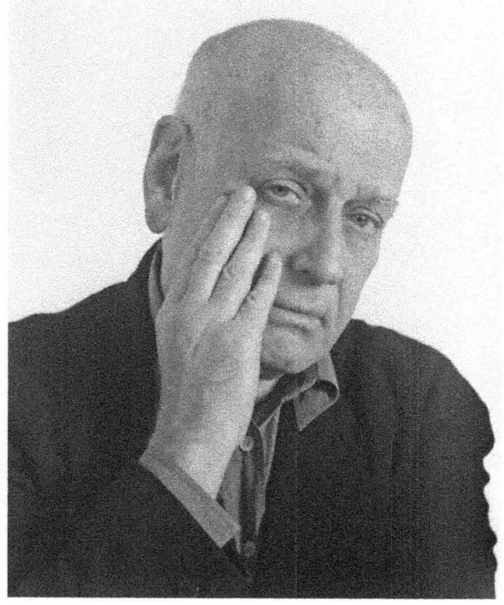

Left: Fig. 8.6 *Alejandro Horowicz. Right:* Fig. 8.7 *Edgardo Cozarinsky* (both Silvio Fabrykant).

cultural product, in multiple contexts that lead us to generalize as to importance and meaning. Fabrykant's, appearing as they do in a photographic exhibit called *Hombres*, open themselves up to the contemporary horizons of knowledge in terms of current thinking regarding gender and the role of the masculine subject in today's society and in terms of the formalities that circumscribe (and, thereby, also allow for strategic transformations) ways at this moment of being a man in Argentina. Concomitantly, the show questions who the historical social agents of the country are and how they conduct themselves, along with who is present and who is absent (**Fig. 8.5**, **Fig. 8.6** and **Fig. 8.7**).

9

Defying the Masculinist Gaze: Gabriela Liffschitz's *Recursos humanos*

One of the guiding axioms of contemporary feminist ideologies is the imperative to refute the masculinist gaze, in general but especially as it relates to the feminine body (essential concepts are surveyed by Draper). It is a refutation that must bring with it a principled dearticulation or deconstruction of the premises — and the privilege and power — of the masculinist gaze, accompanied by strategies to promote an alternative gaze, one that is specifically feminist or lesbian or, if possible, masculine in a nonpatriarchal way. By the masculinist gaze we understand the interpretive contemplation of the body, in a dense process of exclusions and inclusions, of absences and presences, of validated/legitimated and invalidated/delegitimated, such that that body (of a woman, of a child, of a man, or even of a "non-human") is rendered meaningful only insofar as it reinforces the principles of the compulsorily heteronormative patriarchy or can be used to demonstrate what may be considered unacceptable or inappropriate — if not outright threatening — deviations from those principles.

One may view those principles as existing more or less in a fairly codified fashion, or one may view them as inherently unstable and shifting, as a consequence of the vagaries of the patriarchy and power politics. But what is uncontestable is that any strategic definition of

185

the patriarchy brings with it the right to impose a masculinist gaze of the universe and to expect that all will conform to that gaze, all will acquiesce to it, and all will, if only passively, agree to abide by what it confirms and what it disqualifies. Even if one accepts the proposition that the principles of the patriarchy can be a pretty messy affair, either through internal incoherence or strategic compromises, the point is that its privileged discourse sets itself up as beyond defiance.[1]

As has been pointed out in histories of the way in which the masculinist gaze has contemplated women's bodies — has constructed and honed the field of qualified objects — the notion of what is beautiful, sexy, maternal, or lovely has varied considerably. But there can be little doubt that women's bodies, or the bodies of any individual that can be construed as the Other of the masculinist anchor, whether by virtue of gender, sex, sexuality, sexual preference, race, ethnicity, and/or physical capabilities, must ever and always be subject and subordinate to that gaze (see *Writing on the Body* for an excellent collection on the representation of the female body in art; *The Female Body* is a classic reference; see Amador Gómez-Quintero for specific references to Latin American art).

The promotion of the Other is undertaken at the risk of incurring the rejection, the disdain, the anger, and even the actual violence of the owners and agents of the masculinist gaze. The distinction between owners and agents is an important one, since there are those enforcers of the masculinist gaze who are not "natural" possessors of it, such as phallic women or queers who enact so-called homosexual panic. By using the word "natural" here — albeit placing it under erasure through the use of scare quotes — I do not mean to reinvest in essentialist categories. Rather, my point would be that compulsory heterosexualism is fundamentally grounded on essentialist categories, and one must begin the deconstruction of the masculinist gaze by engaging with its inherent essentialism. This point will become important in my subsequent analysis of Liffschitz's photography because of a measure of defiance of the essentialist categories of male and female bodies.

It is not necessary to withdraw from the realization of the varying constructions of the female body by the masculinist gaze to accept the fact that one dominant modern construction has been that of the *Playboy* beauty, whether in the literal terms of the international distribution of the images — the sexist culture — of that magazine or in the extended terms of how the basic image may be inflected by local tastes or vetted through local versions of *Playboy* (see Weyr regarding the cultural institutions created by this magazine; I have been able to discover no ideological analysis of *Playboy*, but see, however, Kipnis on its hardcore cousin, *Hustler*). One can speak of a kernel of the eroticization of the female body that is associable with *Playboy*, but subject to local revisions, or one can speak of the globalization of the *Playboy* model that checks or supersedes local versions of the putatively sexy female body. Yet the result is the same. Not only a legitimated eroticization of the female body in certain terms, but also a standard for that eroticization in terms of general bodily configuration, physical attributes, the self-presentation of the woman as a sexual offering at the disposal of the masculinist gaze and the utilization of that body by sexual acts correlative to that gaze. In general, whatever can be summarized under the heading of the *Playboy* look, which works in semiotic tandem with the masculinist gaze (see Wolf for a standard treatise on masculinist concepts of female beauty). The gaze demands a certain look, and the look invites a certain gaze. Or, to put it differently, the gaze constructs a certain look, and the look confirms the efficacy of the gaze that constructs it.

Gabriela Liffschitz's body, as she exhibits it in *Recursos humanos* (2000) through a series of thirty self-portraits, is an engagement with the dynamics of the masculinist gaze and the look it seeks out/constructs, an engagement that proceeds to constitute a defiance of that dynamics. This Liffschitz accomplishes by putting her own body on display in ways that are reversions of the dynamics of the gaze/look to the degree to which the middle-aged body of the woman, showing a partial mastectomy, is purportedly scandalous to that dynamics. It is a body that is progressively deviant and dangerous to the masculinist gaze, which can only see it as a morbid counterexample of the femininity that compulsory heterosexism would strive to maintain. And it is, therefore, a body that must be anathemized if not directly made to disappear (or, "disappeared," if one may have recourse to the transitive use of the verb as forged in the context of the neofascist disappearance of alleged dissidents during the 1976–83 neofascist regime).

Born in 1963, Liffschitz is in reality only on the cusp of middle age, and in any other context it might almost be considered misleading to speak of her body as belonging to such a cohort. Yet, it is also a major feminist tenet that the masculinist obsession with an infantilized version of the just-pubescent woman is detrimental both to seeing women as fully functioning human subjects (i.e., they are not only little girls as so much sexual putty in the hands of experienced males) and to even seeing women to begin with beyond a certain age. That is, women beyond a certain age begin to disappear from the masculinist gaze, which may only occupy itself with them in a punitive or corrective fashion if they intrude by virtue of a brazen assertiveness. Spanish — and in this it is not all that different from other patriarchal languages — is filled with pejorative, injurious, demeaning slang used to refer to women who do not fulfill the phenotype of the infantilized kitten (*gatita/gatica* is the dominant animal metaphor in Spanish rather than bunny; cf. the English-language adjective "kittenish"; see Suardíaz for a study that makes special reference to Argentine Spanish). The least offensive, but highly generalized, is the epithet *vieja loca* (crazy old dame) to refer to any assertive woman beyond, say, twenty-five years old.[2] If no "sane" Argentine woman wishes to be characterized as a *vieja loca* (just as no "sane" Argentine man could wish to be characterized as a *puto*, a fag), both epithets lend themselves for resemanticization as a form of social protest. In the case of *puto*, there arose in the human rights context of postmilitary and redemocratized Argentina the strategic gay use, as in "Soy puto y me quiero" (I'm a faggot and I love myself). Concomitantly, the daring with which a woman might offer to display her body as a *vieja loca* became an equally significant feminist strategy to counter the repression of the voices of mature women, which occurs via the disappearance of any woman with a "post-prime" body and the mind to go with it (cf. the fiction of Alicia Steimberg, especially *La loca 101*, *Cuando digo Magdalena*, and *La selva* in the area of literature: Steimberg has specialized, one might say, in *locas* in her fiction).

This is more accurately the category into which Liffschitz's body falls. How middle-age she is is not the issue. The issue becomes to what extent she falls outside — beyond the fringe — of the age in which she might be viable as a *Playboy*-type sex icon. The slight bags under her eyes, the hint of wrinkles at her eyes and mouth, the beginnings of problems with skin tone in her arms and thighs, lower tummy wrinkles when she sits, and a decline in the perfection of the curve of her buttocks when she stands: this is a pitiless litany of the affirmation of signs of age in anyone's body. For the model, it is the geography of has-been physical beauty and, therefore, erotic interest for the masculinist gaze. In Liffschitz's case, the record is proleptic, since, by using her body in a parody or mockery of the *Playboy* ethos for the display of the feminine body, Liffschitz implies a prior, if spurious, narrative, that of her body in the narrative of a working sex-symbol model. Liffschitz inserts herself in a mock post–*Playboy* narrative of which there has never been a before, making it impossible to consult a juxtaposition of her body when it was appealing to the masculinist gaze with the body that can no longer be of any interest, except perhaps morbidly, to that gaze (on the female monstrous, see Creed; for the autobiography of a woman coming to terms with what heteronormativity would call her monstrosity, see Grealy).

My catalog of the signs of the decline of the female body is pitiless and would be cruel and demeaning if applied to the body of a woman who wished to hide such a decline through clothes, cosmetics, plastic surgery, and other wiles "de la madre Celestina."[3] The epithet *vieja loca* functions, then, no more, no less, than cruelly and in a demeaning fashion to subject a particular female body to the sort of implacable scrutiny that would lead to its rejection in terms of the patriarchal norms of beauty sustained by the masculinist gaze. Yet, it is this gaze that Liffschitz — at least in a preliminary instance — invokes. I will have more to say below about the revision of the dynamics of the gaze. But suffice it here to insist that the photographer's unyielding self-portraits have as their goal, through the sharp focus of her black-and-white prints, precisely to invite the realization that her body is supposed to have disappeared, supposed to have become an object unworthy of erotic contemplation, supposed to undertake to keep its so-called imperfections out of public sight. In short, this is a body that is, I would allege, not supposed to have been photographed within the masculinist canons of fashion modelling and girlie magazines. I do not mean to imply there is no available audience for *Recursos humanos*, but rather only that it needs to be found, to be constructed, outside the scope of the publications with which it consciously and carefully establishes an intertextual relationship (regarding feminist photography, see Taylor, *Reframings*).

As I have insisted, that context is one of the generic girlie magazine, as represented paradigmatically by *Playboy* in either its iconic original American version or in derivative local ones. Such representations involve images of the woman in naked poses, or in ones that involve the fetishizing of certain items of feminine dress (which can also include the fetish of nonfeminine dress reinscribed within an erotics of the female body). These poses accentuate the female body as at the disposal of the male body: the body exposed to the penetration of the male gaze, which is a metonymy for penetration by the male body. This is all ground-zero feminist analysis of the display of the female body that requires no extensive demonstration or validation here, although one might be reminded that this ground-zero dimension basically includes the utilization of the female body by the male within the genital-privileged boundaries of the heteronormative patriarchy. At the same time, one notes that the masculinist permission for "alternative" utilization of the woman's body are fairly generous. That is, there is no firm line separating the supposedly normal from the kinky, a perception that drives the feminist proposition that pornography and rape, the theory and practice of the abuse of women, while allegedly not sanctified by the heteronormative patriarchy, are inevitable conclusions of the power it accords men over women's bodies. This is the sort of thinking of a radical antiporn feminist like Andrea Dworkin (see Morgan's famous formulation "pornography is the theory, and rape the practice"). I will also return below to the way in which kinky interpretations of *Recursos humanos* are difficult to block, even within the radical feminist proposition that the collection invokes.

The decision by Liffschitz to photograph her nude body with full display, in many of the images, of her pubis recirculates the girlie magazine emphasis on the secondary sexual characteristics of the female body that are part of its fetishizing by the masculinist gaze. Indeed, it would be difficult to know what part of the nude body is not fetishized, and the matter turns more directly on what territories or zones are those that are most conventionally eroticized. These include the buttocks, the breasts, and the pubic area. It is interesting to underscore the fetishizing of the pubis, while noting considerable horror, on the part of the masculinist gaze, for the vagina itself; this horror toward the vagina, as an object of male gaze, is one of the recurring motifs in Eve Ensler's *The Vagina Monologues* (1998), although Ensler makes much of how male horror is translated into women's own revulsion toward the vagina and, then, her redemptive glorification of it. Liffschitz maintains the tenuous distinction between girlie and pornographic magazines in that her pictures show the pubis, but not the vagina or the clitoris; show the buttocks, but not the anus; see also Judy Chicago's vaginal artworks in *The Dinner Party*). In other words, while standard poses of a photography that invites the masculinist gaze are the basis of the images in *Recursos humanos*, there is pretty much an adherence to what might be vaguely described as discreet and tasteful displays of the woman's body.

The reader will have perceived that I have been delaying concentrating attention on what is the truly outrageous dimension of Liffschitz's images, which is the display of her partial left-side radical mastectomy. The parody of the *Playboy* model through the display of her beyond-the-prime nudity is nothing by comparison with the shock of discovering the devastation of that body by cancer. This is a woman whose body is now no longer useful as an erotic image of what is maintained as perfect female nudity, a body doubly shamed by, first, disease and, subsequently, by the surgical invention designed to arrest that disease, and it is a woman who is scandalously shameless in putting the shame of her body on display.[4] There is an extensive feminist bibliography relating to cancer — especially cancer of the breast — and how it is a paradigmatic disease in terms of rendering the woman's body useless for the patriarchal project (Thomson surveys major feminist opinion on physical disability; see the chapter "Fears and Feelings" in Love's legendary manual).

Hysterectomy, for example, renders a woman incapable of fulfilling the prime role assigned to her by the patriarchy, which is the reproduction of the species. By contrast, mastectomy is both a sign of that same incapacitation (because she can no longer breast-feed or can do so only in a much-diminished fashion) and an irreversible depreciation of the dominant visible sign of maternity, the female breast. It is immaterial that a woman can continue to function emotionally and sexually as a woman and can continue to fulfill all necessary maternal roles

(Liffschitz makes specific reference to her young daughter in the decision to create these images [*Recursos humanos* 7]). From a feminist point of view, masculinism denigrates a woman's body, sees it as irretrievably damaged goods, if it has undergone any of these operations for "female troubles." It is a depreciation of the female body that is, from the point of view of a masculinist gaze, compounded rather than ameliorated by the scandal of its representation. The traditional ban on men discussing what is understood as female troubles is not chivalrous discretion; rather it is the censorious silencing of what it is that leaves a woman no longer serviceable to the patriarchal project. Moreover, such troubles were attended to and supervised exclusively by male physicians in their role as agents of the patriarchy.

Liffschitz's body shows minimal scarring—although different lighting in the photographs changes the degree to which scar tissue is visible—and there is little that renders unaesthetic the area from which the breast has been removed. It is essentially nothing less than a profound absence: Liffschitz refers to her absent breast as "la faltante" (6). Yet it is this absence that is most scandalous. It is scandalous because it is a subtraction from what is, in a patriarchal model of complete feminine beauty, the full inventory of female body accoutrements. Vallejos in her article on Liffschitz refers to "la feminidad resumida en las mamas" (2; for histories of views of the female breast see Yalom; Levy; Latteier). It is scandalous, in the case of Liffschitz's body, in the disruption of the symmetry, through strategic bihemispheric pairings, that is often asserted to be a fundamental feature of the body. And, if a total mastectomy achieves its own sort of symmetry, it is, nevertheless, at the cost of augmenting the subtraction of allegedly normal features. And this absence is offensive because it is paraded in the pages of these images—and, moreover, paraded by a woman whose body, in other orders, is beyond the prime of its sexual allure. The decline in sexual allure is compounded by the detail of radical mastectomy, as though in some dreadful way the removal of the breast were an exponentially greater sign of bodily decay.

One way of understanding the way in which women who have had operations for diseases affecting the female body are abandoned by men (and why women must work to conceal that such surgical interventions have taken place) is by seeing it in terms of a momentous disruption of the expectations created by the patriarchal paradigm. Thus, if a man may be shocked by the deviation in a woman's body from that paradigm, a woman may be psychologically devastated by the realization — confirmed by the actual experience — that she will be rejected by men (and even many women) for falling so abruptly away from the paradigm. Liffschitz states in the prologue to her book of photographs that:

> En ese momento [de compartir sus fotos con su médico] me enteré de las dificultades con las que se encuentran muchas mujeres a partir de la operación — sobre todo sexuales, de auto estima y con sus parejas — pero también de los casos en los que las pacientes se niegan a realizar una mastectomía prefiriendo la conservación del pecho a la de la vida. El hecho de pensar que mi trabajo fotográfico pudiera ayudar de alguna forma a mujeres y hombres relacionados con este tipo de operación o cualquier otra mutilación, me dio un impulso invaluable, de alguna manera incluso el cáncer adquirió un sentido [6].

Aging for women is equally a dramatic event for much the same reasons, and a radical mastectomy is nothing less than the violently sudden confirmation of the process of female bodily decline in that one day the breast is there, and the next it is not.

One of Liffschitz's images is particularly useful in this regard in bringing some of these issues together. In the plate on page 29 of *Recursos humanos*, the woman is leaning forward with her arms crossed over her upraised right knee; she is looking into the camera (**Fig. 9.1**). This is the return gaze of the photographic subject, and in the universe of girlie magazines it functions to have the woman being photographed acknowledge, first, the gaze of the (likely) male photographer (who, in turn, is a stand-in for the male spectator) and, second, the contemplation of her image by the male spectator. Whether it is a come-hither look, a bemused look, a defiant look, or whatever, merely suggests options concerning the way in which the subject relates to the gazer. That look may either serve to hold, retain, the spectator's gaze at the expense of his contemplation of the rest of her body, or it may be the point of entry, so to speak, into the process of mapping the female body beginning with the eyes but proceeding to register all of the other territories of the body offered up by the photograph to that gaze. In the process of raising the right leg to be able to prop the crossed arms on it and, in turn, the lowered head on the right arm, the subject brings her pubis directly into view.

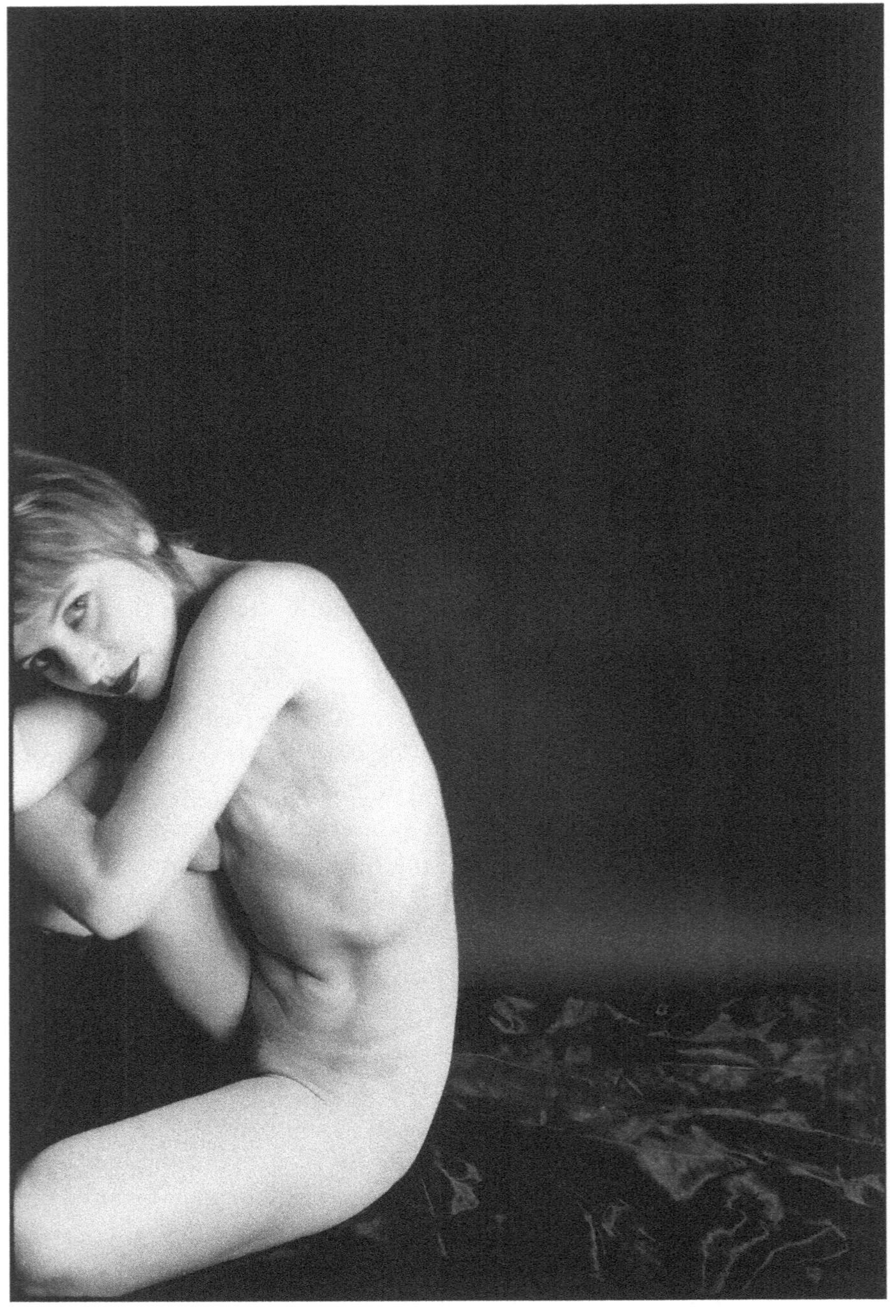

Fig. 9.1 (Gabriela Liffschitz).

But there is something fundamentally "wrong" with this image. Specifically, while the right breast is partially visible below the left arm as it is positioned to support the crossed right one, the position of the left arm is such to fully reveal the startling information that the left breast is missing. Since there is only the hint of scarring visible, it is as though this breast had been air-brushed out, disappeared, a bad visual joke on the woman and, therefore, on the spectator, who presumably will examine the photograph for the mix of aesthetics and erotics to be found in the photograph of what is undoubtedly a very attractive woman. The other thing that is noticeable about this photograph, in the terms of the conventions of girlie-magazine shots, is that it is not properly centered. What the camera sees in such shots is the fullness of the naked female body. I have been using nude up to this point, but now it is time to have recourse to the adjective naked, for the way in which it captures the idea of the vulnerable exposure of human body. Toward enhancing this exposure, the subject is placed squarely and totally in the frame of the shot. Yet the image under discussion has the woman's body bleed off the page to the left (the same side of the body that manifests the crucial absence produced by mastectomy), leaving a black hole on the right side of the frame. There are several images in the book in which Liffschitz utilizes the double technique of the displacement of the body and its off-the-page bleed. The result is to suggest the process of disappearance of the body, as though it were slipping away from the viewer — a powerful objective correlative in the image of the disappearance of the aging, damaged female body from the scrutiny of the masculinist gaze I have spoken of above (see also the image on page 21 of *Recursos humanos,* where the remaining breast is part of the body that is bled off the page: **Fig. 9.2**). In various of these photographs, the woman's body is placed both in positions that replicate *Playboy*-style poses, those that focus on and objectify as fetishes dominant erotic zones of the female body, and in positions that unquestionably expose the absence of the singular fetish of the female breast.[5] Also in several poses, the remaining right breast is hidden (for example, in the image on page 15, by the right hand stretching up to grasp the left shoulder: **Fig. 9.3**), a procedure by which what would normally be exposed fully and gloriously would be the other breast; what is exposed is its absence.

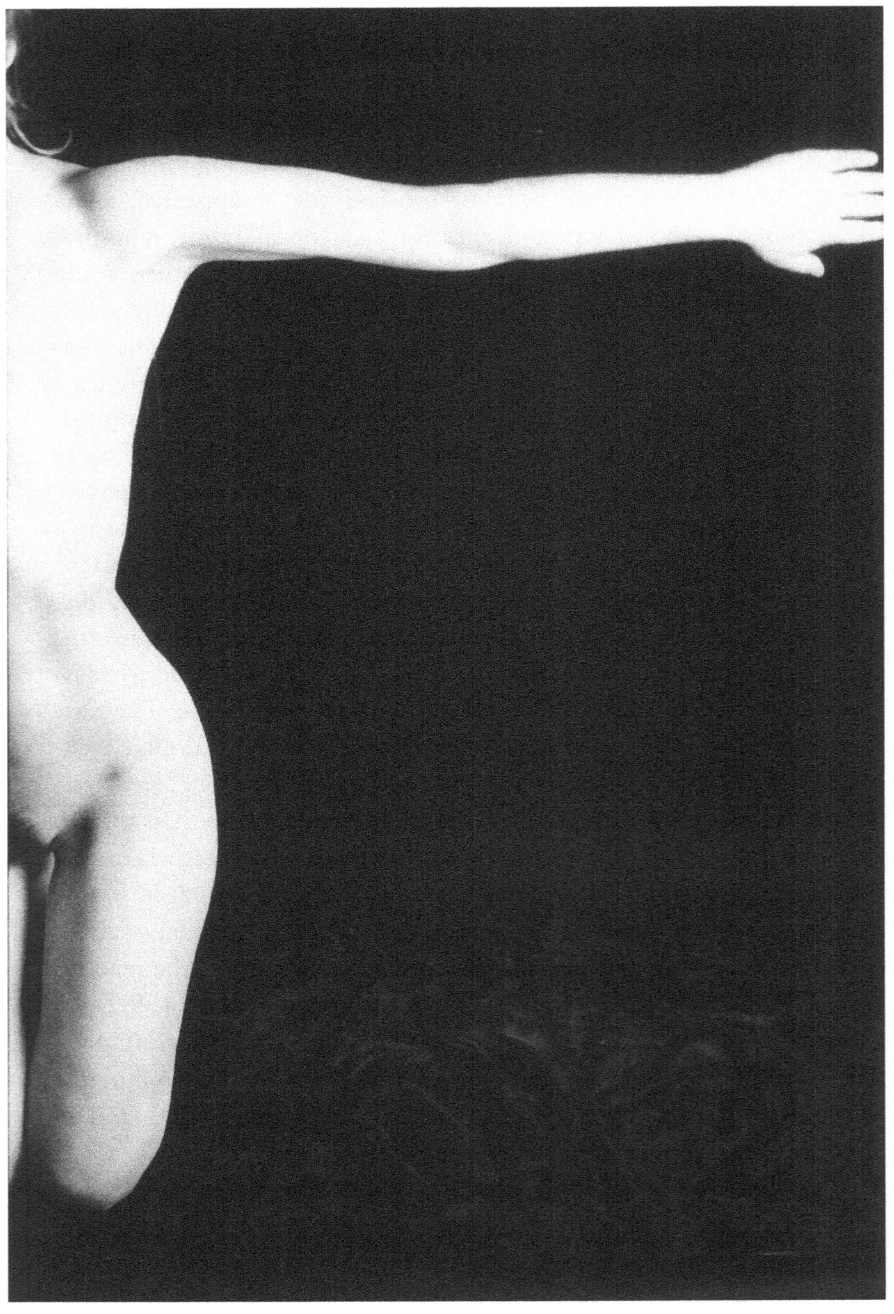

Fig. 9.2 (Gabriela Liffschitz).

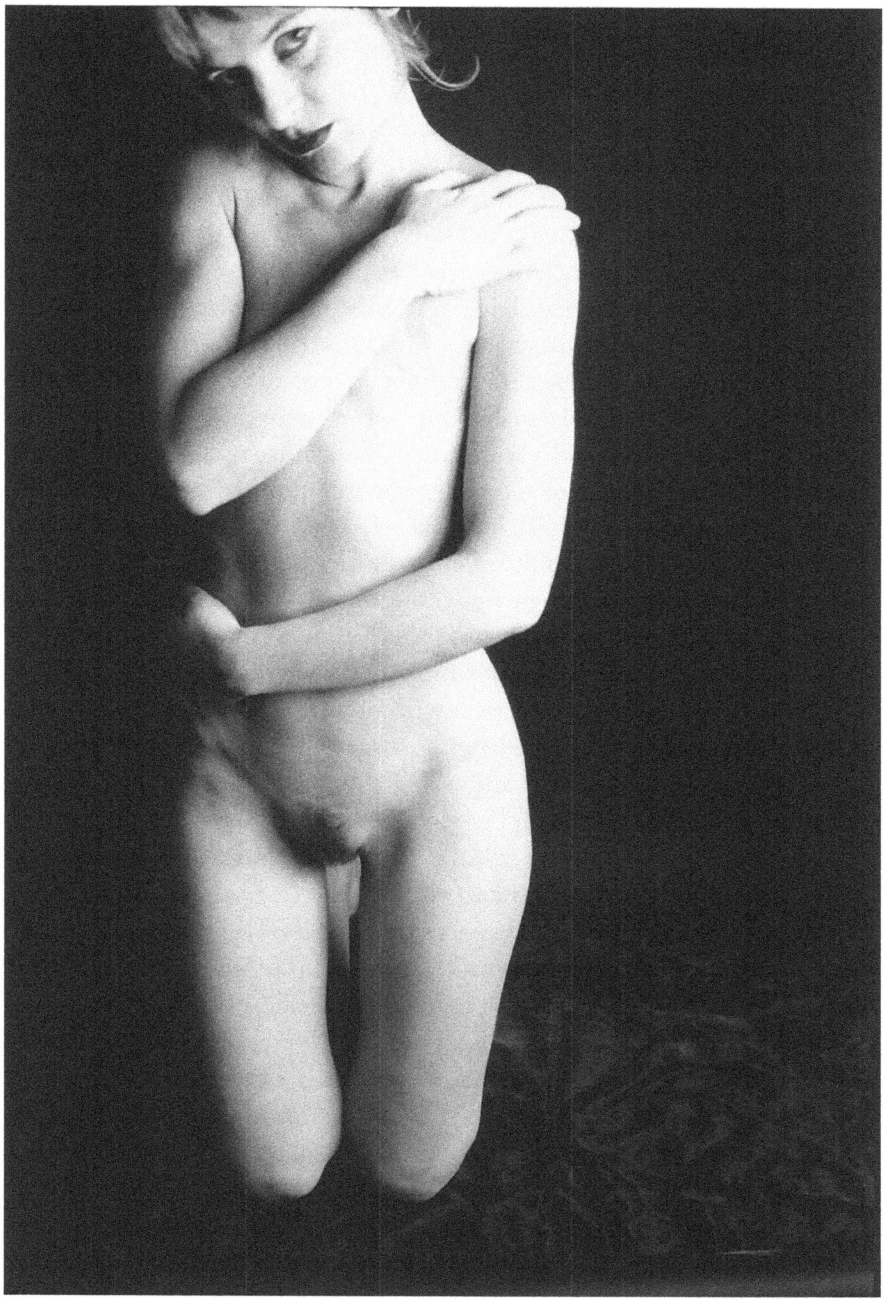

Fig. 9.3 (Gabriela Liffschitz).

In the case of the photograph on page 35, the covering up of the right breast and the leaving uncovered the place where the left breast should be (should, in both its alethic and deontic senses), provides a distinctly androgynous image (**Fig. 9.4**). The androgyny of the body as it is represented here is abetted by the fact that the pubic area is covered and by the fact that Liffschitz's body is quite athletic; moreover, her modified page-boy cut can be interpreted as ambiguous or unisex. Her face is made up, including eyeliner and lipstick, but this is as much the feminization of a male body as it is the masculinization of a female one. Again, there are other images that contribute to the same effect, although this is perhaps the most eloquent one. Reference to the androgynization of the female body by the removal of a major secondary sex characteristic such as the breast, and androgynization enhanced by the defiant display of the body refigured through surgery provides the opportunity to inquire into the way in which the gaze invited by these photographs is concomitantly restructured.

I have been speaking throughout this essay of a congealed or fossilized masculinist gaze, one that is certainly abstract and, to a great extent, overgeneralized, if not simply sheerly hypothetical. Yet there is ample empirical and theoretical writing on the subject of the sort of gaze beckoned or convoked by girlie magazines and their pornographic projections. To be sure, I am asking the reader here to agree to the proposition that pornographic representation of the woman's body is not an alternative form of cultural production, but one that is present *in nuce* in girlie magazines and constitutes a logical extension of the former. This gaze involves expectations based on a paradigm of feminine beauty, sensuality, and erotic appeal and is legitimated by the right to control through the act of contemplation the interpretation of the female body (equally, of the male body, which must conform to its own paradigm within the patriarchal model). It is a gaze that is deducible from the semiotic conditions of the publications in question: one can work back from the images they reproduce and reduplicate in the insistently iterative fashion of popular culture, to construct a model of the sort of ideological consciousness to which they are addressed. To put it in simple terms, the exposure of, say, the female breast in such-and-such a way is meant to satisfy an expectation from the spectator that the female breast will be exposed in such-and-such a way and that it

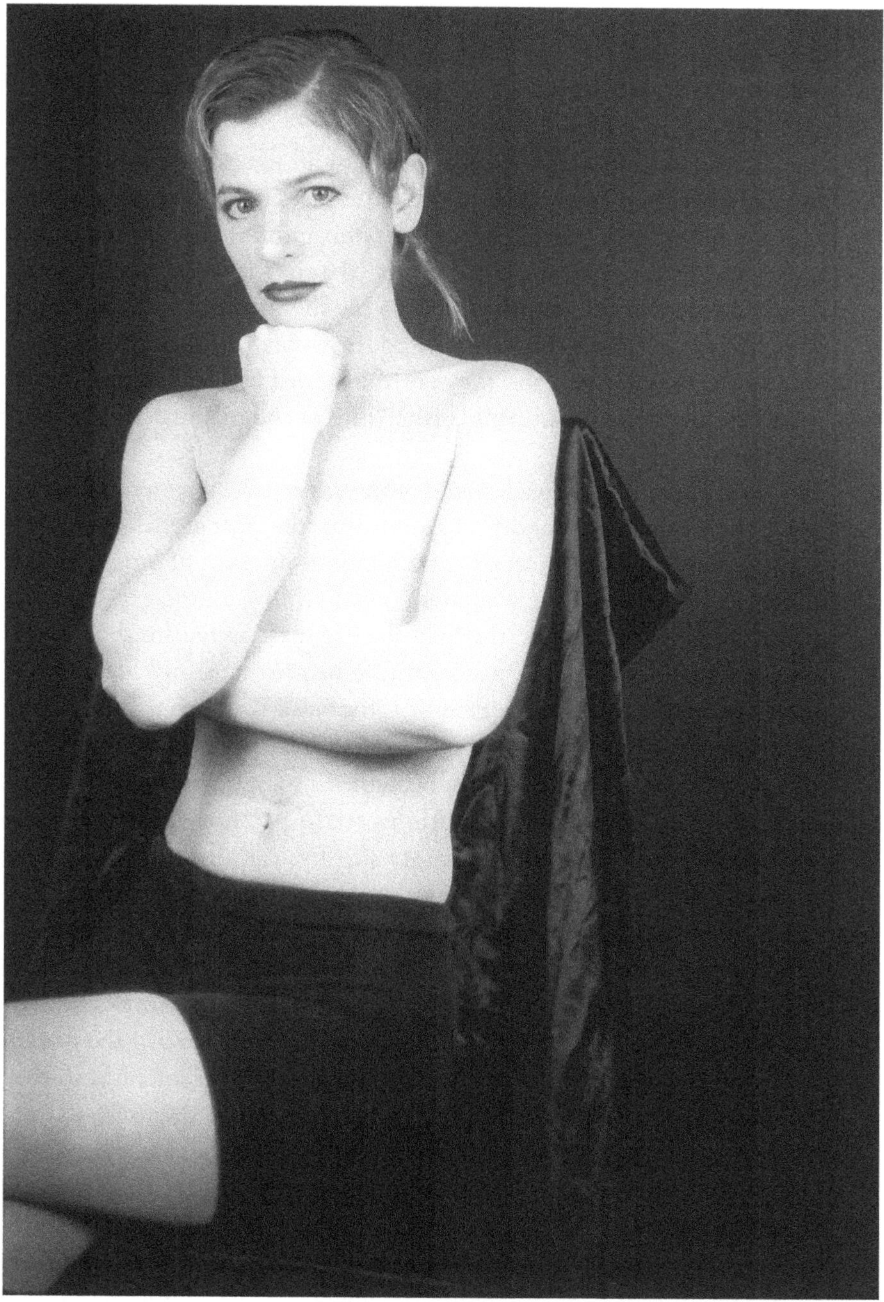

Fig. 9.4 (Gabriela Liffschitz).

will meet certain criteria as to its physical constitution. Such a process of projective semiotic construction yields, in the case of the *Playboy* type of feminine bodily display, what can be labeled the masculinist gaze.

It may not be merely a male gaze: not all males view with a paradigmatically masculinist gaze; and some females (certainly, not all) may gaze in a masculinist way, as part of their obligation to support the patriarchal interpretation of the female body (that is, they may not see these images erotically, but they are likely to see them correctively, in terms of the degree to which they conform to the woman's obligation to support patriarchal norms); and they may be viewed by some lesbians who reinscribe the masculinist details (the "lure of the mannish lesbian" in De Lauretis's terms).[6]

So if there is a congealed masculinist gaze that is reiterated from one girlie magazine to another, confirming the patriarchal paradigm but also allowing itself strategic extrapolations in terms of progressively greater exploitation of the woman's body, building on the exploitation of that body legitimated in the first place by patriarchalism, how does one go about defying and reconstituting or restructuring that gaze? I would maintain that, in the case of Liffschitz's work, that is done by parodying the masculinist gaze and defying its expectations (**Fig. 9.5**). Of course, these expectations can be denied by simply not meeting the demands that the woman fall within certain parameters of age; that the woman fulfill a certain inventory of physical attributes; that the woman strike attitudes that are inviting, seductive, tempting, willing, and forthcoming. To disrupt any one of the criteria of expectation is to fail to serve the model of femininity sustained by the girlie magazines in question. To be sure, certain other optional features may be involved that move the model of the girlie magazine toward the realm of the pornographic, but there is little feminist disagreement as to the sexist and exploitative nature of the former in and of themselves.

Thus, to parody any one, any cluster, or all of these features is to suggest the rejection of the masculinist gaze and a displacement toward alternative gazes. What might these gazes be? It might be difficult, pending a greater concentration of examples than the two dozen or so offered by Liffschitz, to speculate as to where the gaze might go. Suffice it to say that what is fundamental is a *different gaze*. It will be a gaze

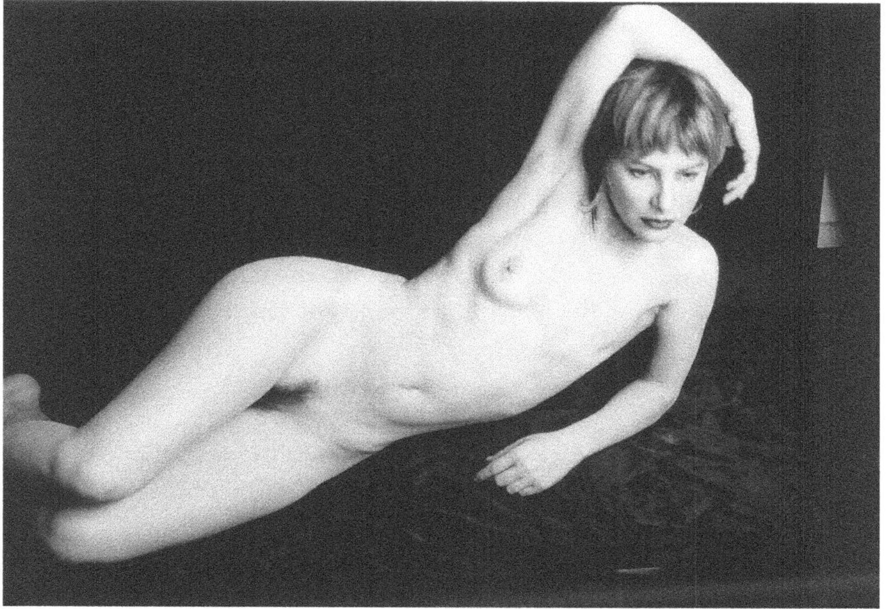

Fig. 9.5 (Gabriela Liffschitz).

that assumes an engagement with the female body — either in general or as specifically exemplified by the subject of *Recursos humanos* — in ways that both refute the sexist and exploitative masculinist gaze and suggest alternative gazes of the body, ones that we can generally call feminist, but might well include the lesbian gaze and a nonpatriarchal masculine gaze as well. Indeed, I would not wish to exclude even those gazes that, while they might re-reify the feminine body, are driven by a fascination with a woman's body that has been restructured in ways that escape the bounds of patriarchal heterosexism.

I would like at this point to take up the matter of supposedly "kinky" responses to Liffschitz's self-portraits. The problem, of course, is what constitutes the kinky. Undoubtedly reference to core parameters of heterosexist patriarchalism would exclude an erotic response to a woman's body with signs of a mastectomy, considering it morbid or perverse. It is better to direct one's sexual energy toward an appropriate objective choice — that is, a woman of presumably healthy reproductive capacities. Such an injunction is along the same line that would block one woman's response to another woman's body: the patriarchal injunction to reproduce the species would gain nothing from such an attraction. To be sure, it is not immediately apparent that a woman with a mastectomy is unable to contribute to the reproduction of the species, even if her capacity for breast-feeding is reduced. But in a semiotic process of investment in corporeal synecdoches, any subtraction of the "standard equipment" for proper mothering is suspect, is an indication of reproductive limitations, if not outright incapacity. Liffschitz writes in the "Prólogo" to her recent collection, *Efectos colaterales*, in which she includes photographs of four stages of her treatment:

> ¿Qué era el cuerpo antes? ¿Antes de ser el protagonista de un relato hasta entonces insospechado? No lo sé, no logro recordarlo porque probablemente no lo haya pensado. No hacía falta. Lo que haya sido antes ha quedado ahora por completo desdibujado, o tal vez es que por primera vez se dibujó un cuerpo ahora: después de haber sido intervenido, revisado, releído, recontextualizado, reinscripto, etc. Ahora tiene el protagónico, digo, se lo ve mucho, como nunca antes había pensado que mi cuerpo podía — era necesario y esperaba — ser visto. Antes jamás me hubiese desnudado ante una cámara, o sí, pero no para hacerlo público. No hubiese tenido sentido. Ahora después de la mastectomía, después de saber aquello por lo que muchas mujeres pasaban — relación a la sexualidad, al erotismo, pero también con relación a su cotidianidad, su imagen, su deseo —, ahora lo tenía. *Ahora era un acto político, ahora era necesario* [no pag.; emphasis added].

However, we need to divide the issue here into two separate categories. On the one hand, there is the possibility, virtually unable to hindered, of a viewer making an erotic investment in these images, despite the ways in which such an investment might contravene the putatively healthy responses of *homme moyen* heterosexuals. There is no way to control erotic responses to any sexual fetish, or, to put it differently, there is no way to predict what might be converted into a sexual fetish, and the Deleuze-Guattari anti–Oedipal proposition has made us aware of how free-ranging and unpredictable erotic energy is, and there is little point, without engaging in authoritarian censorship, to be made in attempting to squelch it. *Recursos humanos* may defy the heterosexist girlie magazine, but it cannot impede other responses, some of which may even be the sort deriving from a masculinist gaze carried to a logically perverse/perversely logical conclusion I have already referred to.

Yet there is a second issue that is even more intriguing, one that is an extension of the feminine and the queer, and that is the erotic investment in Liffschitz's displayed body in ways that shift the grounds of erotic appeal from the supposedly normal, sexy, feminine stereotype of the girlie magazines. An artist like Orlan has deliberately engaged in radical surgery on her body and in radical representations of her body in various stages of reconstruction in order to work toward revised, nonpatriarchal aesthetics and erotics for woman's body, and to count on a spectator that is in appreciate awe of her work (Ince). As a result, it is reasonable to assume that Liffschitz's body, as offered in these photographs, can also become a veneration for a feminist, lesbian, queer gaze that invests that body in something like a range from admiration to loving gratitude, to desire.[7] Indeed, the ways in which Liffschitz's body, as figured in these photographs, can become the object of lesbian desire constitutes the most eloquent defiance imaginable of the heterosexist, masculinist gaze.

Since the whole purpose of this chapter has been to underscore what it is about the self-portraits of Liffschitz's body that goes against the grain of the masculinist gaze, these features — primarily, but not necessarily exclusively — include in very dramatic ways her body, on the edge of middle-age, and, most dramatically, her partial mastectomy: "Incluyo en mi territorio la devastación de la que soy objeto" (Liffschitz, *Venecia* 25).[8]

Appendix:
Photographer Websites

All of the photographers, except for Gabriel Valansi, have websites, and their work may also be viewed at sites belonging to galleries, exhibitions, and publications in which their work has appeared.

Marcelo Brodsky: http://www.marcelobrodsky.com

Sylvio Fabrykant: http://fabrykant.com

Eduardo Gil: http://www.eduardogil.com. Gil's site also includes the work of Gabriel Díaz and Gabriela Liffschitz.

Adriana Lestido: http://www.marcoslopez.com

Marcos López: http://www.marcoslopez.com

Gaby Messina: http://www.gabymessina.com

Chapter Notes

Preface

1. The eleven photographers were Bécquer Casaballe, Gabriel Díaz, Cristina Fraire, Eduardo Gil, Fernando Gutiérrez, Adriana Lestido, Marcos López, Gabriel Valansi, Martín Weber, Marcos Zimmermann, and Helen Zout.

2. Sara Facio, in her essay "De la dictadura a la democracia," discusses the need to assess the deleterious effects on photography of the Argentine military dictatorships: "Es difícil evaluar los daños sufridos por la fotografía argentina durantes las sucesivas interrupciones de la vida democrática del país. Quizás aún no hemos reflexionado lo suficiente sobre el tema" (39). Clearly, censorship and self-cenorship in the print media affected photojournalism and documentary photography, and even in the case of art photography, the very public nature of taking photographs would have been problematical during periods of draconian repression.

Chapter 1

1. I use "reality effect" here advisedly, conscious of Bourdieu's comment in his analysis of photography as a bourgeois art, to the effect that "It is due as much to the social image of the technical object which produces it as to its social use that photography is ordinarily seen as the most perfectly faithful reproduction of the real" (77). It is, moreover, the utilization of photography by the military dictatorship to sell a particular image of Argentine reality that is deconstructed by the work examined in this study. The triumphalism that Gil seeks to undermine in *(argentina)* runs directly counter to the images of a protege photographer of the military like Pedro Luis Raota.

2. Argentines, whether official agents of the government or not, were probably not responsible for these bombings: renewed investigations now point toward an Iranian involvement, although it is not unfair to say that the failure of the police and intelligence operations to make any significant headway in the investigations at the time was virtually criminal negligence.

3. In 2003, Brodsky published in Spain *Memory Works*, a volume of the most important parts of both *Buena memoria* and *Nexo*. Material from *Buena memoria* constitutes part of the representation of Argentina in *Mapas abiertos: fotografía latinoamericana 1991–2002* (222–25).

Chapter 2

1. An earlier version of this analysis of Valansi's photography appeared in *Fisura: revista de literatura y arte* 1.3 (febrero 2003): 27–33.

2. Reference must also be made to the film by Nahuel García et al., *El tren blanco*

(2004), which documents the lives of the *cartoneros* who pick through the rubbish of Buenos Aires at night; as their name indicates, they are principally interested in *cartón* (cardboard).

3. By central core one refers to a combination of the sector descendent from the original settlements, the main administrative and financial installations, and the residential neighborhoods that historically served these installations. This would be, in very broad terms, the part of Buenos Aires east of the Entre Ríos/Callao avenue (all streets in Buenos Aires change name going north and south of Rivadavia, which, by extending east-west from one end of the city, divides it into two dominant spheres; in general terms, the city tends to be more prosperous on the northern side of Rivadavia).

4. Valansi has informed me in a personal communication (August 22, 2002) that the arterial is the Avenida 9 de Julio, which crosses the city, perpendicular to Rivadavia, from north to south (it is the one street that does not change name as it crosses Rivadavia). Valansi says that the image was taken from a plane as it approached the downtown Jorge Newberry airport, although he does not recall whether the segment is north or south of Rivadavia. Because of its jagged line, it is probably the southern section, which shifts somewhat east of its basically straight-line path to avoid the Peronist landmark building, Obras Sociales (in its northward march, the Avenida shifts very slightly to avoid an equally important landmark for the Argentine social elite, the palace that houses the French Embassy).

5. As of this writing, residents, mostly low-income, in the Mexico City periphery of San Salvador Atenco have prevailed against the plans of the Fox government to build a huge new international airport there, a project equally disruptive as that of freeway construction.

6. There are now some "permanently" uncompleted parts of the freeway system as originally conceived in Buenos Aires, which speaks to a combination of poor planning and underfunding. Moreover, there are areas under the freeways, especially on the poor south side, that have been taken over as refuges for the homeless.

7. Originally, the term *cabecita negra* (literally, "black head") referred to people of mestizo/indigenous ethnicity, mostly from the northern provinces, who were brought into Buenos Aires by Perón in the mid-1940s both to provide a cheap labor force for his attempts to industrialize Argentina and, in much heavier ideological terms, to rupture the by then longstanding division of the country into the littoral regions which were of essentially European origin and character (and were, therefore, basically white) and the provinces which still bore extensive evidence of the native peoples of the continent (and were, therefore, essentially "of color").

8. *Cabecita negra* refers to the dark complexion (from the point of view of European-like Buenos Aires) of rural Argentines of indigenous origins; by extension, it also refers to Latin Americans from other countries, especially poorer ones. Thus, the term, in addition to being a racial slur, has ethnic and socio-economic overtones.

9. Valansi has shared with me the delightful fact that these photographs were made with a Kyocera camera that he rescued from being thrown in the garbage.

10. Melamed (22) speaks of the collapse of these business enterprises beginning at the end of 1999 when he refers to the appearance of signs at business establishments that read "Liquidamos Todo" (Everything Must Go) and "Venta Total por Cierre" (Going out of Business Sale); these signs contrast with the flurry of "Gran Inauguración" (Grand Opening) signs at the beginning of the decade.

11. Dani Yako, in his photograph essay, *Extinción: últimas imágenes del trabajo en la Argentina* devotes an entire section of photographs, along with an interpretive presentation by Martín Caparrós, of the extinction of an Argentine television manufacturing company as a consequence of foreign imports: "Televisores" (no pag.).

12. The Citroën appears as a major icon of the socioeconomic identity of the late 1970s family featured in Marcelo Piñeyro's 2002 film *Kamchatka.*

13. Images of Valansi's *Zeitgeist* series are part of the representation of Argentina in *Mapas abiertos: fotografía argentina 1991–2002* (146–47).

Chapter 3

1. Enrique Medina has the narrator protagonist of *El escritor* muse at one point, "[Argentina es] un país donde la corrupción es atractivo turístico" (164; [Argentina is] a country where corruption is a tourist attraction). See Foster on this novel as an exemplar of cultural responses to the Menem period.

2. It is reputed that an Argentine ambassador to Washington in the 1960s replied, when asked why Argentina was the only Latin American country not to receive the Peace Corps, "Does the United States send the Peace Corps to France?"

3. The recent specter of the reelection of Menem as president in May 2003 appeared driven as much by a nostalgia for the prosperity of the early to mid–1990s and the promise of its recapture, as by the lack of other viable political alternatives; as it turned out, this nostalgia vanished in the face of political reality, and Menem withdrew from the race when his defeat seemed assured.

4. One of Gil's most famous images, which does not appear in *(argentina)* because it falls outside the time frame of the dossier, concerns two policemen, assuming very professional stances, guarding a human rights display consisting of the silouettes of the disappeared. Each policeman is stationed at one end of the life-size panel, providing anchoring by members of the security forces, the very same forces that were complicitous in the disappearance of citizens during the neofascist tyranny.

5. Latin Americans can normally move freely from one country to another; what they cannot do is work.

6. One of the concerns in redemocratized Argentina has been the plight of institutionalized psychiatric patients: "As recently as 1985, a team of doctors and jurists published a comprehensive study on the legal status of Argentina's psychiatric patients. The authors ... argued that the national civil code's guarantees against arbitrary or inappropriate hospitalization were unenforceable and often ignored.... The authors concluded that many patients, lost to the outside world, simply became accustomed to hospital life and vanished behind asylum walls (Ablard, 89; the study in question was authored by Cárdenas et al.).

7. I use the rather formal "expectantly" in an attempt to capture the dual meaning of *esperar* in Spanish: "to hope" and "to wait."

8. Gil's photographs extend to the year 2000. By that time, the neoliberalist project had already begun to collapse. The definitive collapse in late 2001 brought with it an enormous outburst of violence born of anger and frustration in the face of frozen assets, failed banks and their disappeared funds, and the closing of numerous businesses whose survival depended on the neoliberalist bubble; thousands of Argentines sought to leave the country for the United States, Europe, or Israel. The signs of the collapse, including the traces of the violence (such as the boarded-up banks whose glass facades had been shattered as part of the assaults of protest), are still very much visible in Buenos Aires and environs, and the frustration, anger, and despair Gil records in the photographs of *(argentina)* have been exponentially greater.

9. The most notable recycling is that of Puerto Madero. Centered around the warehouses that served the large port facility that lies east of Government House and its administrative buildings and the financial center, Puerto Madero had a relatively short life in the late nineteenth century, when it became necessary to inaugurate larger port facilities upriver from downtown Buenos Aires. The facilities at Puerto Madero, including a series of dikes where boats could anchor in waters protected from the vagaries of the mighty Río de la Plata estuary, stood idle for several decades, although they may have been partially used during the military dictatorship. Puerto Madero is now a bustling commercial and residential area, with a mix of recycled buildings and new structures, and the entire area now constitutes one of the approximately fifty official neighborhoods of the city of Buenos Aires. Another important recycled site is that of the old central market: the Abasto, as it is called, is now a major shopping center, owned by the international financier George Soros.

Chapter 4

1. Other important recent films on female senior citizens include Pablo Trapero's 2004

Familia rodante (*Family on Wheels*), Eduardo Mignogna's 2003 *Cleopatra* and his 1996 *Sol de otoño* (*Autumn Sun*; both also starring Norma Aleandro), Santiago Carlos Oves's 2004 *Conversaciones con mamá* (*Conversations with Mom*, starring the magnificent Uruguayan actress, China Zorrilla, who has played many senior women in both film and the theater, most recently the female lead in Marcos Carnevale's 2005 *Elsa y Fred*), and Silvio Fischbein's 1988 *Mamá querida* (*Dear Mommy*).

2. An allied theme is the phenomenon of suicide among seniors, often in recent years as the consequence of the economic disasters that have denied them their pensions or seen them so cut that recipients are reduced effectively to poverty. The topic has not been adequately researched, especially with reference to cultural production, although it is undeniably a corollary to the important study by Diego Melamed, *Irse*, which refers to the reasons why so many Argentines left the country during the final decades of the twentieth century.

3. Another study of considerable interest would concern the representation of "old folk" in the humorous drawings of Quino (pseudonym of Salvador Joaquín Lavado), as much in the narrative strips of *Mafalda* as in the single-panel drawings contained in his extensive list of almost yearly albums. Another interesting cultural source are the albums of drawings and narrative strips by Maitena Burundanera — known only as Maitena — many of which focus on feminist issues regarding age (see the study by Tompkins).

4. Fernando de la Orden also has photographs dealing with *La abuela Lola* (*Granny Lola*).

5. Some images from the show appear in the prestigious photography journal *Aperture* (Messina, "*Grandes mujeres*: Photography").

6. Personal communication from Gaby Messina, August 2004, in Buenos Aires.

Chapter 5

1. There is an eloquent scene in María Luisa Bemberg's film on Camila O'Gorman, *Camila* (1984), in which, as her mother rocks and sews, Camila is lectured by her father on the responsibilities of young ladies as regards marriage. His dia-
tribe is interrupted by a messenger, and when he is once again free to attend to his daughter's education, he asks "De qué estábamos hablando?" His wife responds, "De la cárcel," only to be corrected by her husband: "No, del matrimonio." The mother, without missing beat in either her rocking or her sewing, shoots back, "Es la misma cosa, es la misma cosa." Camila is willing to go to a real prison (and then be executed alongside her improper lover) rather than to submit to the grim incarceration of respectable matrimony.

2. Marco Bechis's 1999 film *Garage Olimpo*, while an execellent film on the subject of the human rights violations of the so-called Dirty War in Argentina in 1976–83, becomes problematical from the point of view of the male gaze of the tortured female body, to the extent that the male gaze of the director watches males torture the female protagonist, María, often with the intervening gaze of male superiors seen watching her torture. Although one could praise the film for focusing on the plight of women during the Dirty War, there is nothing particularly feminist about the film, by contrast to prison narratives by women, such as Alicia Kozameh's *Pasos bajo agua* (1987), Nora Strejilevich's *Una sola muerte numerosa* (1997), Cristina Feijoo's *Memorias del río inmóvil* (2001), Liliana Heker's *El fin de la historia* (1996), and Alicia Partnoy's *The Little School: Tales of Disappearance and Survival in Argentina* (1986); Miguel Bonassos' *Recuerdo de la muerte* (1984) also speaks of women prisoners, although the tone of the text is unquestionably masculinist.

3. *La fuga* tells the story of the (fictional) escape in 1928 of several inmates from the Las Heras National Penitentiary in Buenos Aires. Although the film has a strong element of dirty realism and is devoid of any attempt to romanticize the circumstances of the escapees or their subsequent fates, Mignogna's film is part of an on-going cultural production in Argentina since the return to constitutional democracy in 1983 regarding the conditions and possibilities of individual freedoms.

4. See the taunt by the old Gaucho in the brothel in Carlos Hugo Christiansen's 1979 film version, *A intrusa*, of Jorge Luis Borges's "La intrusa" (from *El informe de*

Brodie [1970]), to the effect that — and I translated from the Portuguese of the film — "spending more than five minutes thinking about a woman is not a manly thing, but rather the sign of a faggot."

5. Mascia-Lees and Sharpe (2) point out the function of the tattoo as indicating that the body is also socially constructed — that is, identified within a system of social semiotics.

6. See Lestido's most recent volume of photographs on mothers and daughters, *Madres e hijas* (2003; see Foster, "Rev. of Adriana Lestido, *Madres e hijas*").

7. One should, however, be careful not to homologize the three groups. Jews and queers were more likely to have been singled out for political reasons; women were more likely to have been victims of the overarching sexism of the security forces.

8. The Chilean artist Eugenio Dittborn in his *Pintura aeropostale* speaks about his interest in recontextualizing police photographs, which he has embedded in several of his canvases: "By citing police photos of criminals and delinquents ... in my work, I've tried to explore a specific and contradictory relationship: the collison between the police camera, the camera that is properly the power of the State working visually, and the faces of small-time Chilean criminals, men and women, who are, mostly, transplanted and impoverished peasants" (13).

Chapter 6

1. The title of the collection is also given in English, as this material has been exhibited, in addition to other countries outside Argentina, in the United States in four different venues, one of which was the comprehensive exhibit of recent Argentine photography at the International Center of Photography in New York in 1999.

Chapter 7

1. There is a Mafalda cartoon — there's always a Mafalda cartoon for the truly important issues of Argentine life — in which Mafalda runs into Felipe on the street. She asks him if he's done his composition for school on national independence. Felipe replies no, because, although he went out for a walk to see if something inspired him, so far nothing has. As he says this, Mafalda is looking around at all the advertisements for foreign products (Lavado, 386).

2. In a reversal of semantic poles, Sara Facio, in her presentation of López's dossier, *Fotografías*, uses "camp" where I would use "kitsch" and, by implication, vice versa: "El mundo que nos descubre Marcos López es más camp que kitsch. La mirada de nuestro fotógrafo tiene el toque de la inocencia" (9). In my usage of "camp," the aesthetic principle of spectacle is self-conscious, ironic, and defiant; "kitsch," by contrast, believes itself to be authentic. If anything, López's critical analysis of Argentine/Latin American culture discovers a principle of kitsch that he puts on display in his photographs. Perhaps in one sense his images are campy, but they begin by recreating what is a world of kitsch.

3. Matei Calinescu's observation is suggestive with reference to the Argentine interest in American products and their "invasion" of the Argentine marketplace during the period of neoliberalism in the 1990s: "The link between kitsch (whose dependence on fads and rapid obsolescence makes it the major form of expendable 'art') and economic development is indeed so close that one may take the presence of kitsch in countries of the 'Second' or 'Third' world as an unmistakable sign of 'modernization'" (226). For Calinescu, kitsch is one of the "five faces of modernity," the other four being modernism, avant-garde, decadence, and postmodernism.

4. The latter has a sunburst in the middle of the second, white, band, between two celestial blue bands, top and bottom, of the flag.

5. Valeria González speaks of how "[López's] reference to pop art, then, does not allude so much to art history as to the process of degradation of local cultures at the margins of the so-called global world" (24).

6. There are numerous ironic uses of "New York" and its phonetic deformations that undermine the presumed cachet of the city and its iconicity vis-à-vis the American experience. See, for example, Angel Muñiz's 1995 film *Nueba Yol* on the Dominican experience in New York.

7. The image I have been discussing so far, often identified as *Carnaval criollo*, is part of the group of López's images chosen to represent Argentina in *Mapas abiertos: fotografía latinoamericana 1991–2002*, 208–11.

8. There is also an opening image in *Pop latino* of *Botella de Inca Kola* (1997); this is an image, as the title indicates, of the bottle unmediated by human agency. Since Inca Kola is of limited distribution in Argentina, as a foreign product, it becomes the disappearing other of the foreign-brand axis Inca Kola/Coca Cola; note the idiosyncratic, non-Spanish, spelling of the former in order not to infringe on the brand supremacy of the American product.

9. "The brand provides a collection of products, some of which only loosely cohere or coexist under the broad corporate umbrella, with an overarching sense of identity and of economic and intellectual mission. The brand is nothing (we might reference our routine, popular encounters with Nike or McDonald's here); it offers itself less as an isolated product to be consumed than as a (totalizing) vision of how we conduct our lives and carry ourselves in the world. The brand is difficult to distinguish from the individual lifestyle (branding's greatest accomplishment is manifesting itself as a lifestyle): a highly pleasurable, seductive, if insidious form of the corporatization of the individual body, community, or, more likely, the targeted constituency, such as youth, or the middle class, or wealthy young professionals. It is the brand that, in the final instance, confers not only status (or identity) but determines the individual's putative worth" (Farred, 126).

10. See the delightful film, the *Gods Must Be Crazy* (dir. Jamie Uys [1980],) built around the consequences of an empty Coke bottle thrown from an overflying plane. Note also that Carlos Fuentes, in an important essay on the Americanization of Mexico, uses Coke's competitor, Pepsi-Cola, as the sign for this foreign invasion, presumably because it tropes better with the Mexican icon of Quetzalcoátl.

11. In another image, López uses what one could call an overly hirsute middle-aged man to display a gourd of maté—a decidedly premodern drink—as though advertising it in the style of mass-marketed beers and colas.

12. López has the following comment to make about Buenos Aires: "Ahora bien, entonces, ¿Dónde ubicarnos dentro de este páramo ventoso, con el río azotando el murallón en plena sudestada, refugiados en un Buenos Aires medieval, acorazado, indigestado por el humo de su propia caldera, por la publicidad y las encuestas falsas, plagado de alarmas, de custodios, de marketing directo y cientos de negocios de pizzas por dos pesos?" (*Al sur del sur: 8 fotógrafos argentinos*, 23).

13. One would not be surprised to learn that, at least in Buenos Aires and some other urban centers, during the much-ballyhooed First-World mentality of 1990s neoliberalism, there was more of a replacement than a recycling economy as regarded products like Coca-Cola; certainly, there was an increased presence of containers that could not be recycled without reprocessing. Some of these changes may hold over into "post-neoliberalism," but they may be too expensive to maintain.

14. Or, as López states so sarcastically in his "Manifiesto de Caracas" that is included in his *Sub-realismo crillo*, "El secreto es callarse, mirar hacia el Norte, hacia la inmensa America, y descifrar lo que te dice el viento" (17; also reproduced as the back cover flap of *Marcos López*).

15. Also identified as *Asado en Mendiolaza*.

16. The fact that Argentines may no longer so easily assemble to affirm their identity through the ritual of the *asado*—beef has become too expensive for the twice-daily consumption it once had, or even the once-a-week-on-the-weekend blowout of more recent times—lends an aura of nostalgia to *Asado criollo*. If, on the one hand, it is a clever framing of the importance of the barbecue for Argentines, it is, on the other, a reminder that such rituals are no longer so easily had. Like a religious persecution of the celebration of the mass, the consequences of neoliberalism and globalization constitute something like the persecution of the celebration of the *asado*.

17. "South" here unquestionably refers to López's Southern Hemisphere origins, but, in the context of his parodies of social and cultural icons, at least in English it evokes the phrase "to go south" = "become

inferior in quality or substance." Thus, the "south of realism" = "the trivialization of realism."

18. It is not completely clear why this should be so. In one sense, perhaps it is because homosociality relies on a hierarchy of power that is disrupted and restructured in the throes of passion. Perhaps it is because most versions of masculine heterosexism are grounded in the belief that sex always involves a domination and submission that would both counter the sociofinancial domination and submission of patriarchal society and produce irresolvably conflicting structurings of it: a man cannot both be the active master in a sociofinancial arrangement and the passive slave in an erotic one. Since women are, in patriarchal heterosexuality, always passive, the "feminization" of one of the men in the homoerotic coupling is radically destablizing. The fact that such a narrative may not be true of all, many, or any homoerotic relationships is a problem of the imagination of patriarchal heterosexuality, not of verisimilar functioning of those relationships. On another level, homoeroticism may involve the threat of a "truer" democracy of human relationships than is possible in patriarchal heterosexuality. This is the Whitmanesque principle, although it is certainly at work in the feminist rejection of the deceits, as regards democracy and social equality, of the patriarchy and its economics of capitalism, as in, for example, ecofeminism. On the other hand, the so-called male homosexuality of ancient Greece (best synthesized by Halperin) is founded on a tight system of male homosociality, whereby the two are not incompatible.

Carrillo discusses "nonsexual homosociality" in the context of homosexual identities in Mexico (358–62).

19. Hence, the Mexican narrative of the two men who wake up in bed together, and one says to the other that he was so drunk last night that he can't remember what happened (a version of this appears in Alfonso Cuarón's 2001 film *Y tu mama también*), or the American war movie motif of soldiers dying in each other's arms. See the Argentine variant on this motif in José Hernández's *Martín Fierro* (Geirola) or the Brazilian one in Bruno Barreto's 1981 film

Beijo no asfalto (Foster, *Gender and Society*, 129–38).

20. Military discipline — and certainly that of other quasimilitaristic organizations like religious orders — may require the weak homoeroticism of homosocialism; see the American motif of "two Marines and a six pack" and the phenomenon of "barracks buddies." The homoerotic pornography of strong homoeroticism is built around such real-life circumstances. The Argentine sociologist Néstor Perlongher insisted on homoerotic — not just homosocial — bonding as a factor in the network of survival among the São Paulo male hustlers he studied.

21. Homosociality among women, of course, works completely differently. While one form of it may be promoted to keep the women entertained — the practice of women assembling in the drawing room for coffee after a meal, while the men remain at table for a cigar and an after-dinner drink — strong female-female bonding is frowned upon as virtually the top of the slippery slope of men-hating and lesbianism. On the other hand, female homosociality is often viewed as an important strategic component, "sisterhood," of women united against male oppression (see the entry on "Homosociality" in Kowaleski-Wallace). Queer sociality would, therefore, have its own dimensions of solidarity, visibility, resistance, and social revindication: "happy together" (see "Homosocialismo" in Mira's encyclopedia in Spanish of queer culture).

22. The importance of meat in Argentine culture and its relationship to violence, homosociality, and homosexual rape was understood as early as the 1830s by Esteban Echeverría, whose short story "El matadero" is a founding text of Argentine fiction (probably written in the late 1830s, but not published until 1871). Echeverría describes the violence surrounding the utilization of beef-eating as a political tool by the Rosas dictatorship, the male homosociality of spaces like the slaughterhouse and the relationship of its denizens to the violent politics of Rosas, and the use of homosexual rape, figured specifically in Echeverria's story but present elsewhere in the period through the use of the corncob (the *mazorca*) as an instrument of terror by

the enforcers of the regime known as La Mazorca. In the relationship between the enforcers and their victim, there is a displaced homosexuality (a bull's pizzle is used in Echeverría's story), and, in their interpretation of the victim as "rapable," there is the understanding of his body as open to feminization or as already feminized — that is, as a male body available for sex at the hands of another (displaced) male body. For the relevance of "El matadero" to the history of homosexuality in Argentina, see Bazán (82–84); Piglia speaks of the violence in Echeverría's story (8–10), and his comments are accompanied by Enrique Breccia's intense graphic representation (10–18). Not all readers would agree that the bull's pizzle is used to penetrate the unfortunate *unitario*, since specific reference is limited to whipping his bared buttocks. However, such same-sex discipline is customarily understood as a form of homoeroticism that may or may not involved subsequent penetration; Bazán clearly understands that rape is involved (82).

23. Serge Brambly, one of Leonardo da Vinci's major biographers, includes a discussion of the latter's homosexuality, and Freud's comments on the subject are famous.

24. One of the two major sequences of Paul Leduc's 1986 film *Frida, naturaleza viva* involves her nurse; one of the final memorable scenes of the film is the same nurse accompanying Frida, who is on a stretcher, into Mexico City's Palacio de Bellas Artes, for her first major exhibition. The nurse is holding aloft a serum bottle.

25. In Peter Medak's 1981 *Zorro, the Gay Blade*, George Hamilton gives a queer twist to the twin motif, when we discover that the supermacho Zorro has a gay twin, known as Bunny Wigglesworth.

26. Historically, gynecology has involved men manipulating women's bodies, and the profession has always attempted to dispel the specter of medical rape in any of its stages by draping the woman so that her body is hidden, by having a female aide present, and by averring that the woman's body is no more than a medical specimen. Yet, a large number of women prefer today female gynecologists (although this does not address the lesbian potential); female proctologists with male patients, mean-

while, remain an essentially non-existent species.

27. Of many possible cultural references, one can think immediately of the doctor/patient relationship in Peter Glenville's 1961 film *Summer and Smoke*, based on the drama of the same name by the gay Tennessee Williams; there is very much of the gay parable about this work in both of its versions, despite the fact that the principal actors are a man and a woman. However, the fact that in the film the doctor is played by the gay British actor Laurence Harvey and his patient by Geraldine Page, who played women-who-might-really-be-gay-men in a number of plays and movies (in 1962, she also starred in the film version of Williams's *Sweet Bird of Youth*), cannot be overlooked: in a still-closeted Hollywood (and Broadway) such formulations were as close as one got to the circumstances of actual gay lives.

28. At least one major American gay play is built around the bathhouse, Terrence McNally's *The Ritz* (1975); it is well known that gay-friendly Bette Midler got her start performing in gay men's bathhouses. The homosocial space of the bathhouse appears in the Mexican Jaime Humberto Hermosillo's 1976 *María de mi corazón* (script by Gabriel García Márquez), and the bathhouse as homoerotic space appears in another Mexican film, Jorge Fons's 1995 *El Callejón de los Milagros*.

29. One of the most significant analyses of homoeroticism within macho hypermasculinity for Latin America is Núñez Noriega's study, devoted to northwest Mexico.

30. The Marlboro Man ads have, for years, sold an image of hypermasculinity, undisturbed by the feminine or the effeminate. However, the death from AIDS of Tom McBride, one of the models for these ads, is a real-world reminder of the homoeroticism always already present in the hypermasculine.

31. Other "penile" compositions authored by López include *En el jardín botánico*, where a parody of Fidel Castro–Che Guevara army-fatigued macho brandishes a plastic pistol that is somewhat flesh-colored rather than gun-metal gray. The way in which Cuba was, throughout the 1990s until the Argentine economic bust of late 2001, a gay Mecca for Argentine tourists is ironic, given

Guevara's notorious homophobia. Walter Salles in his 2003 film *Motorcycle Diaries* plays up Guevara's heterosexual persona by using the Mexican heartthrob Gael García Bernal to play the Argentine; see, on the other hand, the revision of the Korda image in the *Che Gay* poster from the early 1970s (reproduced in Kunzle, 95; Kunzle claims that it is probably British in origin). Casatel-lote, in his excellent commentary on López's work, refers specifically to the parody of Che Guevara (*Marcos López*, 13–14).

32. English does register "merman," although the concept belongs more to the realm of circus sideshow hoaxes than to a centuries-old poetic tradition.

33. A motif that, according to Conner et al. (306), has a lesbian dimension; certainly, the siren that calls men to their deaths at sea is not a very comforting heterosexual formulation.

34. The photographic and filmic record of which is examined by Waugh.

Chapter 8

1. The trope in Spanish is *nunca más*, "never again," which was appropriated at the time of the return to democracy in 1983 from Jewish post–Holocaust rhetoric. It is common to speak of the neofascist military period in Argentine as the Argentine Holocaust, although there are those who object to such an extension of meaning from *the* (one and only) Holocaust centered on the German application of the Final Solution in the extermination of the Jews.

2. For obvious reasons, I am privileging the male pronoun here. It is important to understand, however, than because of the power differential between men and women, the construction of identity is likely to work differently if one is talking about "her" as opposed to about "him."

3. The poster of the show speaks of thirty men, but in reality there were more than thirty images. This essay is based on a CD of twenty-eight of those photographs provided by Fabrykant, who, in a personal communication on August 30, 2004, affirmed that with the passage of time he has become more and more demanding as regards the selection of his images. The CD given to me includes the following names: Alberto Fischerman, film director (deceased);

Antonio Carrizo, journalist for cultural radio; Herminio Iglesias, politician; Astor Piazzola, musician (deceased); Miguel Brascó, writer and journalist; Daniel Czudnowsky, actor; Horacio Altuna, cartoonist; Antonio Ottone, film director (deceased); Guillermo Saavedra, poet and cultural journalist; Leonardo Favio, film director; Mauricio Dayub, actor and dramatist; Amadeo Carrizo, soccer star; Alejandro Horowicz, writer and journalist; Antonio Cafiero, politician; Fernando Sánchez Sorondo, poet; Julio Nudel, actor; Alberto Girri, poet (deceased); Hugo Guerrero Marthineitz, radio and TV personality; Jorge Schusseheim, humorist; Juan Forn, writer; Néstor Tirri, cultural journalist; Abrasha Rottemberg, writer; Adolfo Bioy Casares, writer (deceased); Raúl Alfonsín, former President of Argentina; Ricardo Blanco, design artist; Ulises Dumont, actor; Miguel Rep, cartoonist; Oscar Steimberg, semiologist.

4. Of course, one will remember that there once was a woman president of Argentina, María Esther Martínez (known as Isabel or Isabelita), but there is no known allegation that her presidency (1974–76), which is generally considered to be regrettable and an "accident" of the cynical political engineering of the dying Perón, could be seen to have legitimated the access of women to the Chair of Rivadavia, as that office is metaphorically called. The poet, songstress, and musician María Elena Walsh is quite revered, but she never enjoyed the international prestige of Astor Piazzola. Indeed, the music of the standard tango instruments is universally a male world.

5. The Municipal Prizes in literature are lifetime sinecures awarded for significant creative accomplishment.

6. So much so that, if one preferred to use the traditional word for "maid," *mucama*, in the masculine, it would be necessary to say something like "male maid," *empleada hombre*, since *mucamo*, the masculine form of *mucama*, is conventionally used to mean "butler" (also *mayordomo*).

7. One custom that emerged among most, but not all, men before the return to democracy is the social kiss among men, without any suggestion of homoeroticism (although for some it may carry such an implication). In an image that I include in *Life and Customs of Argentina*, two young

executives who are greeting each other in this manner in the full view of the public street are, nevertheless, still decked out in full accord with the time-honored norms of the financial district (38; the photograph was taken by Eduardo Gil).

8. One must recall that failing to be "sufficiently a man" was enough to bring down on one scorn and a whole array of violent reprisals, as one can see in the treatment of the male subject perceived to be "homosexual." To be less than a man meant to be homosexual, and homosexuals were identified/identifiable by their condition of masculine insufficiency. It is possible to refer here to a broad gamut of cultural productions (see Bazán's history of homosexuality in Argentina, which focuses repeatedly on what is perceived to signal such an abject condition; Sebreli, "Historia secreta," is also useful but limited in scope). Of particular importance for the explicit quality of its visual representation is Enrique Dawi's 1985 film, *Adiós, Roberto* (*So Long, Roberto*), in which being identified as homosexual exposes Roberto to aggressions from every imaginable social sector in ways that are especially interesting from the perspective of film (see Foster, "El homoerotismo"). One must, however, take note of how the epithet *maricón* does not necessarily identify someone who has sexual relations with other men, but rather refers to the individual who fails manifestly to comply adequately with the public profile of "being a man." Hence, the practice of calling a child or young person a *maricón* for evincing momentarily a conduct viewed as not appropriately virile, such as crying. The goal is to correct him with the imperative *No seas maricón* (Don't be a fag); "sissy" might come to mind here, but *maricón*, in the Argentine and general Latin American lexicon, is far stronger and more injurious.

9. The Spanish word *informalidad* means both "informality" and "irresponsibility," an important semantic conjunction as regards a discussion of the codes of masculinity.

10. This is a thorny issue that concerns issues of Argentine racism. Although the majority of the military dictators in the periods 1966–73 and 1976–83 were of direct immigrant descent, notably Italian, the military dictators unquestionably made a point of imposing a type of sober Argentine masculinity, "white" in origin, that excluded those who were seen as "not white" (individuals of indigenous and mestizo descent from the Argentine outback and surrounding countries, the so-called *cabecitas negras* or "black heads") or considered as such by symbolic extension (Jews like Fabrykant).

11. Fabrykant is at work on a new series of Argentine men that will, by his own account (personal communication, August 11, 2006, in Buenos Aires), include many more images like that of Guerrero Marthineitz. The image included here of Roly Serrano, a film and stage actor, is from the as yet unshown new series (Fig. 8.4).

12. I had the honor of being interviewed on my own in the wee hours of the morning on July 5, 1985, in Guerrero Marthineitz's famous television program, which was called *A solas* (*Alone*).

Chapter 9

1. Since these are all basically standard principles of contemporary feminist theory, I have not attempted to document them individually. The best place in Spanish to see these principles expounded and debated is in the Mexican feminist journal, *Debate feminista* (1990–).

2. It is important to note here the resemanticization of this epithet as a badge of courage for the women who, in the late 1970s, began mounting protests over the disappearance of loved ones. Staged outside the Casa Rosada, or Government House, in downtown Buenos Aires, these women were originally dismissed as *viejas locas*, whereupon they assumed with pride the designation *locas*: it may have been crazy of them to voice a public protest against military tyranny during the worst years of the last cycle of repression in Argentina (1976–83), but in that "craziness" lay their courage and the efficacious symbolism of that courage (see Bousquet for one major source of the international familiarity with the phrase "las locas de Plaza de Mayo"). See the definition of *loca* in Garay: "Mujer que ha perdido la razón./Mujer de poco juicio, disparatada, imprudente" (58).

3. The reference here is to the eponymous heroine of Fernando de Rojas's late

fifteenth-century drama, *La Celestina* (also known as *La tragicomedia de Calixto y Melibea*), in which, among other talents, Celestina, a wordly-wise go-between, is a specialist in repairing the ravishments of the body, especially maidenheads.

4. There is an extensive bibliography in English on this topic. In addition to psychological and sociological treatises on the subject (see, especially, *Breast Cancer*, Altman), of particular interest are texts written by feminist cultural figures who have undergone radical mastectomy and/or have had other experiences with cancer that affect their "worth as women." Most prominent among these is Audre Lorde's *The Cancer Journals*. Lorde asserts: "But I believe that socially sanctioned prosthesis is merely another way of keeping women with breast cancer silent and separate from each other" (14). See also Margaret Edson's magnificent Pulitzer Prize–winning play *Wit*, which has been performed internationlly. Weitz discusses the way in which women deal with the balding consequences of chemotheraphy in her chapter "Bald Truths" (esp. 147–55). I recognize this bibliography is emphatically Anglo-American, but I cite it in lieu of equivalent research in Spanish and with reference to the concerns of Argentine women.

5. Neumaier, in her introduction, speaks of how women are objectified by photography: "At any point on the continuum of representation ... women are objectified in a way distinct from the ways in which other groups (men, students, old people, people of color, bankers) are objectified. The determination of a women's sexual desirability by the age and shape of her body is perhaps the most vulgar and common mechanism of the objectification of women facilitated by photography" (2).

6. The lure of the mannish lesbian is not just a lesbian reinvestment in the primacy of male markers for erotic engagement, but as well the nondeconstruction of the male-female binary and the disjunctive and, therefore, singularly distributed signs it defends: women have soft breasts, while men have muscular chests.

7. Thus, the use of twin images from *Recursos humanos* on the cover of the late 2002 issue of *Letras femeninas* (28.1) of the Asociación de Literatura Femenina Hispánica.

8. Another Argentine woman who has suffered from cancer and reported on it, although in a totally different register from that of Liffschitz, is Patricia Kolesnicov. The Colombian singer Soraya (now deceased) also suffered from breast cancer and lent her status as a star to defending the need for early detection and prevention.

Bibliography

Ablard, Jonathan D. "Law, Medicine, and Confinement to Public Psychiatric Hospitals in Twentieth-Century Argentina." In *Argentina on the Couch: Psychiatry, State, and Society, 1880 to the Present,* ed. Mariano Plotkin. Albuquerque: University of New Mexico Press, 2003, 87–112.

Actis, Munú, et al. *Ese infierno: conversaciones con cinco mujeres sobrevivientes de la ESMA.* Buenos Aires: Editorial Sudamericana, 2001.

Afanador, Ruven. *Torero.* Thawil/Zurich, New York: Edition Stemmle, 2001.

Al sur del sur: 8 fotógrafos argentinos. Curators: Valeria González and Marcos López. Madrid: Casa de América, 2001.

Altman, Roberta. *Waking Up/Fighting Back: The Politics of Breast Cancer.* Boston: Little, Brown, 1996.

Amador Gómez-Quintero, Raysa Elena, and Mayra Pérez Bustillo. *The Female Body: Perspective of Latin American Artists.* Westport, Conn.: Greenwood Press, 2002.

Archetti, Eduardo P. *Masculinidades: fútbol, tango y polo en la Argentina.* Buenos Aires: Antropofagia, 2003. Orig. as *Masculinities: Football, Tango, and Polo in Argentina.* New York: Berg, 1999.

Atlas de la República Argentina: incluye reseñas geográficas y cuadro estadístico. Buenos Aires: Librería "El Ateneo" Editorial, 1992.

Avelar, Idelber. *The Untimely Present: Postdictatorial Latin American Fiction and the Task of Mourning.* Durham: Duke University Press, 1999.

Barreda, Fabiana. *La ciudad subterránea.* Buenos Aires: Magna Publicidad, 1998.

Barthes, Roland. *Camera Lucida: Reflections on Photography.* Trans. Richard Howard. New York: Hill and Wang, 1981.

Bazán, Osvaldo. *Historia de la homosexualidad en la Argentina, de la conquista de América al siglo XXI.* Buenos Aires: Marea, 2004.

Bourdieu, Pierre, et al. *Photography: A Middle-brow Art.* Trans. Shaun Whiteside. Cambridge: Polity Press, 1990.

Bousquet, Jean Pierre. *Las locas de la Playa de Mayo.* Trans. Jacques Despres. Buenos Aires: El Cid Editor, 1983. Orig. pub. in French in 1982 as *Les Folles de la Place de Mai.*

Bramly, Serge. *Leonardo: The Artist and the Man.* London: Penguin Books, 1994.

Breast Cancer: A Psychological Treatment Manual. New York: Springer Publishing, 1995.

Brodsky, Marcelo. *Buena memoria: un ensayo fotográfico / Good memory: a photographic essay.* Con textos de / with texts by Martín Caparrós, José Pablo Feinmann [and] Juan Gelman. Buenos Aires: La Marca Fotografía, 1997.

______, org. *Memoria en construcción: el debate sobre la ESMA.* Buenos Aires: La Marca Editora, 2005. Also as *Memory under Construction / Memoria en construcción: el debate sobre la ESMA.* English translations by David William Foster. Buenos Aires: La Marca Editora, 2005.

______. *Memory Works.* Salamanca: Universidad de Salamanca; Valladolid: Universidad de Valladolid, 2003.

______. *Nexo, un ensayo fotográfico de Marcelo Brodsky. A photographic essay.* Buenos Aires: La Marca; Centro Cultural Recoleta, 2001.

Brooker, Peter. *A Concise Glossary of Cultural Theory.* London: Arnold; New York, Oxford University Press, 1999.

Brunk, Terence. "Homosociality." In *Encyclopedia of Feminist Literary Theory*, ed. Elizabeth Kowaleski-Wallace. New York: Garland Publishing, 1997.

Burin, Mabel, and Irene Meler. *Varones: género y subjetividad masculina.* Buenos Aires: Paidós, 2000.

Bustos Domecq, Honorio, pseud. *Crónicas de Bustos Domecq.* Buenos Aires: Editorial Losada, 1967.

______. *Nuevos cuentos de Bustos Domecq.* Buenos Aires: Ediciones Librería La Ciudad, 1977.

______. *Seis problemas para don Isidro Parodi.* Buenos Aires: Sur, 1964.

Cabado, Pablo. *Laminares: Cuba desde 90. Illustratives: Cuba in the 90s.* Buenos Aires[?]: La Marca, 1999.

Calinescu, Matei. "Kitsch." In *Five Faces of Modernity.* Durham: Duke University Press, 1987, 225–62.

Camarasa, Jorge A. *Odessa al sur: la Argentina como refugio de nazis y criminales de guerra.* 2nd ed. Buenos Aires: Planeta, 1995.

Cárdenas, Eduardo José, Ricardo Grimson, and José Atilio Alvarez. *El juicio de insania y la interpretación psiquiátrica.* Buenos Aires: Astrea, 1985.

Carretero, Andrés M. *Chicos de la calle.* Buenos Aires: Corregidor, 1996.

Carrillo, Héctor. "Neither *Machos* nor *Maricones*: Masculinity and Emerging Male Homosexual Identities in Mexico." In *Changing Men and Masculinities in Latin America*, ed. Matthew C. Gutman. Durham: Duke University Press, 2003, 351–69.

Casatellote, Alejandro. *Mapas abiertos: fotografía latinoamericana 1991–2002.* Barcelona: Lunwerg Editores, 2003.

______, ed. "Perdonen el resentimiento." In *Marcos López.* México, D.F.: KBK Arte Contemporáneo, 2004, 5–8, 11, 13–14. Also as "Sorry about the Resentment," 21–22, 25, 26–27, 31–32.

Chicago, Judy. *The Dinner Party.* New York: Penguin, 1996.

Conboy, Katie, et al., eds. *Writing on the Body: Female Embodiment and Feminist Theory.* New York: Columbia University Press, 1997.

Connell, R.W. *Masculinities.* Berkeley: University of California Press, 1995.

______. *The Men and the Boys.* Berkeley: University of California Press, 2000.

Conner, Randy P., et al. *Cassell's Encyclopedia of Queer, Myth, Symbol, and Spirit.* London: Cassell, 1997.

Creed, Barbara. *The Monstrous-Feminine: Film, Feminism, Psychoanalysis.* New York: Routledge, 1993.

Davis, Mike. *City of Quartz: Excavating the Future in Los Angeles.* Photographs by Robert Morrow. London: Verso, 1990.

De Lauretis, Teresa. *The Practice of Love: Lesbian Sexuality and Perverse Desire.* Bloomington: Indiana University Press, 1994.

Deleuze, Gilles, and Félix Guattari. *Anti-Oedipus: Capitalism and Schizophrenia.* Trans. Robert Hurley et al. Minneapolis: University of Minnesota Press, 1983.

Deutsch, Sandra McGee, and Ronald H. Dolkart, eds. *The Argentine Right: Its History and Intellectual Origins, 1910 to the Present.* Washington, D.C.: Scholarly Resources, 1993.

Díaz, Gabriel. *Muertes menores: Minor Deaths.* Buenos Aires, no pub., n.d.

Dillon, Marta. "Amores difíciles." In *Madres e hijas*, ed. Adriana Lestido. Buenos Aires: La Azotea, 2003, 13–15; in English, 179–80.

Dittborn, Eugenio. *Mapa: Airmail Paintings / Pinturas aeropostales.* London: ICA, 1993.

Domenech, Ernesto E. "Fotografías y prisiones." In *Crimen y fotografía.* Buenos Aires: La Azotea Editorial Fotográfica, 2003, 73–83.

Dorfman, Ariel. *The Empire's Old Clothes: What the Lone Ranger, Babar, and Other Innocent Heroes Do to Our Minds.* New York: Pantheon Books, 1983.

Dorfman, Ariel, and Armando Mattelart. *Para leer al Pato Donald: Comunicación de masa y colonialismo.* 5th ed. Buenos Aires: Siglo XXI, 1973.

Dorfman, Ariel, and Manuel Jofré. *Superman y sus amigos del alma.* Buenos Aires: Editorial Galerna, 1974.

Draper, Ellen. "Gaze." In *Encyclopedia of Feminist Literary Theory*, ed. Elizabeth Kowaleski-Wallace. New York: Garland Publishing, 1997, 176–78.

Dreizik, Pablo M., comp. *La memoria de las cenizas.* Buenos Aires: Dirección Nacional de Patrimonio, Museos y Artes, 2001.

Duhalde, Eduardo Luis. *El estado terrorista argentino.* 1st ed. Barcelona: Argos Vergara, 1983.

Dworkin, Andrea. *Intercourse.* New York: Free Press, 1987.

Edson, Margaret. *Wit: A Play.* New York: Faber and Faber, 1999.

Ensler, Eve. *The Vagina Monologues.* The V-Day Edition. New York: Villard, 2001.

Facio, Sara. "Adriana Lestido." In *Leyendo fotos.* Buenos Aires: La Azotea, Editorial Fotográfica, 2002, 87–91.

______. "De la dictadura a la democracia: la memoria cuestionada." In *Leyendo fotos.* Buenos Aires: La Azotea, Editorial Fotográfica, 2002, 39–51.

______. *Fotografía argentina actual.* Buenos Aires: La Azotea Editorial Fotográfica de América Latina, 1981.

______. *Fotografía argentina dos.* Buenos Aires: La Azotea Editorial Fotográfica, 1996.

______. "Lazos eternos." In *Madres e hijas*, ed. Adriana Lestido. Buenos Aires: La Azotea, 2003, 7–11; in English, 175–78.

Facio, Sara, Alicia D'Amico, and Julio Cortázar. *Humanario.* Buenos Aires: La Azotea Editorial Fotográfica de América Latina, 1976.

Farred, Grant. "Crying for Argentina: The Branding and Unbranding of Area Studies." In *Neptantla: Views from the South* 4.1 (2003): 121–32.

Feitlowitz, Marguerite. *A Lexicon of Terror: Argentina and the Legacies of Torture.* New York: Oxford University Press, 1998.

Foster, David William. *Contemporary Argentine Filmmaking.* Columbia: University of Missouri Press, 1992.

______. "Defying the Masculinist Gaze: Gabriela Liffschitz's *Recursos humanos*." In *Chasqui* 32.1 (May 2003): 10–24.

______. "The Dirty Realism of Enrique Medina." In *Arizona Journal of Hispanic Cultural Studies* 1 (1997): 77–96.

______. "Dreaming in Feminine: Grete Stern's Photomontages and the Parody of Psychoanalysis." In *Ciberletras* 10 (2003): 10 pages. http://www.lehman.cuny.edu/ciberletras/v.10/foster.htm

______. "Gabriel Valansi: Neoliberal Nights in Buenos Aires." In *Fisura: revista de literatura y arte* 1.3 (febrero 2003): 27–33. Also in *Significação: revista brasileira de semiótica* 18 (2002): 89–113.

______. *Gender and Society in Contemporary Brazilian Cinema.* Austin: University of Texas Press, 1999.

______. "El homoerotismo y la lucha por el espacio en Buenos Aires: dos muestras cinematográficas." In *Tramas* 6 (1997): 13–42.

______. "Homosocialism ←→ Homoeroticism in the Photography of Marcos López." In *Dissidences* 1 (2005): online Internet 30/08/05 (http://www.dissidences/MarcosLopez.html).

______. "El kitsch argentino: la fotografía de Marcos López." In *Guaraguao: revista de cultura latinoamericana* 8.18 (verano 2004): 79–101.

______. "Masculinidades argentines: *Hombres* de Sylvio Fabrykant." In *Arizona Journal of Hispanic Cultural Studies* 9 (2005): 87–97.

______. Review of Adriana Lestido, *Madres e hijas.* In *Chasqui: revista de literatura latinoamericana* 33.1 (May 2004): 165–67.

______. Review of Enrique Medina, *El escritor, el amor y la muerte: novela.* In *World Literature Today* 73.4 (1999): 703.

______. "Sara Facio as Urban Photographer." In *Buenos Aires; Perspectives on the City and Cultural Production.* Gainesville: University Press of Florida, 1998, 170–94.

______. "Toreros de moda: la fotografía de Ruven Afanador." In *Revista de estudios colombianos* 29 (2006): 6–11.

______. "Women's Society in Prison: Adriana Lestido's *Mujeres presas*." *Journal of Latin American Urban Studies* 6 (Fall 2004): 1–18.

______, ed. *The Redemocratization of Argentine Culture, 1983 and Beyond: An International Research Symposium at Arizona State University, February 16–17, 1987.* Tempe: Center for Latin American Studies, Arizona State University, 1989.

Foster, David William, Melissa Fitch Lockhart, and Darrell B. Lockhart. *Culture and Customs of Argentina.* Westport, Conn.: Greenwood Press, 1998.

Foucault, Michel. *Madness and Civilization: A History of Insanity in the Age of Reason.* Trans. Richard Howard. New York: Pantheon Books, 1965.

Frank, Robert. *The Americans.* Introd. by Jack Kerouac. New York: Grove Press, 1959.

Fuentes, Carlos. "De Quetzalcóatl a Pepsicóatl." In *Tiempo mexicano.* México, D.F.: Joaquín Mortiz, 1971, 17–42

Gambaro, Griselda. *La señora Macbeth.* Buenos Aires: Grupo Editorial Norma, 2003.

Garay, María Cristina. *Diccionario de la discriminación de la mujer en el lenguaje.* Buenos Aires: Editorial Argenta Sarlep, 1994.

Garber, Pablo. "Gabriel Valansi." *libroarte.com.* <http://www.leedor.com/fotografía/gabrielvalansi.shtml

García Canclini, Néstor. *Culturas híbridas: estrategias para entrar y salir de la modernidad.* México, D.F.: Consejo Nacional para la Cultura y las Artes, 1989.

______. *Transforming Modernity: Popular Culture in Mexico.* Trans. Lidia Lozano. Austin: University of Texas Press, 1993.

Geirola, Gustavo. "Eroticism and Homoeroticism in *Martín Fierro.*" In *Bodies and Biases: Sexuality in Hispanic Cultures and Literatures,* ed. David William Foster and Roberto Reis. Minneapolis: University of Minnesota Press, 1996, 316–32.

______. "'Yo tenía un cuerpo': reflexiones sobre la manifestación del Che Guevara" (unpublished manuscript).

Gil, Eduardo. *(argentina).* Buenos Aires: Ediciones Cuarto 14, 2002.

______. *Paisajes Landscapes.* Exhibit catalog. Buenos Aires: Colección Fotografías Argentinas, 2006.

Giudice, Alberto, curator. *Arte y política en los '60.* Buenos Aires: Fundación Banco Ciudad [2002?].

Goñi, Uki. *The Real Odessa: How Perón Brought the Nazi War Criminals to Argentina.* London: Granata Books, 2002.

González, Horacio. "Mármol, imagen y martirio / Marble, Image and Martyrdom." Marcelo Brodsy, *Memory Works.* Salamanca: Universidad de Salamanca; Valladolid: Universidad de Valladolid, 2003, 13–17.

González, Valeria. "Las fotografías de Marcos López en el contexto del arte argentino de los noventa / The Photography of Marcos López in the Context of Marcos López." Marcos López, *Sub-realismo criollo (fotografías color 1993–2003).* Salamanca: Ediciones Universidad Salamanca, 2003, 23–29.

Gorbato, Viviana. *Noche tras noche.* Buenos Aires: Editorial Atlántida, 1997.

Graziano, Frank. *Divine Violence: Spectacle, Psychosexuality, & Radical Christianity in the Argentine "Dirty War."* Boulder, Colo: Westview Press, 1992.

Grealy, Lucy. *Autobiography of a Face.* Boston: Houghton Mifflin, 1994.

Guagnini, Nicolás. "Entrevista / Interview." Marcelo Brodsky, *Memory Works.* Salamanca: Universidad de Salamanca; Valladolid: Universidad de Valladolid, 2003, 117–23.

Gutiérrez, Fernando. *Treintamil.* Buenos Aires: La Marca, 1997.

Gutman, Matthew G., ed. *Changing Men and Masculinities in Latin America.* Durham: Duke University Press, 2003.

Halperin, David M. *One Hundred Years of Homosexuality and Other Essays on Greek Love.* New York: Routledge, 1990.

Hollanda, Francisco Buarque. *A ópera do malandro.* 2nd ed. São Paulo: Livraria Cultura Editora, 1979.

Huyssen, Andreas. "Memory Sites in an Expanded Field: The Memory Park in Buenos Aires." In his *Present Pasts: Urban Palimpsests and the Politics of Memory.* Stanford: Stanford University Press, 2003, 94–109. Also as "El arte mnemóico de Marcelo Brodsky / The Mnemonic Art of Marcelo Brodsky." Marcelo Brodsky, *Memory Works.* Salamanca: Universidad de Salamanca; Valladolid: Universidad de Valladolid, 2003, 7–11.

Ince, Kate. *Orlan: Millennial Female.* Oxford: Berg, 2000.

Invernizzi, Hernán, and Judtih Gociol. *Un golpe a los libros: represión a la cultura durante la última dictadura militar.* Buenos Aires: EUDEBA, 2002. See also the exhibit catalog *Un golpe a los libros 1976–1983: una producción de la Dirección General del Libro y Producción de la Lectura.* Buenos Aires: DG Libro, Secretaría de Cultura, Gobierno de Buenos Aires, 2002.

Jameson, Fredric. "Metacommentary." In *The Ideologies of Theory: Essays 1971–1986.*" Minneapolis: University of Minnesota Press, 1988, 1.3–16. Orig. *PMLA* 86.1 (1971): 9–18.

Jelin, Elizabeth, and Pablo Vila. *Podría ser yo: los sectores populares urbanos en imágenes y palabra.* Photos: Alicia D'Amico. Buenos Aires: Centro de Estudios de Estado y Sociedad; Ediciones de la Flor, 1987.

Kipnis, Laura. "(Male) Desire and (Female) Disgust: Reading *Hustler.*" In *Cultural Studies,* ed. Lawrence Grossberg, Cary Nelson, and Paula Treichler. New York: Routledge, 1992, 373–91.

Kolesnicov, Patricia. *Biografía de mi cáncer.* Buenos Aires: Editorial Sudamericana, 1999.

Kowalski-Wallace, Elizabeth, ed. *Encyclopedia of Feminist Literary Theory.* New York: Garland Publishing, 1997.

Kunzle, David. *Che Guevara: Icon, Myth, and Message.* Los Angeles, UCLA Fowler Museum of Cultural History, in collaboration with the Center for the Study of Political Graphics, 1997.

Larraya, Fernando Pagés, org. *La bacanal de los niños: antropología del chico de la calle.* Buenos Aires: Seminario de Antropología Psiquiátrica, 1998.

Latteier, Carolyn. *Breasts: The Women's Perspective on an American Obsession.* Binghamton, N.Y.: Haworth Press, 1998.

Lavado, Joaquín Salvador. *Toda Mafalda.* Buenos Aires: Ediciones de la Flor, 1993.

Leibovitz, Annie. *Women.* Essay by Susan Sontag. New York: Random House, 1999.

Lestido, Adriana. *Madres e hijas.* Buenos Aires: La Azotea Editorial Fotográfica, 2003.

_____. *Mujeres presas.* Buenos Aires: Impresa Latingráfica, 2001.

Levy, Marvyn. *The Moons of Paradise: Some Reflections on the Appearance of the Female Breast in Art.* New York: The Citadel Press, 1965.

Liffschitz, Gabriela. *Efectos colaterales.* Buenos Aires: Grupo Editorial Norma, 2003.

_____. *Recursos humanos.* Buenos Aires: Filòlibri, 2000.

_____. Review of Eduardo Gil, *(argentina). Chasqui: revista de literatura latinoamericana* 32.1 (May 2003): 128–29.

_____. *Venecia.* Buenos Aires: Ediciones Ultimo Reino, 1990.

Lihn, Enrique. *Batman en Chile, o el ocaso de un ídolo, o solo contra el desierto rojo.* Buenos Aires: Ediciones de la Flor, 1973.

López, Marcos. *Fotografías.* Selection and introduction by Sara Facio. Buenos Aires: La Azotea Editorial Fotográfica, 1993. New ed., 2006.

_____. *Marcos López.* México, D.F.: KBK Arte Contemporáneo, 2004.

_____. *Pop latino: fotografía y textos.* Buenos Aires: La Marca Editora, 1999.

_____. *Sub-realismo criollo (fotografías color 1993–2003).* Salamanca: Ediciones Universidad Salamanca, 2003.

Lorde, Audre. *The Cancer Journals.* Special ed. San Francisco: Aunt Lute Books, 1997.

Love, Susan M. *Dr. Susan Love's Breast Book.* Reading, Mass.: Addison-Wesley Publishing, 1990.

Luís, José, and Pedro Luís. "Pedro Luis Raota." www.raota.com (accessed 5–27–03).

Magialardi, Silvia, and A. Bécquer Casaballe, eds. *Buenos Aires: una visión fotográfica.* Buenos Aires: Fotomundo; FM Tango; Ediciones Culturales Argentinas, 1992.

Manrique, Jaime. "Legs." In *Eminent Maricones: Arenas, Lorca, Puig, and Me.* Madison, University of Wisconsin Press, 1999, 3–38.

Mascia-Lees, Frances E., and Patricia Sharpe. "Introduction: Soft-Tissue Modification and the Horror Within." In *Tattoo, Torture, Mutilation, and Adornment: The Denaturalization of the Body in Culture and in Text,* ed. Frances E. Mascia-Lees and Patricia Sharpe. Albany: State University of New York, 1992, 1–9.

Mattoso, Glauco. *O calvário dos carecas: história do trote estudiantil.* São Paulo: EMW Editores, 1985.

Maturi, Aníbal. *Los chicos de la calle.* Buenos Aires: Editorial Galerna, 1987.

Medina, Enrique. *El escritor, el amor y la muerte: novela.* Buenos Aires: Planeta, 1998.

Melamed, Diego. *Irse: cómo y por qué los argentinos se están yendo del país.* Buenos Aires: Editorial Sudamericana, 2002.

Messina, Gaby. *Grandes mujeres.* Catalog. Text by Juan Travnik. Buenos Aires: Foto-Galería, Complejo Teatro de Buenos Aires, 2004.

______. "*Grandes mujeres*: Photography by Messina." In *Aperture* 178 (Spring 2005): 70–79.

Mira, Alberto. *Para entendernos: diccionario de cultura homosexual, gay y lésbica.* Barcelona: Ediciones de la Tempestad, 1999.

Morgan, Robin. "Theory and Practice: Pornography and Rape." In *Word of a Woman: Feminist Dispatches, 1968–1992.* New York: W.W. North, 1992, 78–89.

Mueller, Andrew. "Chernobyl veinte años después." In *Brando* (abril 2006): 90–99, 128. Photographs by Gabriel Díaz.

"Mujeres presas con sus hijos—Adriana Lestido." http://www.zonezero.com/exposiciones/fotografos/lestido.default2.html.

Myths, Dreams & Realities: Contemporary Argentine Photography. Exhibit catalog. Houston: Houston Center for Photography; Pan American Cultural Exchange [1999?].

Neumaier, Diane. "Introduction." In *Reframings: New American Feminist Photographies*, ed. Diane Neumaier. Philadelphia: Temple University Press, 1995, 1–12.

______, ed. *Reframings: New American Feminist Photographies.* Philadelphia: Temple University Press, 1995.

Nuestras estancias. Argentine ranches. Cincuenta estacias representativas de la República Argentina. Buenos Aires: Casa Pardo, 1968.

Nunca más: informe de la Comisión Nacional sobre la Desaparición de Personas. Buenos Aires: EUDEBA, 1984. Translated into English: *Nunca más, the Report of the Argentine National Commission on the Disappeared.* With an introduction by Ronald Dworkin. New York, Farrar Straus Giroux, in association with Index on Censorship, London, 1986.

Núñez Noriega, Guillermo. *Sexo entre varones: poder y resistencia en el campo sexual.* 2nd ed. México, D.F.: Coordinación de Humanidades, Programa Universitario de Estudios de Género, Instituto de Investigaciones Sociales; Hermosillo, Son.: El Colegio de Sonora; México, D.F.: Miguel Angel Porrúa Grupo Editorial, 1999.

Olalquiaga, Celeste. *The Artificial Kingdom: On the Kitsch Experience.* Minneapolis: University of Minnesota Press, 2002.

Olsen, Tillie, Julie Olsen Edwards, and Estelle Jussim. *Mothers & Daughters: An Exploration in Photographs.* New York: Aperture Foundation, 1987.

Orden, Fernando de la. "La abuela Lola." In *Fotomundo* 411 (septiembre 2002): 54–56.

Panera Cuevas, F. Javier. "Marcos López (fotografías en color 1993–2003) / Marcos López (Colour Photography 1993–2003)." Marcos López, *Sub-realismo criollo (fotografías color 1993–2003).* Salamanca: Ediciones Universidad Salamanca, 2003, 9–14.

Perlongher, Néstor. *O negócio do michê: prostituição viril em São Paulo.* São Paulo: Editora Brasiliense, 1987. Reissued in Spanish as *La prostitución masculina.* Buenos Aires: Ediciones de la Urraca, 1993.

Pianca, Marina. "La política de la dislocación (o retorno de la memoria del futuro)." In *Memoria colectiva y políticas de olvido: Argentina y Uruguay, 1970–1990*, ed. Adriana J. Bergero and Fernando Reati. Rosario: Beatriz Viterbo Editora, 1997, 115–38.

Piglia, Ricardo. *La Argentina en pedazos.* Buenos Aires: Ediciones de la Urraca, 1993.

Piscano, Margarita. *El triunfo de la masculinidad.* Santiago de Chile: Surada, 2001.

Prignano, Ángel O. *Crónica de la basura porteña: del fogón al cinturón ecológico.* Buenos Aires: Junta de Estudios Históricos de San José de Flores, 1998.

Prongher, Brian. *The Arena of Masculinity: Sports, Homosexuality, and the Meaning of Sex.* London: GMP Publishers, 1990.

Ramírez, Mari Carmen. *Cantos paralelos: la parodia plástica en el arte argentino con-*

temporáneo / Visual Parody in Contemporary Argentinean Art. Con textos de / with texts by Marcelo E. Pacheco [and] Andrea Giunta. Austin: Jack S. Blanton Museum of Art, University of Texas at Austin; Buenos Aires: Fondo Nacional de las Argentinas, Argentina, 1999.

Raota, Pedro Luis. *Faces of Life*. Buenos Aires: Escuela Superior de Arte Fotográfico, 1983.

Rapisardi, Flavio, and Alejandro Modarelli. *Fiestas, baños y exilios: los gays porteños en la última dictadura*. Buenos Aires: Editorial Sudamericana, 2001.

Rathje, William, and Cullen Murphy. *Rubbish! The Archaeology of Garbage*. Tucson: University of Arizona Press, 2001.

Rich, Adrienne. "Compulsory Heterosexuality and Lesbian Existence." In *Blood, Bread, and Poetry: Selected Prose, 1979–1985*. New York: W.W. Norton, 1986, 23–75.

Riesman, David. *The Lonely Crowd: A Study of the Changing American Character*. New Haven: Yale University Press, 1950.

Salgado, Sebastião. *An Uncertain Grace*. Photographs by Sebastião Salgado; essays by Eduardo Galeano and Fred Ritchin. New York: Aperture, 1990.

Sánchez de Balcero, Inés. *Cultura y marginalidad urbana: estudio antropológico entre los trabajadores de la basura*. Bogotá: Universidad de Bogotá Jorge Tadeo Lozano, 1999.

Santos, Lidia. *Kitsch tropical: los medios en la literatura y el arte en América Latina*. Madrid: Iberoamericana; Frankfurt am Main: Vervuert, 2001.

Sarlo, Beatriz. *La batalla de las ideas (1943–1973)*. (With the collaboration of Carlos Altamirano.) Buenos Aires: Ariel, 2001.

______. *Escenas de la vida posmoderna: intelectuales, arte y videocultura en la Argentina*. Buenos Aires: Ariel, 1994.

______. *El imperio de los sentimientos, narraciones de circulación periódica en la Argentina (1917–1927)*. Buenos Aires, Catálogos Editora, 1985.

Scalabrini Ortiz, Raúl. *Los ferrocarriles deben ser del pueblo argentino*. Buenos Aires: Editorial Reconquista, 1946.

______. *El hombre que está solo y espera*. Buenos Aires: Gelizer, 1931.

Scobie, James R. *Buenos Aires: Plaza to Suburb, 1870–1910*. New York: Oxford University Press, 1974.

Sebreli, Juan José. "Historia secreta de los homosexuales en Buenos Aires." In *Escritos sobre escritos, ciudades bajo ciudades, 1950–1997*. Buenos Aires: Editorial Sudamericana, 1997, 275–370.

Sedgwick, Eve Kososky. *Between Men: English Literature and Male Homosocial Desire*. New York: Columbia University Press, 1985.

Seligmann-Silva, Marcelo. "Catastrophe and Representation: History as Trauma." In *Semiotica: Journal of the International Association for Semiotic Strudies* 143.1–4 (2003): 143–62.

Shua, Ana María. *La muerte como efecto secundario*. Buenos Aires: Editorial Sudamericana, 1997.

Sontag, Susan. *Regarding the Pain of Others*. New York: Farrar, Straus and Giroux, 2003.

Steimberg, Alicia. *Cuando digo Magdalena*. Buenos Aires: Planeta Biblioteca Sur, 1992.

______. *La loca 101*. Buenos Aires: Ediciones de la Flor, 1973.

______. *La selva*. Buenos Aires: Alfaguara, 2000.

Suardíaz, Delia Esther. *Sexism in the Spanish Language*. M.A. thesis, University of Washington, 1973.

Suleiman, Susan Rubin. *The Female Body in Western Culture: Contemporary Perspectives*. Cambridge: Harvard University Press, 1986.

Taylor, Barry. *Palpable Signs: Contemporary Women Photographers.* London: Scarlet, 1999.

Thompson, Michael. *Rubbish Theory: The Creation and Destruction of Value.* Oxford: Oxford University Press, 1979.

Thomson, Rosemarie Garland. "Physical Disability." In *Encyclopedia of Feminist Literary Theory*, ed. Elizabeth Kowaleski-Wallace. New York: Garland Publishing, 1997, 307–08.

Timerman, Jacobo. *Preso sin nombre, celda sin número.* Barcelona, El Cid Editor, 1981. Cover title: *El caso Camps, punto inicial.* Trans. Toby Talbot as *Prisoner without a Name, Cell without a Number.* New York: Knopf, 1981.

Tompkins, Cynthia. "Las <<mujeres alteradas>> y <<superadas>> de Maitena Burundarena: feminismo Made in Argentina." In *Studies in Latin American Popular Culture* 22 (2003): 35–60.

UNICEF. *Declaración de los derechos del niño [comentada por Mafalda y sus amiguitos para el UNICEF].* Bogotá: Editorial Retina, 1977.

Vallejos, Soledad. "Lolas a la vista." http://www.pagina 12.com.ar/2001/suple/Las12/01–01/01–01–12/nota-4.htm

Viñas, David. *Qué es el fascismo en Latinoamérica.* Barcelona: Editorial de La Gaya Ciencia, 1977.

Waugh, Thomas. *Hard to Imagine; Gay Male Eroticism in Photography and Film from Their Beginnings to Stonewall.* New York: Columbia University Press, 1996.

Weitz, Rose. *Rapunzel's Daughters: What Women's Hair Tells Us about Women's Lives.* New York: Farrar, Starus and Giroux, 2003.

Weyr, Thomas. *Reaching for Paradise: The Playboy Vision of America.* New York: Times Books, 1978.

Wolf, Naomi. *The Beauty Myth.* London: Chatto & Windus, 1990.

Yako, Dani. *Extinción: últimas imágenes del trabajo en la Argentina.* Textos de Martín Caparrós. Buenos Aires: Grupo Editorial Norma, 2001.

Yalom, Marilyn. *A History of the Breast.* New York: Alfred A. Knopf, 1997.

Index